DISSIDENTS OF LAW

Dissidents of Law

On the 1989 velvet revolutions, legitimations, fictions of legality and contemporary version of the social contract

JIŘÍ PŘIBÁŇ
Cardiff Law School, University of Wales, UK
Faculty of Law, Charles University, The Czech Republic

Routledge
Taylor & Francis Group
LONDON AND NEW YORK

First published 2002 by Ashgate Publishing Company

Reissued 2019 by Routledge
2 Park Square, Milton Park, Abingdon, Oxon, OXl 4 4RN
52 Vanderbilt Avenue, New York, NY 10017

Routledge is an imprint of the Taylor & Francis Group, an informa business

A Library of Congress record exists under LC control number:

ISBN 13: 978-1-138-73707-5 (hbk)
ISBN 13: 978-1-315-18556-9 (ebk)

Contents

Acknowledgements

I wish to thank all friends and colleagues who helped me during my work on this book. I am particularly grateful to Prof. David Campbell from the Cardiff Law School, University of Wales, for his detailed comments and extensive editorial work. Prof. Roger Cotterrell from the Queen Mary and Westfield College, University of London, Prof. David Dyzenhaus from the University of Toronto, Prof. Peter Fitzpatrick from Birkbeck College, University of London, and Prof. David Nelken from the University of Macerata provided me with a number of extremely helpful comments on the whole project. Prof. Václav Bělohradský from the University of Trieste and Prof. Costas Douzinas from Birkbeck College, University of London, helped me to clarify concepts and ideas elaborated in the sixth and seventh chapters. Dave Burnett from the Cardiff Law School, University of Wales, and Prof. Pavel Holländer, Justice of the Constitutional Court of the Czech Republic, provided me with comments on the third and fourth chapters, while Prof. Gunther Teubner from the University of Frankfurt generously commented on the fifth chapter and Prof. Phil Thomas from the Cardiff Law School, University of Wales, helped me with drafts of the second and seventh chapters.

I am also very grateful to my students in the courses 'Developments in the Modern Legal Positivism' and 'Post-structural Legal Science' which I was teaching at the Faculty of Law, Charles University, in the summer semesters of 1999 and 2000. Their insights and thoughtful interpretations of the problems analysed in this book were extremely valuable for me.

The same must be said about students in the seminar 'Post-modern Jurisprudence', which I was leading at the University of Pretoria in the spring of 1999, and the course 'Human Rights in Central Europe', which I was teaching at the University of San Francisco in the summer of 1999.

My final and special expression of gratitude must go to my colleague and friend James Young from the Cardiff Law School, University of Wales, with whom I spent many hours discussing the whole project and who provided me with great moral support during the work on this book.

Editorial Note

Some parts of the text and concepts have been taken and elaborated from the following articles and texts:

- Přibáň, J. (1997), 'Beyond Procedural Legitimation: Legality and Its "Infictions"', 24 *Journal of Law and Society*, pp. 331-49.

- Přibáň, J. (1998), 'Doing What Comes Naturally, or a Walk on the Wild Side?: Remarks on Stanley Fish's Anti-foundationalist Concept of Law, Its Closure and Force', 9 *Law and Critique*, pp. 249-270.

- Přibáň, J. (1999), 'Legality and Legitimacy after the Velvet Revolutions', in J. Přibáň and J. Young (eds), *The Rule of Law in Central Europe: The Reconstruction of Legality, Constitutionalism and Civil Society in the Post-Communist Countries*, Ashgate Publishers, Aldershot, pp. 29-55.

- Přibáň, J. (2001), 'Legitimitation Between the Noise of Politics and the Order of Law: A Critique of Autopoietic Rationality', in J. Přibáň and D. Nelken (eds), *Law's New Boundaries: The Consequences of Legal Autopoiesis*, Ashgate Publishing, Aldershot, pp. 104-22.

- Přibáň, J. (2002), 'Moral and Political Legislation in Constitutional Justice: A Case Study of the Czech Constitutional Court', 8 *Parker's Journal of East European Law*, n. 1.

- Přibáň, J. (2002), 'Legalist Fictions and the Scientific Legitimation of Law', 15 *Ratio Juris* [forthcoming].

1 Introduction

I have developed the thoughts and notions contained in this book over a long time. The project dates right back to the mid 80s, when I started my law studies at the Faculty of Law of Charles University in Prague. The communist regime seemed solid and the Czech communist leaders understood the magic word 'perestroika', introduced by the Soviet leader Michail Gorbachev, in a way which strengthened their own power at that time.

Being a law student, I was especially interested in the subjection of the system of positive law to the totalitarian communist ideology and the political domination of the Party. Law had been commonly defined in textbooks as 'the will of the ruling class'. But though 'the working class' ruled, its will was announced by the highest Party bodies. The reduction of law to the symbolic level of totalitarian ideology and to the real governmental power of the Party bodies posed the problem of the general degeneracy of the social and political context of positive law. The core concepts of modern politics such as the people, democracy, the rule of law and legality were 'improved' in the newspeak of communist ideology as the working people, people's democracy, socialist rule of law and socialist legality.

The symbols of modern government had been supplemented and changed in order to serve the totalitarian domination of the Party. All spheres of social life including law were subsumed within this framework of ideological legitimation. Communist ideology defined the conditions of legitimacy and legality was determined by this definition. The supremacy of ideological legitimacy could be seen in all branches of positive law and legal education.

This personal experience initiated my interest in the problem of legitimacy and legality. I started reading 'semi-legal' authors like Max Weber, Carl Schmitt, Hermann Heller, Jürgen Habermas and Niklas Luhmann. This reading became a student enthusiasm. I quickly realised that the problem of legitimacy and legality was one of constitutive topics of modernity, communist totalitarianism being the characteristic excess of the project of modernity.

It was also interesting to read the 'illegal' texts of dissidents in which the problem of legitimacy played a key role, too. The essays of Václav Havel sought to establish the legitimation field and define the strategy of the anti-communist dissent. The main aim of dissident strategy was to pull down the 'facade of legality' of communist power, which blurred its repressive character. Dissidents used the concept of socialist legality to expose the repressive character of the communist regime and its ignorance of both national laws and international legal obligations. The dissident strategy involved both legalist and natural or moral rights arguments.

After the anti-communist revolutions of 1989, the whole of Czech society started the historically unprecedented process of transformation from the totalitarian into liberal democratic society. The topic of legitimacy and legality was frequently discussed in public debate. Revolutionary social change was beset by the problem of the persistence of communist legality in the hectic lawmaking of the new, democratically elected Parliament. Was communism legal or illegal? If it was legal, was it possible to prosecute its representatives for political crimes? If it was illegal, how is it possible that the communist party, which never gave up its ideology, can continue to work in the new liberal democratic conditions and overtly challenge the new political regime?

These questions were not merely academic and did not preoccupy only the new political elites. Revolutionary change posited the basic necessity of legitimating the emerging legal system of the post-communist society. However, it has proved impossible to establish post-revolutionary legality as the sovereign legitimation framework. The attempts to do so made by the Parliament and the Constitutional Court of the Czech Republic are highly controversial and show the incommensurability of the legal and political function of these bodies.

Law and politics started to differentiate. Legality ceased to be able to make the claim to be the sovereign ideology which would have provided it with complete legitimacy. The Velvet Revolution and subsequent political and social developments effectively took a strong commitment to pluralism as their code. Accepting this code, it is possible to understand the whole revolutionary process as a process of belated modernisation, the primary goal of which was to get rid of the vocabulary of a sovereign ideology.

Legitimacy by legality and its limits

Does this modernisation process of the differentiation of social life, a part of which is the differentiation and separation of law and politics and therefore of legality and legitimacy, automatically mean the self-legitimation of law, as if proposed by, for example, the social theory of autopoietic systems? One of the main aims of this book is to provide a negative answer to this question despite of accepting many elements of the procedural notion of the legitimacy of law which is inherent in the autopoietic theory of law.

Certain external political conditions of the democratic rule of law system (*Rechtsstaat*), such as the democratic character of the legislative bodies, the protection of human rights and freedoms and the recognition of the principle of the separation of powers and its codification in the constitution, are the basis of the legitimacy of liberal democratic political domination and positive law. However, it is evident that law established on these political conditions can never achieve complete legitimacy because legitimacy is both a matter of *a priori* principles and social belief. Anti-liberal and anti-democratic elements are therefore an internal part of the liberal democratic system of the rule of law. In pluralistic societies, there is no way to establish a unified belief and achieve solid legitimacy.

Legitimacy is an open matter. Consequently, legitimacy must be transformed into legitimation procedures. The topic of legitimacy becomes the topic of legitimation. The legal protection of political principles no longer has primary importance. It is more important to create the procedures which will enhance the chance of social acceptance of legal regulations. In this book, I will nevertheless seek to prove that concern with legitimacy belongs neither exclusively to the legal system nor to a political system separated and distanced from the legal system. The topic of legitimacy and legitimation is inseparable from legality and every legitimation eventually looks for its transformation into legal legitimacy. At the same time, legitimacy is not an issue internal to law, for it emerges rather from the tension and difference between positive law and its social environment. Legitimacy is irreducible to legal procedures because it can also mean resistance to and denial of positive law. The anti-communist dissent is evidence of this difference between legitimacy and legality.

In the liberal democratic societies, then, legality paradoxically becomes more legitimate when it opens a space for various legitimation strategies and in this way denies its sovereign position within political discourse. The original liberal notion of the rule of law as a state in which law governs political power and society has disappeared. Law must adopt a more reflexive stance towards social and political plurality. *Legitimacy by legality* is conditioned by legality's power to secure this plurality. Consequently, *legitimacy directly depends on legality's power to redefine itself as something other than the sovereign legitimation discourse of contemporary liberal democratic societies.* This goal may be achieved only by the transformation of political principles, formulated in the language of legality, into procedures, which, by legal means, secure the plural, open space of liberal society.

The contemporary relationship between legality and legitimacy is a relationship of homogeneity and heterogeneity. Legality seeks to establish a common political space and perform the function of social integration. In current social conditions, however, legality is required to promote plurality, even a plurality of legitimation and delegitimation strategies focused on legality itself. This paradox of the liberal democratic rule of law, criticised for instance by Carl Schmitt, turns out to be a constitutive element and condition of legitimacy in the contemporary post-modern situation. Legality must have 'gaps' and abandon the concept of sovereignty if it wants to keep its legitimation force.

Legality and its fictions

The role of legal theory in analysis of the legitimacy of legal rational political domination is another important problem analysed in this book, specifically as it arises in the development of the legal and political systems of post-communist societies. Legal theory is unique because its analytical function involves normative judgments about the system of positive law. Although it pretends to be an analytical and value-free scientific discourse, legal theory seeks to influence the processes of lawmaking and the enforcement of law and thus the construction of legal reality. Legal science creates 'the nature of law'. Legal theory constructs the true nature of law and reflects law's real functions in the modern society. In order to understand the legitimacy of law and political domination, it is necessary to analyse this constructive and reflexive power of modern legal theory.

The construction of scientific discourse about law turns on an ability peculiar to legal science, to construct *fictions*. Scientific discourse about law, the primary function of which is the analysis of positive law, is possible only when these fictions are formulated. The scientific, analytical enterprise of jurisprudence depends upon an artificial construct which must reformulate legal reality in order to make its scientific description possible. The logically pure crystals of legal theory are conceivable only on the basis of a fictitious notion which belongs to the sphere of imagination as it exceeds the limits of analytical thinking. Legal fictions are ubiquitous in legal communication and may be traced back to Roman law. These fictions, for instance the fiction of a legal person are an internal part of legal logic and pragmatics.

The importance of legal fictions was emphasised by Jeremy Bentham, Rudolf Ihering and, more recently, by Lon Fuller. Fictions create an artificial reality which must be applied to an existing legal case or dispute in order to come to an authoritative decision. The artificial reality of fictions establishes pragmatic steps within the framework of the 'real' reality of positive law. This book is not concerned with any particular legal fiction existing in the various branches of different legal systems. It is more concerned to show that legal theory, in order to fulfil the demands of scientific, independent and true discourse about positive law, must shape itself against the background of some constitutive fictions. These fictions are the general artificial constructs supporting the claim of modern law to be a rational, logically coherent and hierarchical system which operates independently of (and on) other normative orders and social systems.

The main purpose of fictions in modern, legalist, positivist theory is to set up the paradigmatic conditions for the 'right' answer to the question: 'What is law?'. They have a constitutive and legitimation function within the paradigm of legal science because they are the basis of all analyses and definitions of positive law. This is exactly the function of Hans Kelsen's fiction of the basic norm, Jeremy Bentham's fiction of the political sovereign, or Thomas Hobbes's older concept of the social contract. Rudolf Stammler's fiction of the just law, later used by Gustav Radbruch, had a similar, although not so significant impact on legal science.

It was precisely Radbruch's formula, according to which law must correspond to the principle of justice, that resonated strongly in the post-communist systems of positive law. As in Germany after 1945, post-communist countries after 1989 sought to use this formula in order to punish past political crimes which could not be regarded as criminal under communist legislation. Radbruch's formula, which makes the fiction of the just law being the condition of law's validity, had a marked impact in precisely those historical periods of complex political and legal change in which the problem of legitimacy and legality is extraordinarily urgent.

The legitimation fictions of legality constructed by analytical jurisprudence and legal positivism turn on the type of close link between thinking and language described by Friedrich Nietzsche and later, in late modernity, worked out by Ludwig Wittgenstein in his *Philosophical Investigations*. Such fictions exhibit the extent to which modern analytical thinking depends on language metaphors. Wittgenstein's thesis that 'language bears the thinking' (Wittgenstein, 1980: par.329) and processes of thinking can have a meaning only in language is evidenced in the fictions of legal science.

The three 'F' thesis: legitimations as fictions

If one accepts that the grammar of legal theory and philosophy as the general science of law is established by some fiction, it is necessary to change radically one's perspective on the possibility of giving a scientific legitimacy to positive law. Legalist legal theory obviously represents the attempt to legitimate scientifically the system of positive law. This science is unique in that it seeks both to be a science about law and science directly connected to the functions of positive law. Legal science seeks to become a part of the system of positive law. The scientific legitimacy expressed by legal theory and philosophy is to be founded on the sources of rationality internal to modern law. Legal science as a legitimation strategy is a self-legitimation strategy produced by the system of positive law.

This whole cycle of the modern system of positive law, legal positivist philosophy and scientific legitimacy is however disrupted by the existence of *grammar fictions* which constitute legal science as a legitimation strategy claiming the sovereign right to answer the question about law's nature. Fictions are 'the outside' of legalist methodology, but also, paradoxically, its foundation and therefore the foundation of legal science as a whole. Imagination becomes the foundation of scientific legitimacy.

The whole legitimation process in legalist and positivist science, which originally was to legitimate legality by use of the internal rationality of the legal system, eventually can be seen to have *fictitious foundations*. Saying that, we should avoid the danger of seeking to place the fictions in the realm of fakes or falsity because we identify scientific truth with reality, correctness and the true nature of things. Fictions stand *beyond truth and falsity*. They are not a false discourse about the political and legal systems and their rationality. Those fictions constitute the very possibility of speaking about law and politics as systems and orders.

Both legal experts and the subjects of political and legal systems use fictions in order to link concrete legal regulations with the more general principles of civil society and moral values. Fictions shape the semantic field from which legitimacy emerges and in which legality encounters its social and intellectual environment. Fictions therefore represent a very important pragmatic element of the system of positive law.

I should like to reformulate Talcott Parsons' analysis of the existence and legitimacy of any social order by extending his demonstration of their reliance on the double 'Fs' of force and fraud. The existence of a legitimate order in modern political society is not ultimately secured by force and fraud but rather by a fiction, which constructs legitimacy through a permanent process of social communication and domination. This *thesis of the third 'F'* is one of the central topics of the whole book.

The legitimation fictions of legality constructed by legal science are not alone. Fictions are to be found beyond the world of scientific legitimation strategies. It is possible to find grammar fictions elsewhere in society. These all put forward different narratives to justify existing or emerging social structures, or to dismantle them and substitute them for different structures. Every legitimation fiction seeks to provide a unifying interpretation and reflection of social reality. The social world produces a need for belief in legitimacy in those living in it. Social solidarity and unity is necessary for the reproduction of the social world. People must consequently create coherent narratives which provide the social world with meaning based around certain unifying symbols, and thus secure solidarity between those living in it (Berger and Luckmann, 1967: 135f.).

The social contract and dissent

Providing the social world with legitimacy means giving it meaning and attributing value to it and its component structures. Legitimation means giving meaning and order to an originally chaotic and unstable world. Fictions must exist, and their function is by no means limited to the social sciences. Modern political societies derive their existence mainly from the fiction of the social contract, which involves other fictions, first of all the fictions of the people and the general consensus or will. Fictions determine modern notions of political order and social integrity. This book starts with an analysis of these constitutive fictions of modern politics and law and their contemporary transformations.

The fiction of the social contract has a unique meaning. At the beginning of modernity, it worked as the foundation of political and moral unity. The general consensus established by this contract was to secure the integrity of modern political society. Unlike the fictions constructed by legal positivism, however, the fiction of the social contract does not construct a completely neutral framework for modern political culture, in which political rules might be subjected to some 'master principle'. It reproduces the paradoxical structure of modern political life in which establishing the generally binding framework is to be constituted by particular expressions of the individual wills of every party to the contractual act; that is to say, by every citizen of the political community.

This paradoxical interplay of generality and particularity, unity and plurality, or consensus and resistance, is fully exposed in the contemporary social and political situation, which might be characterised by the dismantling of political sovereignty and the permanent pluralisation of the public sphere. The procedural aspects of the social contract, which gradually replace the processes of generating universal political principles on a contractual basis with the processes of social and political pluralisation and particularisation, play a more important role. These processes, however, can never lead to a completely pluralistic situation. For the conditions of the liberal democratic rule of law system, it will be argued, inevitable is the *centre-periphery* loop in which all legitimation strategies and fictions of legality and political domination have to be constructed.

Legitimacy as a general belief that the existing political institutions are right cannot be coherently established within the framework of the social contract or any other fiction. The most important source of the legitimacy of contemporary liberal democratic societies, which were established on the one principle of the rule of law, has become the plurality of legitimation strategies and fictions. The purpose of fictions is to establish general validity, yet no fiction can fully succeed in this process of universalisation of the particular. Temporary success would lead only to a bigger crisis of legitimacy of political domination and law in contemporary liberal democracies.

The fiction of the social contract has maintained its exceptional ability to keep persuasive force not only by shifting from the consensual model with its emphasis on normative integrity to the heterogeneous and pluralistic model in which compromise and conversation become primary goals and strategies. It has also shown as extraordinary persuasive power to generate and create parallel structures for other legitimation and de-legitimation fictions. If legitimacy means attributing meaning and order to a chaotic world, the fiction of the social contract, if heterogeneity and plurality in the very process of negotiating the contract by diverse participants are emphasised, has the power both to establish the order and produce the chaos. Political and legal systems are unimaginable from their outside, but it is to that outside that the legitimation claim of the creation of 'order from noise' refers.

The formation of legitimacy as a process of legitimation and the shift in the meaning of the social contract fiction opens the problem of dissent as one of the many (de)legitimation strategies in contemporary politics and law. Dissent is one of the most important such strategies because it, more than any other strategy, demonstrates that it is impossible for legality to sustain the status of being the sovereign basis of legitimation, which it is given in contemporary liberal democratic politics. Dissent has a strong pluralisation effect and refers to parallel vocabularies which dismantle the neutralising power of legality and the identification of legitimacy with legality. The importance of 'gaps' in legality as a condition of its legitimacy is manifested by dissent. The current interpretation of the social contract, which is inseparable from the concept of 'gap' legality and its inability to define the sovereign condition of legitimacy, arises as a consequence of the extraordinary force of the strategy of dissent. Dissent cannot become the new foundation of a system of legitimate political domination and law. Dissent points to the limits of legal legitimacy by standing outside those limits, persuasively challenging the sovereign claim of law and thus paradoxically secures its legitimacy in the liberal democratic conditions.

The main argument of this book may, then, be summarised as our new understanding of the social contract: the social contract requires that the legitimacy of any system of law and political domination must be constantly re-negotiated. This process is the unconditional responsibility of those living or wishing to live under the contemporary liberal democratic rule of law. Extraordinary force of this responsibility is manifested in the strategy of dissent.

....

The structure of this book has its horizontal and vertical levels. At the horizontal level, I seek to analyse the fictitious character of every legitimacy and legitimations which emerge within the sphere of politics and in the context of modern social sciences and legal theory. The uniqueness of the fiction of the social contract, which I return to in the final chapter, is given by the fact that it has the capacity to reflect on both centring and decentring tendencies which are present in the process of legitimation.

At the horizontal level, I also analyse the 1989 revolutionary changes in the Central European communist countries and the influence of the anti-communist dissent as a (de)legitimation strategy. The descriptions of the revolutions and dissent are used as starting points leading to the general arguments and conclusions about the concepts of legality and legitimacy. The concept of dissent is exceptionally important for the whole work because it encapsulates the notions of difference, uniqueness and heterogeneity that stand against the unifying, centring and homogenising force of legality.

At the vertical level, I elaborate the argument about transformation of the concept of the legitimacy of law and political domination. The original modern concept of legitimacy as principles and foundations of law and politics has been transformed into the concept of systemic and procedural legitimation. Consequently, it is necessary to formulate the whole problem of legitimacy as a functional interdependence of the legal system and its legitimating social environment. The fiction of the social contract may be used and reformulated so that it reflects the heterogeneous conditions of contemporary democratic societies.

The book is divided into seven chapters starting with this introduction. The second chapter focuses on the modern fictions of the sovereign people and general will which are directly connected to the fiction of the social contract in its originally unifying and homogenising social function. These fictions stand behind the democratic legitimacy of modern political domination and law and eventually lead to the concept of the people as being both politically and morally sovereign. The second part of this chapter therefore analyses Habermas' discourse theory which respects such legitimation pattern. The description of the 1989 anti-communist revolutions, then, shows how these events effectively dismantle the fiction of the sovereign people and general will in their modern unifying sense.

The third chapter focuses on legal theoretical responses to the modern principle of legitimacy by legality. Legal theory constructs its own fictions and seeks to provide the scientific legitimation of modern law. However, the attempt to define internal conditions of the legitimacy of law failed. Contemporary legal positivism assumes the moral legitimation of law and creates the fiction of the just law as the principle unifying the internal rationality of legality and the political morality of liberal democratic societies. The main purpose of the fiction of the just law remains the same: to maintain legality as a sovereign legitimation framework.

The fourth chapter analyses the role of contemporary legalism and the fiction of the just law in the 1989 revolutionary events and subsequent transformations of post-communist societies into the liberal democratic regimes. After the general introduction, this chapter draws on the analysis of the decision-making process of the Czech Constitutional Court and its definitions of the legitimacy of the democratic and constitutional rule of law. The fiction of the just law and criticisms of legal formalism play a decisive role in the Court's judgments. Social effect and controversies accompanying the Court's judgments nevertheless reveal the impossibility of conceiving legitimacy as a problem of the sovereign interpretation and principles to which law and political domination must be subject.

The fifth chapter critically analyses the theory of autopoietic social systems. This theory benefits from the abandonment of relating the problem of legitimacy to the concept of political sovereignty. It comes with a procedural perspective in which legitimacy is transformed into the permanent processes of legitimation. The main argument of this chapter may, then, be summarised: it is impossible to reduce the legitimation procedures to the legal system, as suggested by the theory of autopoiesis, because legitimation always exceeds the system of law and involves its social environment.

The following sixth chapter concentrates on the unifying function of legality and its limits in relation to the social environment of the legal system and existing plurality of legitimations. Legality cannot support its legitimacy by confirming its sovereign status. This legitimacy is strengthened by the 'gaps' in legality and by the fact that legality is exposed to the pressure coming from its periphery and social environment which creates different legitimations as calls for socially comprehensible law. The second part of this chapter, then, takes the anti-communist dissent as an example of the strategy which moves the problem of legitimacy beyond the legal system and refuses to reduce this problem to the matters of political sovereignty and transcendental critique of legality. The dissident pragmatic use of the rhetoric of human rights shows this change of the problem of legitimacy.

The final seventh chapter returns to the fiction of the social contract and involves a synthesis of the arguments and conclusions elaborated in the previous chapters. The fiction of the social contract is formulated in such a way which makes it impossible to found legitimacy in authenticity and define the legitimation process as a permanent communication between the legal system and its social environment. This communication runs at the level of different (de)legitimation fictions. Instead of consensus, the communication gives priority to the acts of conversation in which plurality and heterogeneity have the same legitimating effect as the consensually established unity of political community.

2 Legitimacy Without a Sovereign People

Modern difficulties with legitimacy

In this chapter, I will discuss *democratic legitimacy of political domination* and the character of a legal system based on such legitimacy. Any modern democratic society is closely connected with the fiction of the social contract, which involves two other fictions: the fiction of the people as the sovereign holder of political power and the fiction of an achievable general consensus which determines the sphere of politics and public life in general.

The legitimacy of modern political domination and law involves contradictory hopes and fears. On the one hand, it is a typical feature of modernity that many of its ambitious goals and hopes may be realised only by political actions. The fiction of the people as politically sovereign is based on the ultimate concept of men as the masters of their world. The characteristic modern goals of liberation and progress can be understood only in a close relationship to politics, political institutions and decision-making processes. Moreover, the general will of the people must not be arbitrary or contingent. Democratic legitimacy must be accompanied by expert legitimacy. Democracy and expert knowledge are not necessarily contradictory, as it might appear from many criticisms of modern bureaucratic government. The generality of the people's will calls for the universal impersonal voice of an expert. According to Auguste Comte, experts must become politicians and thereby realise the utopia of positivism. Scientific method shall reveal moral and political truths, which must be recognised by everyone in the same way as mathematical and biological truths. In social processes, no arbitrariness may be accepted. The voice of an expert must rule, reveal social truth and purposes and define normatively the intellectual context, which must be accepted and shared by all.[1]

On the other hand, modernity also gives rise to the fear that social development does not go the right way and humankind, instead of realising 'the ideals of humanity', has created pathological forms of social life which will lead to decline and catastrophe. Modernity gives rise to the fear that humankind will not have enough wisdom to stand up to the demands of modern knowledge and ethics established on it. When Francis Bacon claimed that knowledge is power, he formulated the main idea of modernity that possession of knowledge would be the moral justification of political power. Every political power will appeal to this knowledge in order to justify its steps. The will to knowledge (Foucault, 1990) organises the power structures of modern world.

Although modern experts support such a vision, they often fear that the modern social development is not right and write essays on the decline of morals or civilisation in order to stop this pathological decline. For instance, Axel Honneth says that modern social philosophy is concerned with definition, analysis and the overcoming of pathological social processes (Honneth, 1994: 3ff.). This concept of social philosophy and sociology may be traced to Rousseau's contract model and belief that human nature is degraded in political conditions, or to Marx's analysis of 'alienation' as the dehumanisation of the modern world. It also is to be found in the more recent theories of Charles Taylor and Michel Foucault.

Axel Honneth's genealogical interpretation is too reductionist and its attempt to disclose a pattern in the development of modern social philosophy does not respect the specific nature of and the fundamental differences between the works of individual modern philosophers. One fact is nevertheless obvious - the widespread *ethos of social research*, the goal of which is to stop, heal and warn against the pathological development of modern humankind. Sociology wants to provide modern social, political and moral order with *scientific legitimacy*. It wants to participate actively in shaping the social order and to protect that order from what it calls irrational prejudices and unscientific ideological beliefs which hide the true nature of modern societies.

Modern social science does not want only to analyse pathological social phenomena; it also wants to treat them and keep 'the social body' in a good

---

[1]For one of many interpretations of Auguste Comte's positivism, see I. Berlin, 'Two Concepts of Liberty' (Berlin, 1969).

and 'healthy' condition. With some authors, for instance Karl Marx or Karl Mannheim, this ethos is very strong and essential; with others, like Max Weber and Raymond Aron, it is rather weak and marginal. It is as if the history of modern times was the history of social crises and sociology was both its expression and its treatment.

How is it possible to say that some social phenomena are pathological, while others are treated as healthy, organic and beneficial? Is the real purpose of scientific discourse to define the border between order and disorder? Are social stability and unity the final goal of any sociological research? Are there any constructions within the paradigm of social sciences, which are to produce this unity and stability? Prior to Honneth's interpretation of the modern history of social and political philosophy, the claim that a history of modern social sciences is the history of struggle with social decline was analysed by the Czech philosopher Jan Patočka in one of his *Heretical Essays* entitled 'Is Technological Civilisation Decadent, and Why?' Patočka refused to conceive social decline only in terms of moral judgment and sought to understand it as ultimately an existential part of the intrinsic nature of human life (Patočka, 1996: 96). Patočka's analysis also involves a critique of sociological objectivism and decisionism, which is always only 'a perspective *from without*' (Patočka, 1996: 98).

Patočka denies the possibility of giving a scientific legitimacy to modern social order and its political system. No science, be it sociology or legal theory, can describe and understand the complexity of modern world. This inability paradoxically leads to an ever greater effort of social sciences to rule in their own field, thereby achieve the status of a sovereign explanation of all problems existing there.

According to the logic of the modern social sciences, law may be stated only in legal language. Economics must be discussed exclusively in economic categories. Criminality ceases to be a crime and becomes a matter of social deviance. It is therefore extraordinarily important to understand how these objectifications emerge in the different fields of social sciences and into what *fictitious constructions* these objectifications are transformed in modern legal and political philosophy and sociology.

The legitimacy of legal rational political domination becomes the crucial question in modern societies because all claims to such legitimacy unite these societies at the symbolic level and make it possible to speak about society as if it were a whole, a system, or even an organism. Legitimacy is understood as a problem of unity and coherence, which turns out to be the most difficult problem in particularised and pluralistic societies. The attempts of sociology and political and legal philosophy to address this problem raises further problems such as the nature of law, political power, violence and force and ideologies dominating in modern societies.

Democratic legitimacy is an extraordinarily complex and contradictory topic because its claim to legitimacy is based on its general acceptance and universal consensus as an ultimate ethical value. Legitimacy therefore always raises moral issues.

The People - a sovereign of political power and morality

In *The Structure of Social Action* (Parsons, 1949), Talcott Parsons analyses the Hobbesian problem of the existence of social (political) order and asks why *force* and *fraud* are insufficient to establish it. Parsons poses this question in the archetypal modernist fashion by opposing force and fraud to rational persuasion. Rational arguments generate generally acknowledged values, conceived as obligations, and thus make modern social order possible (see, for instance, Honneth, 1993: 163-5). Parsons's perspective reminds Durkheim's sociology of morality and involves elements of purposive rationality typical of Hobbes's philosophy (see Habermas, 1987b: 210ff.). Sovereign political power is subject to a clearly defined moral obligation to enforce natural law in political society. This is the purpose of the social contract, which gives birth to Leviathan. Due to universal nature of the social contract, this political obligation achieves the character of a *universal moral convention*. One of the finest elaborations of this aspect of the social contract is Locke's political and legal theory.

The purposive rationality and the natural rights of individual political actors presupposed in modern theories of the social contract effect a great change in political, legal and social philosophy. *The fiction of the social contract* means that the problem of social or political order is the subject of a general communication among social actors which is to establish a solid social and political environment on the basis of consensus. This communication must not be impaired by any relation of subjection (as is the natural state) or domination. Under such circumstances, this communication is able to construct a legitimate political order and law.

Rational political communication is conceivable only when a new political subject, free and capable of voluntarily accepting contractual obligations, is defined. The fiction of the social contract is closely tied to the modern idea of citizenship and the concept of a moral person. Modern contractual theories are sometimes described as an expression of the civil thinking and philosophy of the 18th century (Honneth, 1993: 181). For instance, Ferguson's essay on civil society demonstrates how the two different political cultures and moralities - of enterpreneurs and soldiers can coexist on the basis of the soldiers being persuaded by the enterpreneurs to give up brute force in political life and accept the enterpreneurs' culture as beneficial for themselves. Ferguson, like Hobbes, gives a fundamental importance to the enterpreneurial (civil) persuasive power based on the advocacy of purposive action, which is finally adopted by a military class and thus leads to the establishment of the new civil society. Civil society is simply more beneficial for and therefore acceptable to everyone and on this basis becomes a legitimate political order (Ferguson, 1996).

The main theme of all these modern notions is the legitimacy of a new political sovereign, *the people.* The contractual way in which people create the political order, power and government is to establish and support the social harmony and agreement in the uncertain conditions of emerging modern societies. *Political consensus* therefore becomes the main mechanism of legitimate political domination.

The people can achieve a sovereign power only when general consensus is possible. However, this consensus does not have the form of a commonly shared tradition, because the contractual fiction replaced it with purposive rational communication concerning the conditions and limits of the commonly shared political world. Traditional or religious consensus is replaced by the consensus which emerges from the procedures of persuasion and is a product of rational argumentation. Dissent, conflict and struggle are regarded as the results of fundamental misunderstanding (Honneth, 1993: 293-4). The primary purpose of social contract theory was the constitution of the consensual politics, which would give the new political sovereign volitive and normative unity.

Nevertheless, this consensus cannot be understood purely in terms of the procedures of purposive rational negotiations. As analysed by Emile Durkheim, Max Weber and many others, every consensual mechanism must have its own normative framework. Even modern, civil, consensual society must have some moral integrity which sets limits to permissible communicative procedures and therefore to the permissible ways of achieving consensus.

The people are at the apex of modern political domination. The people can act as a body because individual citizens are capable of agreement and therefore of a uniting rational consensus. Political consensus cannot be only a product of the procedures of political decision-making, and its function is also the establishment of a coherent moral environment. The existence of this fact is usually referred to as the *democratic legitimacy* of modern political order and law. The belief that legitimate government must have the consent of its citizens is a truism, yet it is a very ambiguous and contradictory belief. Taken to its extreme, the ideology of consensus could well lead to a collapse of democratic political institutions, because not all our power mechanisms are subjected to the limited consensual technique of the majority decision-making (Dworkin, 1985: 37). Consensus cannot be reduced to the will of the majority government because such will is susceptible to momentary and arbitrary political influences. Besides any such empirical consensus, it is necessary to establish a more general normative framework of cultural and moral rights which would have the power to preserve the stability and coherence of modern political society.

Consensual democracy is not only a form of government; it is also the principal modern cultural value. Consequently, democratic legitimacy based on consensus must be divided into *empirical* consensual legitimacy and *symbolic* consensual legitimacy. Whilst empirical legitimacy can be measured statistically as refers to the extent of empirical public support of government, symbolic legitimacy refers to the *a priori* values and principles consented by all reasonable people and respected independently of the momentary political will of citizens.

Democracy has a strong symbolic meaning. When, in his Gettysburg speech in 1863, Abraham Lincoln famously talked of the government 'of the people, by the people, for the people', he did not mean a technique of government but rather a rich ultimate value, which must always be respected in modern political life.

Modern political domination is always based on the concepts of the people and sovereignty. But the French and American revolutions are good examples of the difficult tension between these two concepts. The first condition of their existence is a normative framework which can be consented by all people and is common to all people. This condition, however, immediately raises the problem of how the conceptual constructions of the sovereign people and its general consensus can be realised in practice. In the revolutionary France of 1789, the idea of the sovereign People became the main mechanism of both the stabilization and destabilisation of the political situation and clearly dominated the political language. Francois Furet writes that:

> No one believed it, though everyone professed to do so, since everyone was speaking in the name of the people. Nor did anyone have the power to create that consensus, even among those who might be called the 'men of 1789', and who were in agreement about the society and the kind of political regime they wanted. There was an essential instability inherent in revolutionary politics, as a consequence of which the periodic professions of faith concerning the 'stabilisation' of the Revolution unfailingly led to renewed bursts of revolutionary activity (Furet, 1981: 47).

To replace the old monarchical legitimacy with a new democratic legitimacy required political imagination. Legitimacy by the people and its general will turned out to be the most suitable for the idea of republicanism. In the future, it was claimed, the people will always be the final constitutive element of legitimacy. In his work 'What is the Third Estate?' (Sieyes, 1963), Sieyes expressed a contradiction which has always been present in the ideas of the sovereign people and democratic legitimacy. The people must include all individuals in a political nation, but the expression of its will can be the product only of the principle of political representation. There is an unavoidable tension between the people's will and the representation of this will in political bodies. The question '*Who is the people?*' implies a deep instability, because the concept of the people's general will, which is to establish the fictitious politically homogeneous environment, cannot face the heterogeneous reality of civil society. Stability turns into instability, security into insecurity.

Who are the people? Every attempt to answer this question and every definition instantly commits high treason against the interests of the people. The people, like Jehovah, can never have a concrete form or personification. Therefore, everyone who declares him/herself to be the will of the people becomes immediately a traitor and a counter-revolutionary (Žižek, 1991: 263ff.). Sieyes tried to avoid this ideological trap by dividing power into *constitutive* and *constituted* power. This distinction has become the basis of many modern political theoretical conceptual frameworks including the system for the democratic rule of law worked out in the historically first decision of the Constitutional Court of the Czech Republic (see especially the fourth chapter of this book). In this distinction, the people constitute the power and representative bodies are constituted powers which must follow the sovereign will of its constitutor - the people's will. The people imposes its will upon representative political bodies and acts as the ultimate political sovereign, and its actions can claim legitimacy because they are backed by the general will. The people replaced the king and aristocracy in the sovereign position and became the empirical sovereign through its political representatives.

This empirical position is possible only if the people are conceived as one body with one general will. Unity is possible only at the symbolic level. At the level of real empirical politics, this unity of the people is always 'damaged' by the heterogeneity of the will and actions of the people's representatives and by their particular political interests. The sovereignty of the people and democratic legitimacy are the pre-political foundations of the constitution of every modern political society. Nevertheless, they cannot be expressed in empirical political life otherwise than in the form of established representative bodies. Democratic legitimacy and its concepts of the people and the general will therefore oscillate between the stability and instability, between the sovereignty and high treason.

The problem of democratic legitimacy is postulated as a problem without a solution in its founding concepts. Legitimacy must have an empty form. This form, however, can never be fully legitimate. It has generality, yet it lacks the unity of the general will.

....

The metaphysical notion of the general consensus of the people must transform itself into concrete political and legal procedures and, at the same time, the *a priori* principles of formal procedural justice must be transformed into real democratic government. The speculative Enlightenment ideal central to modern thinking must be transferred into the sphere of practical politics and government.

In ancient Greek political philosophy, democracy was conceived as a form of government which did not necessarily have any moral value. In the

Enlightenment and during the revolutions, the opposite development gradually prevailed. Democracy had to be transformed from a metaphysical and moral ideal into the form of government and political power (Arendt, 1990: 225). Modern political domination presupposes democratic legitimacy in the sense of constructing all power, decision-making and enforcement from the will of citizens and all political institutions (directly or indirectly) being linked to the popular vote/will.

In order to avoid the tyranny of government without rules, it is necessary to define the people's power by political procedures and limits and subject democracy to the idea of republicanism (Arendt, 1990: 164-5), which involves respect for civic and individual freedoms (Kant, 1970: 98-9). But not even these limits and procedures can provide democratic political society with stability and long-term existence (Sartori, 1987: 186-7). Political power, enforcement and sanctions are not enough for the existence of any political society. This society is not built only on a system of command. It is built on political obligations (Plamenatz, 1968) and therefore on a voluntary commitment that cannot be secured by mechanism of political enforcement and sanctions. Political obligations maintain the integrity of political regimes.

This voluntary act refers us back to questions of moral integrity. Giovanni Sartori says that it is this political obligation which finally makes political domination legitimate. He understands the crisis of legitimacy as a crisis of authority and defines authority in terms of moral influence (Sartori, 1987: 187). Legitimate democratic domination has consequently *a double structure*: together with procedures of general vote and elections, which realise the idea of the people as political sovereign, and other electoral and appointment procedures within the framework of constitutional democratic regime, there must also be a general moral consensus on the acceptance of the structures and functions of democratically established political institutions. Democracy is both a technique of power and a moral condition with common ideals. Legitimacy then may seem to be provided by this second structure of general value consensus, which supports the legitimacy of democracy as a legally defined technique of power.

Popular government is to be founded on *the morality of the political people*. The people must be both a political and a *moral sovereign*. Consensus must be both procedurally technical in terms of power politics and moral in terms of cultural values. Consensus must overlap the heterogeneity and plurality of political society (Rawls, 1987). Because the idea of the people's sovereignty implies the process of the universalisation of government, democratic morality also has become universal, as is suggested in the wide acceptance of the concept of natural or human rights.

Democratic government, with procedures of political justice which emphasise individual rights and the consensually founded space of universal public morality, are also characteristic of those contemporary political theories which refuse to base justice and political order from some a priori notion of good. The main purpose of John Rawls's theory of justice, which is probably the most popular current political theory constructed from the social contract fiction, is to constitute, on the basis of the minimum consensus, a public political morality which would be able to provide an integrative framework for modern democratic societies. Within this framework, different comprehensive religious, philosophical and moral doctrines may coexist (Rawls, 1993: 36).

In Rawls' theory one quickly recognises the modern configuration of the sovereign will of the people, universally valid political morality, and consensually integrated political society. Unlike ethical liberalism, which primarily links justice to the moral category of good,[2] Rawls' liberalism defends a proceduralist position according to which people create a political society on the basis of contract and a notion of what is politically right but not morally good (Rawls, 1972). This is how 'justice as fairness' is realised. It is a concept of justice which can be agreed by all reasonable people if they do not have any knowledge about their real social position. Reason is universal and every individual, if s/he is to be a political actor, is a person capable of rational judgment. Reason is the entitlement of individuals to act as moral persons and negotiate with other people.

In Rawls's version, the democratic will and the people's sovereignty are derived from Kant's moral and universally valid category of the moral person and therefore Rawls is closer to the ideas of republicanism than to some organic notion of the people. Rational procedures cannot, however, function only as a cold political mediation, behind the borders of which there would be a chaotic and pluralistic world of private beliefs and ideologies. Political institutions are founded on the principle of *fairness* and contribute to the moral integrity of modern democratic societies and

---

[2]John Rawls treats the works of Joseph Raz or Ronald Dworkin as typical of ethical liberalism (Rawls, 1993: 135).

the establishment of democratic public culture. Even a democratic regime must win the support and trust of those subject to it. It can be secured only by the acceptance of the rationality of government, which can be consented by citizens of modern democracies and therefore established as binding public reason (Rawls, 1993: 212ff.).

In spite of the recognition of the plurality of ideologies, doctrines and private beliefs of citizens, the sphere of politics is identified with a moral integrity which rests on an all-embracing consensus about the political principles of fair decision-making. Rawls summarises his ideas about the legitimate liberal order in the following words:

> [o]ur exercise of political power is fully proper only when it is exercised in accordance with a constitution the essentials of which all citizens as free and equal may reasonably be expected to endorse in the light of principles and ideals acceptable to their common human reason. This is the liberal principle of legitimacy. To this it adds that all questions arising in the legislature that concern or border on constitutional essentials, or basic questions of justice, should also be settled, so far as possible, by principles and ideals that can be similarly endorsed. Only a political conception of justice that all citizens might be reasonably expected to endorse can serve as a basis of public reason and justification (Rawls, 1993: 137).

The political decision-making procedures established on the notion of justice as fairness depend on general consensus in order that government is supported by more than the threat of sanctions. A common democratic political morality established through practical reason must be formulated which might provide government with legitimacy. This morality creates the culture of civil society on which all modern constitutional democracies are based (Rawls, 1999: 134).

In the narrower context of examining the relationships between the legislator and citizens, Rawls defines the conditions of legitimate political domination and law in these words:

> [T]hus when, on a constitutional essential or matter of basic justice, all appropriate government officials act from and follow public reason, and when all reasonable citizens think of themselves ideally as if they were legislators following public reason, the legal enactment expressing the opinion of the majority is legitimate law. It may not be thought the most reasonable, or the most appropriate, by each, but it is politically (morally) binding on him or her as a citizen and is to be accepted as such. Each thinks that all have spoken and

> voted at least reasonably, and therefore all have followed public reason and honored their duty of civility.
>
> Hence the idea of political legitimacy based on the criterion of reciprocity says: Our exercise of political power is proper only when we sincerely believe that the reasons we would offer for our political actions - were we to state them as government officials - are sufficient, and we also reasonably think that other citizens might also reasonably accept those reasons (Rawls, 1999: 137).

The legitimacy of modern liberal democracies in Rawls' contractual model remains derived from the universal reason binding 'all reasonable beings' and normatively framing the limits of politically acceptable behaviour. Political consensus is built on this reason and contributes to the moral and rational integrity of modern democratic societies. It is instructive to see how Hobbes' and Ferguson's notion of reciprocity as the political basis of stable government is still central to current contractual theories of political liberalism.

The people may be the political sovereign only if its will can both be expressed in the structures of law and create the common framework of political culture and the moral principles of civil society. The overlapping consensus must be present both in the mechanics of government and the principles of civil society. Citizens have a duty to accept and unite in what is politically reasonable (Rawls, 1999: 132). This means that the moral life of modern democratic civil societies is not established on some essentialist concept of good, but rather on the good emerging from rational procedures and concept of fairness in its moral and political sense.

Sovereignty of discursive ethics?

The modern concept of legitimacy, which emphasises consensus, unity and universality, has two aspects - legal and moral. Political domination must be expressed in the impersonal language of the law in order to satisfy the demand of universality and general validity. Legality is the only technique of government, which can provide modern political domination with legitimacy. Law's legitimacy, however, does not come automatically and the legitimating scheme of the constitutional and democratic rule of law itself must rest on the concepts of the people's sovereignty and basic human rights (Habermas, 1987b: 178). Political morality underpins legal legitimacy. The legal system rests on the people's morality and consensus.

The constitution has the ultimate legal force, taking precedence over legislation, and must express the fundamental consensus about the principles of democratic political morality.

Human rights are not exclusively legal concepts for they also express the moral integrity of modern civil society. All the institutions of a constitutional democratic state should be obliged to protect this integrity. Hannah Arendt tells us *On Revolution* that the constitution is to create *novus ordo saeclorum* and 'conserve' the revolutionary process threatening to end in chaos (Arendt, 1990: ch. 4-5). Revolution contains the destructive element which is necessary to break up the old political order, but which also represents a potential threat to the new, emerging institutions inspired by revolution.

Revolution and the will of the people expressed in it must be melted and transformed into constitutional rules for the exercise of political power which respect human freedoms and civil rights. This is the only way to unite the post-revolutionary society and give legitimacy to the political institutions which emerge after the revolution. To escape the danger of the permanent revolution, revolution must become conservative. The French Revolution, according to Arendt, represents the first alternative, the permanent revolution, while the American Revolution represents the second one, the conservative revolution. The creation of *novus ordo saeclorum* is the most important task for all modern revolutions. The republican constitution, such as the Constitution of the United States of America, must limit the will of the people and turn it into 'cold' constitutional principles and legal rules.

Any legitimacy must then oscillate between the democratic will and its legal manifestation and limits. The democratic is defined and formalised in the constitution and its laws. The constitution and its laws must make the principles and techniques of democratic government the source of its legitimacy. Consensus and generality stand behind modern legality and form its moral political basis. On the other hand, this basis can have its concrete expression only through the language of constitutionality and legality.

……………………………………

One of the most complex theories of the legitimacy of the modern project of political domination undoubtedly is Habermas' theory of communicative reason, in which political communication undistorted by domination is shown to precede the democratic collective will formation and institutions of the rule of law/*Rechtsstaat*. Habermas refuses to conceive of the modernisation of politics only in terms of techniques of legality and criticises Max Weber for the 'elitism' of his concept of legitimacy by legality (Habermas, 1997: 73). The abstract structure of legal rules defining political domination and the rational character of administration are not sufficient to generate citizens' belief in their legitimacy. According to Habermas, in Weber the integrative function of law is too closely linked to bureaucratic domination, and therefore the inner rationality of modern law is sundered from judgments of citizens as the subjects of law and political power.

Although Weber also conceived of legal rationality in a moral practical sense, Habermas argues that he failed to take seriously an ethical formalism in his account of domination and legitimacy. Habermas argues that Weber's concepts of legitimacy and legality did not resolve the duality between autonomy of a unifying legal rationality and the general acceptance and belief that legality is right; such a duality of internal meaning and externally imposed discipline is, however, present in every legitimate domination.

Habermas also criticises the concepts of the legitimacy and the autonomy of law in Luhmann's systems theory as entirely ignoring this duality because it fails to understand law as an instrument of consensus formation and therefore turns the subjects of legal procedures into powerless elements that must learn to accept those procedures (Habermas, 1992: 579). Though the legal system's independence may be guaranteed only by law's internal rationality expressed in autonomous procedures, it is impossible to ignore that there are relationships between law and politics and law and morality even in highly complex modern society. According to Habermas, the rationality of law cannot be only a matter of law (Habermas, 1992: 580).

In what is it possible to identify the foundations of social integrity, if, as Habermas claims, the Hobbesian problem does not have a purely legal solution? Habermas' answer is the *communicative action*. In the same way that Emile Durkheim identifies the *conscience collective* and Talcott Parsons cultural symbolic unity as the basis of value consensus, so Habermas regards communicative action and communicative rationality as the normative and procedural foundation of post-conventional modern society. It is to eradicate the modern tension between system and life-world which leads to the crisis in legitimacy of modern political domination and the welfare state.

According to Habermas, modern society is pluralistic and differentiated to such an extent that its institutions are permanently challenged by the threat of dissent. The constituent parts of the life-world differentiate into autonomous systems of politics and economy. The life-world itself becomes pluralistic, its unity falls apart, and the space of possible dissent grows. The life-world is increasingly rationalised, split into fragments and colonized by different social systems with specific procedures and modes of communication (Habermas, 1987b: 324-5; Habermas, 1997: 27-8). Dissent and fragmentation are understood as pathological in that they limit the possibilities of social communication and thus weaken social integrity. Communicative action therefore aspires to the pre-dissensual sphere which is intrinsic to a coherent life-world. This world is symmetrically ordered around communicative everyday practice and the socio-historical network of communicative action (Habermas, 1997: 80). General communicative rationality overcomes the fragmentation of life-world.

According to Habermas, communicative action originally belongs neither to the world of moral norms nor to the world of strategic and purposive rational action. Nevertheless, some moral view of the world is present in it because it expresses *the principle of discourse*, which posits social communication free of domination and therefore requires principle of democracy and the democratic formation of political will. Discourse and communicative action are the sources of the legitimacy of law and the form of political domination in modern democracies (Habermas, 1997: 121). The legitimate rule of law/*Rechtsstaat* assumes the separation of powers and principle of impartiality in legislation, yet its legal procedures must also correspond to the democratic will formation and the people's will should correspond to the discursive principles that make communicative action and rationality a practical possibility (McCarthy, 1996: 1083). At this stage, law meets morality and politics and post-conventional modern society, according to Habermas, can integrate.

Habermas' *Legitimation Crisis* (1976) focuses on the problem that in late capitalist societies the demands on the state and its law lead to a lack of legitimacy and consequently to a crisis of political domination and authority. The political system can, up to a certain level, produce conformity by giving various compensations to sections of the populace, but there comes a point of crisis when the demands for compensation exceed the capacity of the system. Habermas believes that a lasting response to this crisis cannot be based on ever more complex economical and political strategy but must directly address the loss of normative force by the state. Consensus can be achieved only on the basis of recognition of general interests that may be communicatively shared (Habermas, 1976: 108). Respect for the conditions of communicative reason therefore must serve as the foundations of a sovereign discourse which unites the pluralistic political society, secures its integrity, and provides it with legitimacy.

Communicative action has supremacy over the system rationality of late capitalist society and eventually exposes its norms and values to the ultimate truth (Habermas, 1976: 95). This truth is the criterion of correctness which is immanent in continued communication and autonomous on any cognitive claims. According to Habermas, communication cannot be reduced to the purposive rationality of the contractual model in which all sides can negotiate even on the basis of irrational motives. These norms and values are recognised in the discursive procedures of mutual communicative actions and, therefore, unlike traditional values and norms, may always be questioned (Habermas, 1976: 105). The environment of discourse and communication nevertheless is clearly defined as a social unity with cultural integrity taking place in a defined space for public discussion.

The principle is necessarily regarded as *discourse ethics* and creates the universal foundation of political order and law which it provides thereby with legitimacy. Those claiming that their arguments are valid must subject those arguments to the procedures of rational general will formation and accept the rules of argumentative practice. Consensus is based on the *a priori* structures and strategies of communicative rationality. Values, interests, purposive choice of strategies and instruments are framed within communicative rationality, the moral political claims of which are universal.

Concepts such as consensus, compromise, agreement etc. have their roots in universal argumentation, in its structures, and its relations to the notion of correctness, but also, as Robert Alexy claims, to the notion of cognitive truth (Alexy, 1989: 187ff.). Alexy argues that discursivity is not only a matter of dialogue and communication. It also involves a set of monologues about the rules and norms which must be adopted by everyone who wants to participate in practical rational argumentation. All social discourses (pragmatic, ethico-political, moral, juristic or negotiative) have their final explanation in the communicative rationality, which is to be the ultimate foundation of the public world of politics and therefore also a necessary condition for the functioning and legitimacy of political and legal systems.

Political order and law are the systems with their own internal rationality. However, the extent of their legitimacy is finally dependent on the extent to which these systems are diffuse and open to moral discourse (Habermas, 1992: 565). Habermas' claim that there is a common basis to morality, law and politics is certainly not another naturalist or moralist theory which defines a moral content of law and places it above the positive law. This universal morality of communicative reason is already contained in the internal rationality of law (Luhmann, 1996: 898) and politics and has a purely procedural nature. This morality cannot have the strategic nature of the empirical legal system, but formal procedural morality and empirical legal process should be in a relationship of mutual control (Habermas, 1992: 568).

In this context, Habermas draws a distinction between morality and legitimacy:

> the expression 'legitimacy' designates the specific kind of prescriptive validity that distinguishes law from 'morality'. Valid moral norms are 'right' in the discourse-theoretic sense of just. Valid legal norms indeed harmonize with moral norms, but they are 'legitimate' in the sense that they additionally express an authentic self-understanding of the legal community, the fair consideration of the values and interests distributed in it, and the purposive-rational choice of strategies and means in the pursuit of policies (Habermas, 1997: 155-6).

Legitimate law must satisfy the claims of universal discourse morality and rationality. Habermas wishes to supplement the legal procedures of the constitutional rule of law system with the more fundamental procedures of the communicative rationality, which also are formal and so can provide contemporary complex societies with moral universalism. The democratic collective will formation is not merely a legal technical matter but must be situated in the broader structures of social communication and the civil culture of consensus and understanding. The procedures of democratic legislation can embrace both communicative and juristic rationality. The collective will is shaped both instrumentally and on the basis of the values of communicative rationality (and therefore democratically and without political imposition and domination). This is absolutely essential for the legitimacy of law (Habermas, 1992: 565, 569ff.).

....

Habermas believes that democratic procedures must be founded on the broader practical rationality of communicative action and discourse ethics which will furnish the possibility of a general consensus. In his theory, democratic will formation based on the discourse principle is a mixture of prescriptive contents and the Weberian value-neutral concept of political domination (Rasmussen, 1996: 28). Dissent is only a side effect and risk accompanying communication in modern societies. Even the concept of human rights, which is as important as the democratic principle (which, according to Habermas, may itself be derived from discourse ethics), appears to be only an expression of cultural and political consensus.

This concept of legitimate political domination and the rule of law may be summarised thus: the internal rationality of law and the legitimacy of legal procedures is not an exclusive matter of law; it is rather based on the procedures of communicative rationality which can claim universal moral validity and binding force. The legitimacy of legal procedures is established by the openness of law toward the moral demands of communicative action. Such moral legitimacy must grow from public engagement based on a common will of individuals to participate in political communication. It is this communication that has the power to establish legitimacy and trust in political and legal institutions.

Habermas makes powerful attempt to remove the tension between democratic procedures of the collective will formation (which realise the idea of the people's sovereignty) and the concept of human rights, which originally were not derived from the democratic collective will but were justified by the ideology of inviolable natural rights recognised through human reason able to comprehend a universal ethics. In Habermas' theory, human rights are not conceived in this Kantian transcendent sense. They are formulated against the background of the universality of procedures and rules established by the discourse principle and communicative rationality. However, human rights in this way are intimately linked to the idea of public discourse and democracy.

The moral basis of human rights in traditional natural law is replaced in the discourse theory by their discursive definition, which means that they become just a product of the collective will. The basic tension inherent in the modern rule of law is thereby resolved in favour of the principle of the sovereignty of the discursive procedures, which diluted the principle of the people's sovereignty. The autonomy of the concept of human rights is reduced to the public world of discourse subject to *a priori* rules and limits of political and moral consensus.

The notion of social and political emancipation, so intrinsic to Habermas' political ethos, is imaginable only as a form of *integration* into the collective processes of communication within the environment of homogeneous values. This precedence of social integration and subjection of heterogeneity to the unified discursive environment has been criticised as 'the collectivisation of reason' (Weinberger, 1996: 172).

During the 90s, Habermas significantly moved away from his original solution to the legitimation crisis of late capitalism. The notion of one unifying discourse entrenched in practical reason and communicative force was gradually replaced by a recognition of discourse plurality and a search for those discursive procedures which would be able to neutralise this plurality and thus create legitimate political conditions and law. But though discourse compatibility seemingly is an improvement upon discourse unity (Habermas, 1997: 167), Habermas continues to oscillate between the 'heterarchy of relative discourses' and 'erecting the hierarchy of a super-discourse' (Teubner, 1996: 907).

The purpose of the discourse procedures is to unite the heterogeneity of discourses and create a common political space with generally binding rules. These procedures respect the specific nature of different discourses, yet they have the power to subject them to one communicative framework. A moral legal super-discourse is thus being born which limits and normatively defines the external impact of all particular discourses.

The modern drama of the struggle between autonomy and subjection is given yet another form here. Habermas seeks to resolve the struggle by giving priority over the internal logics of different discourses to discourse procedures. These procedures are superior because they have universal validity and lead to the formulation of general political goals. The Enlightenment paradox of the individual who is free and has civil rights only on condition that s/he subjects her/his actions to universally binding rules or procedures retains its original structure in Habermas' social and legal philosophy. The rejection of the Kantian transcendental philosophy only makes it necessary to understand universality in close relation to the collective processes of democratic communication and decision-making. The goal of communicative rationality is consensus and the processes of communication necessarily imply a norm which may be imposed upon those who do not share the ideal of the communicative commonwealth (Welsch, 1996: 117, 119).

In comparison with the legal procedural model of legitimacy, the problem of legitimacy is expanded from anonymous procedures of law into the democratic political institutions and their subjection to the rules and procedures of communicative reason. Habermas claims that compromise reached through negotiation is only one of many ways that can set up collective goals. But this implies that there must exist a consensus about value orientations, which makes it possible to compromise different interests and resolve interpersonal conflicts (Habermas, 1989: 145). It is consensus and not compromise which secures the integrity of the social fabric. And this consensus requires subjection to the regime of truth/correctness as revealed in universal communicative rationality. The democratically formed collective will is to embrace the principle of the recognition (and if necessary the emancipation) of heterogeneous opinions and conflictual beliefs. The basis of that will is, however, a unity which makes it possible that we are all able to agree and reach consensus in the public world of politics. Unity turns out to be necessary when the political and social world is to be constructed from the grand fiction of the people and established through the participation of the individuals of this world.

In Habermas' theory there is certainly no place for Rousseau's romantic concept of the people as one organism with its own will, for in that theory the people were 'diluted' into procedures (Habermas, 1997: 463ff.). The procedures in which the people are present which can claim sovereignty because of its formalistic, moral, universal character, are the procedures of communicative rationality able to integrate society, avoid the threat of dissent and still keep the acceptable level of heterogeneity and plurality. In order to keep *democracy* legitimate, it does not have to be the people's democracy, but rather *communicative* democracy. Instead of the narrow concept of democratic legitimacy as a state founded on democratic procedures of power distribution, Habermas comes up with the concept of decentralised discursive legitimacy which recognises the segmentation of civil society. Discourse procedures form the democratic collective will at all levels of civil society and the state is only one of many social institutions which must respect those procedures in order to conform to the demands of legitimacy. Legitimacy is not a matter only of the character of the institutions of political domination. It is primarily a matter of the discourse procedures, the validity of which goes beyond state and law into every field of civil society (for further discussions concerning the discourse theory see also Rorty, 1998: 307-26).

The sovereignty of the discourse principle and communicative rationality borrows the characteristics of the sovereignty of the people (Cohen, 1999: 385-416). In spite of all the moral warnings which led to the attempt to free individuals from system dependence by placing law between system (as an institution) and life-world (as a structure of action), *the individual remains a functionary of the whole* in the regime of discourse procedures. Kierkegaard's characterisation of modernity as a condition of atomisation when people (though in mutual relations) act as isolated individuals and are not concrete living people may well be applied to Habermas' communicative procedures, although his original goal was to integrate the elements of authentic political community into the political and legal systems. If an individual does not want to participate in the process of universalisation, s/he either remains outside the sphere of politics, or is forcibly absorbed by it by the normative power of communicative rationality. Upon entering this sphere, s/he becomes one of many elements of the communicative masses.

Discourse ethics distinguishes between the private and public freedom. However, differences between the processes of the individual and collective will formation do not play an important part in the securing of legitimacy. Legitimacy is finally always a question of the collective will formation which must occur according to the pre-existing procedures of discourse freed from any domination and enforcement. The differences existing between different formations of different wills and strategies in the contemporary social conditions have no impact on the discursive concept of legitimacy as the procedural unity of the political space. Habermas did not resolve the modern political puzzle. He transferred it from legal procedures into the world of communication and discourse procedures based on the democratic consensus.

On the road to mega-polis

The determination of policy towards political consensus turns on the answer to two questions: is consensus in contemporary heterogeneous and pluralistic society possible? And is consensus necessary for the preservation of that society and its culture? Addressing this second question leads one further to ask whether the goal of every politics and law is to overcome diversity and plurality in order to create an integrated space, the constituent principles of which are universally acceptable and therefore able to generate the social and political consensus which makes law and political domination legitimate and enforceable. Might it not rather be the case that political institutions and the system of positive law generate plurality and is not this plurality their constituent element? To answer 'yes' would imply that the pursuit of consensus so typical of the modern liberal democracies should be turned upside down. The primary purpose of political and legal institutions would not be so much to secure the minimum integrity, but rather to produce the maximum plurality.

The discourse theory of law and politics needs communicative rationality, which presupposes a certain collectivity, in order to formulate a category of general norms on which the legitimacy of law and political order can be based. This collectivity is a highly idealised form of democratic community in which the process of political decision-making is not distorted by asymmetries of power. Its universal foundation requires that it be located in the rhetoric of the people, although it is defined in terms of the procedure through which all actors sharing the discourse and constructing a consensually established democratic collective will.

According to Habermas, the ability of actors to achieve consensus in their discourse is a necessary condition required for them to pass judgments concerning the truth or falsity of statements expressed in the discourse. Collective decision-making is a criterion of truth (Habermas, 1984: 219). Are those who refuse to or who cannot participate in this communication and collective will formation denied the ability to decide upon truth? Do disagreement and dissent, which certainly are important moments of the dynamic of modern society, have any legitimacy in this condition? What is the role of Kant's independent critical thinker *(Selbstdenker)* in the community, in which all steps are oriented to the general consensus and the purpose of communication is a unification of statements?

Ota Weinberger's legal positivist critique of 'discursive collectivism', which is close to the left-wing political ideas, assumes that the normative powers of reason cannot be determined by collective decision-making because they have an *a priori* character in the Kantian sense (Weinberger, 1996). Another legal theoretical critique of discourse theory, but one which is politically conservative, emerges from Richard Posner's polemic with Bruce Ackerman. Posner rejects Ackerman's theory of rational discourse as the legitimating foundation of political order, law and individual rights. Like Weinberger, Posner objects that legitimation by rational discourse and the participation of people in it

> makes the status of idiots and children - even of adults who are not sufficiently intelligent or well educated to be able to debate issues of political legitimacy – problematic (Posner, 1990: 336).

Habermas' concept of discourse ethics and Ackerman's dialogical concept of legitimacy (which is significantly influenced by Habermas) assume a participation in collective procedures which leads to a consensus able to claim a universal binding force. The two main objections may then be summarised as follows: not everybody wants or can participate in this process and some norms and obligations are valid independent of whether they are the product of the consent of people as political actors. Discourse and consensus as its consequence cannot be the sovereign foundation of political and legal norms.

Posner rejects every such attempt to subject law and its procedures to other fields of social practice and thinking, in this case to political consensus (Posner, 1990: 126). The validity of law and its decision-making processes are independent of political consensus, which is always merely a temporary expression of the will of the more powerful in democratic society. Consensus cannot legitimate the validity of law. The ideal speech situation, which secures the formation of a domination-free political consensus in Habermas' theory, has no implication for the validity of a legal norm forbidding murder. Law has much more complex sources of normativity and cannot be subjected to the political consensus.

The discursive coalition of legitimacy and universality also faces another objection, that the declared universality and legitimacy of political consensus is only one of many voices in the contemporary situation of cultural heterogeneity and political pluralism. The crucial question may be then summarised: is it possible to take the consensus concerning cultural values and social norms as an overarching political strategy in contemporary liberal democracies and their legal systems?

R.A. Dahl explores this aspect of democracy through his concept of *polyarchy* (Dahl, 1971). Polyarchy recognises that democracy involves a very high level of control of the administration and public office bureaucrats, which may be exercised by individual citizens and groups in their differences, uniqueness and heterogeneity. In democracy, plurality appears to have at least the same importance as unity. Making it impossible for anyone to occupy and rule the public space absolutely and against everyone secures the openness of that sphere. Liberty and limited government are secured by the subjection of political domination to political criticism from many different perspectives. Constant tension and confrontation between different political beliefs and goals seem to be the typical feature of contemporary liberal democracies. The obvious failures of the consensual political mechanisms of majority will decision-making only emphasise the fact that every political will is actually particular and contingent and there is no moral coherence in current social conditions.

The well known tension between democracy as normative ideal and democracy as a fact is easily recognisable in the polyarchical vocabulary of contemporary liberal democracies. Polyarchy is an unpredicted consequence of the sovereignty of the people. The people can rule only when it can express its will. However, at the moment of its expression, there is no guarantee that this will is going to be united. Discourse ethics is to serve as such a guarantee of unification, but its normative structures in fact do not work and contemporary democracies rely on the pluralistic condition of polyarchy in which no opinion is universally generalisable and always has only a socially limited validity. Instead of the general will, it is plurality and the unlimited nature of particular political wills that constitutes the empirical politics of contemporary liberal democracies. The emphasis on democratic consensus present in the discourse theory turns out to be inadequate.

Against this background, it seems that the ideal of the Greek *polis* as a closely tied and culturally and politically homogeneous community is irrelevant to current conditions. Instead of the ideal of *polis*, contemporary people are challenged by a globalised *mega-polis* (Sartori, 1987: 26). The collective bodies of contemporary democracies cannot and do not satisfy both the demand that they express the will of the whole community and the demand that they contribute to the self-perfection of every member of this community. No expression of the political will can claim universal validity. Nowadays, collective democratic decision-making must give up such ambitions. It would even be a highly dangerous business to attempt to revive the principle of the unity of a community or people as an organic collectivity. Contemporary *mega-polis* is not a single organism. It is a highly abstract construction, the structure of which initiates atomisation, depersonalisation and anonymity. One of the main languages of these structures is obviously the language of legality (Unger, 1996).

Contemporary democratic societies have lost the power to cultivate wo/man in her/his individuality and adjust individuals to the universal ideal of humanity. However, the ideals of individuality and autonomy still exist in *mega-polis*. They ceased to enjoy paramount status as political goals, but they persist as a consequence of liberal democratic politics, which cannot do other than maintain respect for them. *Mega-polis* is not dominated by the distinction of the private and public worlds, in which the public means integrity and the private means plurality. In other words, it does not have any criterion or leading principle according to which it would be possible to establish Rawlsian reasonable pluralism (Rawls, 1993: 36; Rawls, 1999: 11). The public of *mega-polis* is itself pluralistic and differentiated to such an extent that it is unclear what is particular and general. The public world of politics and law of liberal democracies is actively invaded by different ideologies and comprehensive moral and religious doctrines and their influence is not limited, as conceived by liberals like Rawls, by some democratic government integrated by public reason and legitimated by the overlapping consensus. Serious limitations on the influence of consensus are often generated by the very fact of political plurality and the impossibility of utterly dominating other doctrines in a fair political contest. In other words, plurality itself is a regulative principle of the life of *mega-polis*.

Mega-polis is 'cold', but its structures make it possible to accommodate many different communities which can co-exist with each other. Autonomy, independence, plurality and heterogeneity are its main features. *Mega-polis* is not an anonymous machine extinguishing all moral and educative demands of *polis*. Due to the self-restraint of its own political ambitions, this machine can have benign moral consequences because it opens a space for different life-worlds and individual fragments of experience. These life-worlds open new possibilities of solidarity and political or legal culture which is not entirely subject of the ideal of political unity. *Mega-polis* itself paradoxically and indirectly becomes a moral product.

Revolution without the people

In its recent history, Europe has witnessed a unique set of political changes which, though taking place in former totalitarian societies, has raised the general problem of the heterogeneity of liberal democratic order. The revolutionary changes in Central and Eastern Europe in 1989 obviously have blown apart whatever legitimacy was left to totalitarian systems. They also have disclosed the limits of the legitimacy based on consensus of the democratic rule of law. In order to assess what, if anything, remains legitimate in the idea of the collectivity of the people as the modern political sovereign in the contemporary situation of growing social heterogeneity and pluralisation, it is essential to analyse the 1989 revolutionary events in communist countries. It is necessary to emphasise the fact that totalitarian communist regimes called themselves ‘people’s democracies’. The concept of the people was exploited by those regimes for ideological purposes. Why, then, did the people’s democracies cease to exist? What ideological shifts accompanied the fall of communism? What decisive discursive and strategic moments lay behind the revolutionary changes of 1989?

Every revolution raises the fundamental question of what remains legitimate and what can no longer be treated as legitimate. The importance of political legitimacy is revealed in the revolutionary gap separating the past from future. Legitimating strategies applied during revolutions define the framework of the future space of politics and thus overcome the instability caused by revolutionary processes. The revolutions of 1989 contained their own sources of legitimacy which significantly differed from common notions of democratic legitimacy, the people’s will and general consensus. Those sources of legitimacy cannot be reduced to discursive procedures because communicative rationality and consensus represented only one of many revolutionary strategies and that particular one had only a limited impact on the whole process of revolution and subsequently on the establishment of the new system of political domination and law. The 1989 revolutions radically changed our basic understanding of the possibilities of political legitimation because they were not accompanied by any legitimation fiction having a sovereign constructive role in the normative framework of new political order. The fiction of the people's sovereignty and its general will, which determined all prior modern revolutions, could not stand as a unified political vocabulary and therefore functioned only as one of many revolutionary elements in these events of 1989.

It is possible to describe the revolutionary changes in the former Soviet bloc countries as one common process only at the level of journalistic simplification or very insensitive political analysis. Though there were many features common to the revolutions in all former Soviet bloc countries, it is essential to stress that each had its own specific socio-political, economic and legal dynamics.

The changes in Hungary were dominated by political decisions taken by the communist party and political opposition groups were integrated into a coordinated process of political transformation. Political opposition emerged as a deliberate consequence of the reformist efforts of the communist party élite (Stokes, 1993: 78f.). This élite initiated liberal democratic political changes in the belief that this move would bring it advantages in the new political conditions which were to be brought about by political reform.

In Poland, Solidarnosc and the Catholic Church represented strong popular political opposition which had to be respected by the communist system and which, when the international political situation changed in the late 80s, could apply strong pressure for the transformation of the one party political regime (Stokes, 1993: 102f.). Unlike the Hungarian communists, Polish communists always grudgingly responded to political pressure by making concessions to the popular anti-communist resistance movement.

Unlike the gradual reform which took place in Hungary and Poland in the late 80s, culminating in the dissolution of the totalitarian system during 1989, the political regimes in Czechoslovakia, East Germany, Romania and other Soviet bloc countries remained inflexible during this period, in which their ruling party élites were unwilling to make any political changes. Revolutionary changes in those countries were concentrated into a shorter time. The fall of the Berlin wall remains probably the biggest, the most emotional, and most popular symbol of all the 1989 changes in the European Soviet Bloc countries.

The fall of communism in Poland, Hungary or Czechoslovakia is impossible to explain by reference to stereotypical images of modern revolution. Though in Czechoslovakia, unlike in Poland and Hungary, the changes occurred very quickly under the direct pressure of crowds in the streets, some politicians and revolutionary leaders refuse to refer to those events as the revolution. A famous Czech novelist and dissident Ludvík Vaculík even preferred to talk about 'the coup of nice people against nasty people'.

This statement stresses the fact that the former totalitarian regime met with primarily a moral condemnation and not the total political confrontation which is more typical of modern revolutions and leads to the eradication (political or even physical) of representatives of the former regime. After 1989, it was most important to transform 'wicked' legal and political systems (for the concept of 'wicked legal systems' see Dyzenhaus, 1991) into the 'decent' liberal democratic societies and this involved the social integration even of those who represented the former regime. What, then, was the nature of the change, which overthrew the communist regime, until then thought to be omnipotent, its coercive power and control ubiquitous, but no shop-window was broken? Did this represent something unique and new in modern history?

The most surprising fact about the whole revolutionary process in Czechoslovakia and other countries of the former Soviet Bloc was the absence of the people in the ideological discourse of the revolution. It may appear quite absurd to imagine a modern revolution without the fiction of the people as the sovereign political actor that pulls down and re-builds political institutions. Political modernity was born in the moment when political reality ceased to be regarded as a product of tradition and came to be regarded as a product of human will. Modern politics is always an expression of the will of the people and every revolution must therefore call for democratic legitimacy. What other than the will of the people can make a revolution in modern social and political conditions? In modern revolution, the people create their political institutions on the ruins of the old regime and against its power and therefore create new institutions *ex nihilo* in the theological sense (Schmitt, 1985b).

With regard to Czechoslovakia, the claim that the people were absent from the revolution also might seem indefensible. The resounding phrase of the seventeenth-century Czech scholar Comenius 'People, your power has returned to you', which was quoted by T.G. Masaryk in his inaugural address as first President of Czechoslovakia in 1918 and used in Marta Kubišová's famous 1968 pop-song reacting to the Warsaw Pact invasion, became one of the most popular slogans of the Velvet Revolution and was used by Václav Havel in his New Year's address after he had been elected President of Czechoslovakia in December 1989.

It is therefore no surprise that the historian and journalist Timothy Garton Ash named his book about the revolutions of 1989 *We the People* (1990). He himself, however, shows a high sensitivity for the specific character of those events when drawing historical parallels with other modern revolutions (Garton Ash, 1990: 131ff.). Who were the people, then, who made the 1989 revolutions possible? Was it the ultimate agent in human history, as understood by some modern political thinkers, or can we see a change in the meaning of this concept when sufficiently carefully examining the inner logic of the revolutionary changes of 1989?

To illustrate this problem, I think it is useful to recall what people marching through the Leipzig streets in October 1989 were chanting. They were chanting 'Wir sind das Volk (We are the people)'and at the same time 'Wir sind ein Volk (We are one people)' (Stokes, 1993: 140). This grammatical duality and tension between the definite and the indefinite article reflects, in my view, the whole complicated and sometimes contradictory nature of the 1989 revolutions. Obviously, these revolutions were an open political protest against the totalitarian communist regime which denied people any access to and participation in political life. People demanded free elections, the separation of political powers, and civil rights, in sum, the well known institutional framework of western liberal democracy. People called for the reconstruction of the western model of liberal democracy which had been hidden behind the 'Iron Curtain' and which, unlike the Soviet model of people's democracy, seemed to work. In that sense, people were, of course, the people who asked for a liberal democratic and constitutional regime and therefore for the sovereignty through free elections and representation.

How should one understand, however, the slogan 'We are one people'? Its German formulation may be understood in terms of call for one united nation, which had been forced to live in two separate states and now called for its reunification. This demand already exceeds the institutional framework of democracy, because the political people, *demos,* is formulating its political goal in terms of the reunification of a separated *ethnos.* Such a demand involves the danger of a nationalist and holistic concept of politics which has always been the problem of modern German political history. However, the slogan 'We are one people' also indicates that the word 'people' does not necessarily need to have a sovereign political meaning and can refer to a much more differentiated and complex cultural framework and community. People do not have to be grammatically defined only by the definite article. The indefinite article may well point to the heterogeneity and vagueness of the whole concept of a/the people. The political catastrophe of modern European history was then, when the people as *ethnos* subjected all the functions of the politically sovereign people, *demos*, to a unity of the state on the basis of blood and soil, not constitution and citizenship.

But similar references to 'people' instead of 'the people' could be heard, for instance, in Budapest or Prague. Unlike a sovereign subject of history called 'the people', people originally formulated their goals in a more existential and moral language and accused the communist regime of constant lies and propaganda. People refused to live any longer like 'laboratory rabbits' for the project of real socialism and communism (Garton Ash, 1990: 50, 71ff.). In this sense, people demanded something more than simply political reform. They demanded to be freed from totalitarian politics. They were fed up with ideological lies and communist politics with its various '-isms' (Urban, 1990: 124-6). They wanted to live a decent life as people in their singularity, uniqueness and autonomy.

The open and polyarchical space of the forum

When talking of the absence of the people, the concept of the people should be understood as an historical agent, united in one social and political vision, which is to be brought into being. People in the former Soviet Bloc countries did not have to use as much political imagination in their revolutions as did the French or the American people in theirs two hundred years ago, because the model of the political institutional framework they were asking for already existed in the western liberal democracies (compare Dahrendorf, 1990). To talk about the absence of the people is not to ignore the quest for democratic legitimacy by the velvet revolutions. It is rather to perceive the 1989 events as a quest for a number of parallel legitimations, without any overall legitimation scheme. Liberal legitimation could seem dominant at some stage, yet it was accompanied by many other alternatives, from the ethnic nationalistic to the communitarian.

The events of 1989 took on a significantly pluralistic nature in the way they dismantled communist totalitarian systems. The common ideological denominator of this revolution was purely negative. It was to get rid of communist ideological lies (Garton Ash, 1990: 136). Some scholars even speak about the 'revolutions against the Revolution' (Arato, 1993: 673) because they denied the logic of modern revolutions. Slogans chanted during the general strike or written on banners lacked any unifying ideology, complex political programme or propaganda. A plurality of and differences between popular political rhetoric were characteristic of the Velvet Revolution in Czechoslovakia. On streets and squares there was not the people, rather there were different people with different demands and ideals, united only by the repugnance they felt for the communist regime. The only common thing connecting people in November 1989 was a total disgust with the regime which, although it provided them with a minimum level of welfare and economic security, robbed them of those crucial civil rights, which constitute the main political or rather existential condition of every liberal and decent society. This condition, as Orwell put it in *1984*, consists of the freedom to say that 'two plus two equal four'. According to Winston Smith, the hero of *1984*, all other freedoms may be derived from this simple 'pre-political' freedom. This existential motif characterised the negative political will of the Czechs and Slovaks, of the Hungarians, Poles, Germans, and of the other nations in former communist Europe.

People demanded the reconstruction of those political democratic institutions, which owe their very existence to the concept of the sovereign people, but at the same time were rather cautious about using the term 'the people' in the ideological framework and discourse of the revolutions. The reason lies in the fact that this concept was so heavily exploited by communist ideology and propaganda and legitimated so many political crimes committed by the communist regimes. In communist systems, the Party élite always spoke in the name of the people, but in fact permanently humiliated people's dignity. The names of the revolutionary organisations themselves are a good illustration of this revolutionary hostility to the people. Instead of the cliché of the people, they used 'forum', which connotes an open public space to which there is unrestricted access and certainly no pre-existent definition of those who are permitted to speak in such a space.[3]

---

[3]In Hungary - The Democratic Forum; in German Democratic Republic - The New Forum; in the Czech Republic - The Civic Forum; in Slovakia - The Public Against Violence.

The 1989 revolutions provided further confirmation of the fact that every modern political ideology must respect the idea of the popular government, even the totalitarian and authoritarian ideologies of communism, fascism and Nazism. The importance of democratic legitimacy even to dictatorships was analysed for instance by Franz Neumann who said:

> [S]ince modern totalitarian dictatorships arise, almost without exception, within and against democracies (weak though the democratic structures may have been), the totalitarian clique has to assume the shape of a democratic movement and to retain this facade even after it has come to power. In other words, it is forced to practice the ritual of democracy even though the substance is totally denied (Neumann, 1964: 244).

During the 1989 revolutions, a new caution about the vocabulary of democracy emerged. This was only partly caused by the previous exploitation of this vocabulary in communist ideology, in which the use of words like the people and people's democracy had given rise to a monopoly of political power and enormous political repression.

The velvet revolutions were not then conceptualised so much in terms of the sovereign power of the people, but rather in terms of freedoms and autonomy of those who make up the people. The sovereign people disappeared, and was replaced by a strategy demanding pluralisation and autonomisation of different forms of life (for similar conclusions see, for example, Preuss, 1993: 639-60).

The 1989 revolutions posed an historic challenge to the former conception of legitimacy in the terms of the centralised model and unifying fictions of modern society. They were initiated by decentralizing efforts. The original legitimacy of these revolutions was negative, because they were first of all successful attempts to escape from a highly integrated repressive system, which sought, like other modern political systems, to legitimate itself democratically, although the concept of the sovereign people had been supplemented by the concept of the 'working people'.

This negative attitude which necessarily followed from the revolutionary attempt to escape from the totalitarian system was already evident in the round-table talks which started radically to change the political situation in Poland and Hungary during 1989 and later became a typical feature of the revolutions in other East European communist countries (Elster, 1995). Neither the communist governments nor the dissidents had democratic legitimacy in the round table talks because they did not participate in those talks as elected representatives of the people. The communist governments did not hold political power because they had won a free election contest. The dissident groups enjoyed the spontaneous (and later organised) support of the public, but they also had not passed the test of free elections which would have provided them with a strong democratic mandate. The main purpose of the round table talks was a transformation of politics through the establishment of political and social plurality and the creation of a system of checks and balances between different branches of constitutional power. The legitimacy of the round table talks was entirely based on the pragmatic necessity of changes to the system, and these changes were designed and drafted by élite and expert groups of negotiators.

The revolutions gave a pluralistic character to the concept of the people. The identity of the people as the constitutor of political power ceased to be based in unity and consensus. The people's identity was defined in terms of plurality and heterogeneity. In January 1990, there were about two hundred political parties and movements in Czechoslovakia, which illustrates how fascinated people were by the possibility of social and political plurality and how important the process of differentiation was at that time. The communist party's support eventually stabilised at only between 12 and 15 percent, and those traditional parties formerly organised in the National Front[4] were left with limited political influence. The dominating political organisation in two republics of the Czechoslovak federation was the Civic Forum in the Czech Republic and the Public Against Violence in Slovakia (Bankowicz, 1991: 157ff.). The original structure of the Civic Forum as a revolutionary organisation articulating political demands against the communist power emerged from the fact that the people in the sense of organic unity and discursive force was absent from the Forum. The Forum's organisation was heavily decentralised and in fact anyone, anywhere (in factories, schools, administration, or army), could decide to form a local unit of the Civic Forum together with other

[4]The National Front was an organisation ruled by the Communist party, in which other political parties, namely the Socialist Party (its programme before February 1948 was founded on the ideas of social redistribution and the protection of national identity) and the People's Party (a Christian Democratic party with support mostly in rural areas) were forced to unite after 1948. After 1989, those parties emancipated into independent political forces, again, but only the People's Party survived and its support is between 8 and 10 percent.

individuals critical of the communist regime. Dissidents allied with critical communists, intellectuals allied with workers, students allied with artists, Catholics allied with atheists, and neo-liberal economists allied with adherents of 'socialism with human face', all those people cooperated within the Civic Forum and Public Against Violence organisations.

In the first weeks of the Velvet Revolution, informality of structure was the main characteristic of both revolutionary organisations because their primary task was to bring together all who were critical of the communist regime and who wanted to support revolutionary changes. The Prague Coordination Centre of the Civic Forum became a centre because of its strategic location in the capital and due to the authority earned by the former dissidents, striking university students and courageous artists who had called for the general strike and had opened theatres for public discussion until then strictly prohibited by the communist regime (Garton Ash, 1990: 89ff.). Theatre stages became political forums where anybody could speak and nobody was subjected to the strict procedural logic of the majority will. There was always a space for promulgations of and argument between different opinions. This was the main reason why all Civic Forum organisations soon started to split, which itself eventually turned out to be an extremely positive consequence of the strategy of plurality and heterogeneity.

The Civic Forum involved the structures of polyarchy and initiated their establishment in the new political condition. The important and unique role of the Civic Forum was to dismantle the institutions of communist power. Later, the revolutionary force of the Civic Forum was turned into a process of natural restructuring and differentiation of society. The Civic Forum had to be torn apart and disappear so that its inner plurality of vocabularies and political differentiation could be transferred to the newborn world of democratic politics. The spontaneously emerging polyarchy which was an important political weapon of the Forum as a revolutionary organisation was adapted by an entire political society. The absence of a sovereign political vocabulary in the Civic Forum stimulated the creation of pluralistic political conditions and allowed the necessary confrontations between political opinions and ideologies and between emerging political programmes.

The adoption and differentiation in 'normal' political programmes and ideologies began with the approach of the first free parliamentary elections in June 1990. These elections undoubtedly had a very strong impact on the subsequent character of the process of generating political ideologies, propaganda, sophisticated programmes and strategies. The structure of the Civic Forum came under a growing tension which was intensified by the local elections in the autumn of 1990. A year later, the whole revolutionary organisation split and disappeared from political life in post-communist Czechoslovakia. As Gale Stokes states about the post-revolutionary development in all post-communist countries:

> In the place of the antipolitical leaders have come dozens of professional politicians of all stripes, many considerably less attractive than the historians, philosophers, and musicians that the velvet revolutions brought forth (Stokes, 1993: 256).

The revolutionary movements of the Civic Forum in Czechoslovakia, the New Forum in German Democratic Republic, and Solidarnosc in Poland played an enormous role in the struggle against the communist system, and their structure indicates that they had the one very important general characteristic of being anti-bureaucratic movements opposed to bureaucratised power structures. They represented a different form of participation in political life; different from the communist one party model, but different also from traditional liberal democratic systems with their bureaucratised political parties. I believe that this is a consequence of their main function during their dissident activities and also during the revolutionary processes, which was to show that there is an alternative to seemingly omnipotent political systems. In the Czech lands, the Civic Forum developed very quickly during the revolution, from the dissident nucleus, from which it took a lot of its ideas, principles and strategies, into a mass social and political movement. It is no surprise then, that the first leaders of the Civic Forum were famous dissidents and intellectual opponents of the communist regime.

The early stage of the 1989 velvet revolutions, be it the round table talks in Poland and Hungary, or the demands of the revolutionary organisations in Czechoslovakia and German Democratic Republic, was characterised by its strong effort to weaken the old regime as much as possible. However, this regime was still strong enough to lead political negotiations and could not be overthrown by a classic revolutionary destructive action (Arato, 1993: 681). The original pre-revolutionary dissident attempt to achieve the maximum of changes possible in the existing political situation, gradually turned into a strategy of the peaceful transfer of power, the organisation of free democratic elections, and the establishment of a legal system protecting fundamental human rights and freedoms. Instead of there being a revolutionary creative act *ex nihilo*, there was a gradual transformation of the totalitarian systems into a set of liberal democracies, which, moreover, were able to incorporate former representatives of the totalitarian power as common actors of democratic politics.

The round table talks and the revolutionary forums did not rely on modern revolutionary legitimacy with its exalted 'either, or' structure. The exclusion of the representatives of the old regime from the new political condition were not goals of the velvet revolutions. Negotiations and compromise took the place of a radical revolutionary action. The plurality of opinions and voices did not exclude communists, but rather made them only one of many parties in the new emerging political system. This rejection of the permanent revolution and support for the rule of law meant that the confrontation with the totalitarian past did not occur in the way understandably favoured by the angry 'revolutionary people' and this caused significant political complications of a different character in each country. It is nevertheless true that this strategy manifests a strong continuity with the attitude held by dissidents and human rights activists in the formerly communist Eastern Europe.

Existential revolutions? or 'How much is the ferry to England?'

All the communist regimes in the Soviet bloc were permanently scared of a possible revolt by intellectuals and considered this social group to be a dangerous threat to its very existence. People like Kolakowski, Michnik, Lukacs, Konrad, Patočka or Havel, who could hold very different views but always were independent of and critical about official ideology and power, had an enormously important 'subversive role' and enjoyed natural authority and prestige amongst the public for their ethical and intellectual views. The political and, first of all, ethical views and opinions of dissidents also had a great influence on the character of the revolutions in their first period.

It is slightly to exaggerate, but it is nevertheless entirely possible to say that the most crucial revolutionary demand and first political and ethical goal of the revolutions was simply a renewal of the possibility of 'living in truth'. Timothy Garton Ash even calls 1989 'the year of the truth' (Garton

Ash, 1990: 131). Living in truth, originally Franz Kafka's expression, the ethical and civil importance of which was testified to all Czechoslovak and other Soviet bloc countries' dissidents, does not obviously mean living in the only ultimate objective truth. It also does not mean subjecting one own's life to the procedural criteria of rightness and truth, as in the Habermasian discourse theory, or to the aesthetic criterion of authenticity. The demand to live in truth escapes every judgment and communicative procedure which seeks to define binding normative criteria of truth.

When Habermas speaks about *'Die Einheit der Vernunft in der Vielheit der Stimmen' (the unity of reason in the plurality of voices)* (Habermas, 1990: 84), he means that the unity comes first and that the plurality of individual voices is derived from this. In order to achieve a voice, one must accept the procedures of communicative rationality. In the discourse theory, the individual as an autonomous person is defined by external standards and civil subjectivity cannot escape from the unity of reason. Human rights are then always treated as a product of the process of democratic will formation and cannot be formulated from the individual's perspective. According to the discourse theory, social emancipation and human rights are identical (Habermas, 1990: 102).

It would be ridiculous to criticise Habermas' discourse theory for not corresponding to reality. The discourse theory does not pretend to be a 'realistic' descriptive theory. It constructs the conditions for the validity and legitimacy of political system and law. Discourse procedures and the ideal of social communication freed from asymmetries of power represent a normative demand on politics and law in post-conventional, modern society. Discourse procedures function similarly to the general will fiction, being a theoretical construction from which the legitimacy of political domination and law is derived. An argument merely that the 1989 anti-communist revolutions had dynamics other than this one therefore cannot be sufficient for the critique of this theory. A critique of the discourse theory must prove that the empirical revolutionary process gave rise to a normative framework and legal fictions which went far beyond the limits of the discourse theory.

As is apparent from its normative character, the discourse theory is another attempt to give a *scientific legitimation* to politics and law. In his legitimating discourse, Habermas seeks to convince us that the problem of legitimacy still must be conceived in terms of social integrity and universally binding rules. On the other hand, the legitimation strategies and normative demands which were developed during the velvet revolutions, showed the limits of the normative power of discourse and its ability to secure social unity and integrity. Legitimation by means of discursive procedures has lost its universality and therefore its power to generate political consensus.

The 1989 velvet revolutions proved that no discourse has the power to declare itself universal and sovereign and therefore to claim to be the normative basis for political institutions. There is no actual voice or discourse which can speak in its name and define its normative framework (Feher, 1993: 705-9). Democracy speaks in many voices. As was shown by the development and the dissolution of the democratic forums in the post-revolutionary conditions, these voices are normatively clustered in political parties and organisations, while other voices, also democratic, refuse to enter this world of institutionalised politics and remain outside it. *In the post-1989 societies, then, preservation of heterogeneity has priority over the construction of the unified discourse framework of liberal democracies.*

Although Habermas acknowledges the importance of the private spheres of the life-world for the legitimacy of law and speaks about the interdependence of private and political autonomy, the relation between the public and private sphere is not balanced in discourse theory. The equal right to an autonomous private life is strengthened and accompanied by equal rights and activism in the sphere of political autonomy. Without political equality, there is no private autonomy (Habermas, 1996b: 777, 784). In order to secure the legitimacy of law, it is necessary to preserve a reciprocal relationship between private and public autonomy, but it is how the political power is regulated, and whether the regulating constitutional framework corresponds to the free discourse framework, that ultimately decides the law's legitimacy.

A command of the political vocabulary and engagement in the public structures of civil society is essential for a citizen to protect the private sphere of his/her life-world. What originally seems to be a balanced relation between the private and political autonomy in Habermas ultimately collapses as the compliance with discursive procedures regarded as the decisive condition for the legitimation of law and the protection of private freedoms. Private autonomy only generates political discussion. The problem of legitimacy is decided by political communication through approved discursive procedures. The private sphere may generate claims to legitimacy, but the public political sphere has the decision-making power founded on the procedures for communication among different types of discourses.

Communicative rationality undoubtedly inspired the establishment of the round table talks and negotiations between the communist power and dissidents. The absence of freedom of expression and democratic political discussion had been finally acknowledged even by the communist élite as one of the reasons that the communist totalitarian system was in crisis and it was this that led it to communicate with the political opposition. The political strategy of the round table talks was a necessary rational background of the whole revolutionary transformation, yet it is not the only strategy and vocabulary. The purpose of these talks was not to achieve consensus and agreement but rather to find some acceptable way to create the conditions of political plurality and difference. Later, these conditions found their form in the structure of the revolutionary 'forum' organisations. Forum represents a much more radical and heterogeneous condition in which communicative rationality represents only one of many political strategies and vocabularies. The legitimacy of the new political order obviously emerged with the help of communicative rationality, but this rationality cannot serve as the foundation of this order and its legitimacy.

Habermas seeks to fetter and undermine the anonymity of modern social systems, including legal system, and impersonal conformity with universal communicative rationality, recognition, and discourse ethics present in manifold social discourses and establishing the political world. However, this systemic conformity is replaced with the communicative rationality conformity, although it is defined as an open and democratic structure. On the other hand, living in truth does not mean any subjection. It means 'only' the possibility of individuals mapping their personal horizons and limits and thereby experiencing their singularity as autonomous beings with individual interests and goals. Living in truth is not symmetrical and conceivable from the structures of even handed communication. Such living is asymmetrical and embraces the possibility of living within the heterogeneous space of many little 'truths', together with them and in their neighbourhood. Individuals do not have to understand those truths from the position of truthfulness, but they can and have to respect them due to the simple fact that they belong to other human beings.

Universality emerges from the experience of uniqueness and difference. Such heterogeneity obviously is a danger to every totalitarian structure.

The Velvet Revolution in Czechoslovakia and other communist countries had exactly this strong pre-political, pre-constitutional, existential aspect, with roots in the dissident call for the individual autonomy of every human being and the possibility of human authenticity both in general and political sense.

In this context, the Velvet Revolution was Havel's existential revolution in spite of all possible criticism that it failed because of the failure to achieve a political state without bureaucratic, instrumental and purely technical structures. Living in truth, formulated in negative terms, means a possibility to escape from the evil which destroys the human individuality and singularity, constantly measures individual's actions and thoughts and exposes him/her to the light and judgments of the outside world of politics and ideology. The Velvet Revolution was a rebellion against such evil, which builds the walls in the cities and heads of its non-citizens. It was the event during which 'history has outdone Shelley, for poets were the acknowledged legislators of this world' (Garton Ash, 1990: 136).

This existential dimension of the Velvet Revolution is nicely illustrated by Garton Ash mentioning his conversation with a taxi-driver from East Berlin who asked him in November 1989: 'how much is the ferry to England?' (Garton Ash, 1990: 63). A couple of weeks ago, this question would have been pointless, indeed absurd, because the taxi-driver could only dream about such a trip abroad, but then it had regained its common meaning. This question is a matter which does not finely distinguish between politics and constitutionality, or explore duality of the private and public world. It precedes every possibility of politics.

In the political sense, this question is a critique of that quasi-private world of consumerism, which was guaranteed to subjects by the late communist system on the condition of the consumers non-interference in the sphere of politics. It has turned out that no system of social welfare can gain stability by denying human rights and freedom in return for a minimum of social and economic protection.

The 1989 revolutions involved the demand for democratic government and the common liberal private/public distinction in its political, constitutional and legal sense had to be reconstructed in the post-revolutionary societies. Both aspects of liberal democracies were present in the revolutions. However, those revolutions also involved something that escapes every vocabulary of human rights and democratic procedures, as known for instance from the constitutional documents. They included the demand for autonomy and freedom from the political. This freedom is not a freedom or right only in the legal sense, because it precedes every system of law and is asymmetrical to it. It is beyond the limits of legal language and political structures. Totalitarian systems therefore must systematically fight against it. It is not secured even by the procedures of communicative reason.

We may formulate this freedom in the words of Kundera's Sabina, who says in *The Unbearable Lightness of Being*:

> behind Communism, Fascism, behind all occupations and invasions lurks a more basic, pervasive evil ... the image of that evil was a parade of people marching by with raised fists and shouting identical syllables in unison (Kundera, 1984: 100).

It is the evil, which deprives individuals of their privacy. It deprives them of their singularity, intimacy and the possibility of authenticity, constantly measures their actions and thoughts and exposes them to the light and judgments of the outside world. All totalitarian regimes systematically deprive individuals of their intimacy. It is their main political target. Is the discursive criterion of rightness which emerges from the transformation of the people to communicative rational procedures an effective protection against this evil?

Intimacy is the sphere of the singularity which ignores the rules and judgments of any audience. The distinction of the private and public world vanishes in it because intimacy knows only the autonomy of the individual unrelated to subjection to a universal game which would be controlled by an *a priori* chosen audience. When individuals call for living in truth, they do not assume an audience. On the other hand, communicative procedures already assume a certain type of audience: the people. Is not finally even the people produced and constrained by the procedures of communicative rationality susceptible to the evil which characterised totalitarian regimes and their ideologies? Is not this evil latent in the very principle of the people's sovereignty? Does not Sabina's nightmare describe the ambivalence and possible threats not merely of communism but of democratic legitimacy as such?

Communicative procedures and discourse ethics are sovereign because they correspond to the processes of democratic political will formation. The universality of discourse ethics is derived from the idea of democracy. Because the sovereignty of discourse ethics and communicative procedures are legitimated democratically, law and politics must be subjected to them. This is why we may say that the procedures and principle of discourse is both in law and above it. Discourse theory seeks to neutralise the weakness of formal legal legitimacy by incorporating universally valid procedures of communicative rationality into the sphere of legal procedure. Universality and democracy coincide, legal correctness and political rightness derive from the procedures, the main purpose of which is to represent the sovereign people and its general will. Discourse theory assumes that the legal system is able to draw on non-legal procedures, which are more legitimate and general than law.

This theoretical approach is characteristic of all attempts to make the legitimacy of law depend on law's correspondence to universal values. That which is legitimate must have a legal form, but this form must contain something that goes beyond its framework. The 'smaller' world of legality must partake of the 'bigger', universally binding world of discourse ethics. The system of law must express the much broader system of cultural values, democratic consensus, etc. The system of law is therefore exposed to a tension with other normative systems. Two normative systems meet here, the legal one with a limited validity and the legitimating one with a general validity. The more general must fit into the more specific, yet it must not destroy its specific features.

This centralised model of legitimacy must lead to the contradictions in the validation of norms within the legal system. It is unclear whether a norm is valid because it is legally binding, or because it has accommodated the features of a more general legitimate order. Legitimacy understood as a matter of values and subjection of the legal system to a more general normative framework necessarily evokes the question whether it is possible to formulate such a framework in contemporary, complex societies.

The velvet revolutions of 1989 have weakened the centralised model of legitimate political domination and law because they could do without the unifying consensus and ultimate fiction of the sovereign people. The rule of law and liberal democracy were victorious in the 1989 revolutions. The revolutions were restorations of the constitutionally founded rule of law which would respect human rights and carry out the functions of representative democracy through a separation of powers. Human rights were the main inspiration of the revolution and then formed its institutional framework. One important stage of the revolutions ended when the resulting constitutional systems incorporated respect for human rights through the principle of the due process of law and recognition of international human rights treaties. Human rights and freedoms denied to the people living under real communism were given constitutional and legal recognition in the new political conditions.

In this sense, the revolutions had something of *a liberal legalist character* and lacked the radical democratic action. The constitutional legalist framework was a 'natural' outcome of a long-term social and political movement at the beginning of which had been the dissidents' struggle for human rights. Human rights and the protection of political freedoms had to be entrenched in the post-revolutionary constitutional documents and this imposed a legalist approach on the revolutionary changes. Moreover, democratic legitimacy did not have any foundationalist influence on this revolutionary legalism.

The rule of law and the constitutional protection of human rights and freedoms won the confrontation with political totalitarianism, but it also had to recognise its limited, politically problematic nature. The acceptance of the liberal democratic principles and rule of law can hardly represent new foundations for our times, as is claimed by Francis Fukuyama in his popular Hegelian concept of the end of history and victory of liberal democratic and market societies over their enemies (Fukuyama, 1992). Every post-communist country could develop in many different ways from an autocratic and national populist to a liberal democratic state. It is hard to say whether we are experiencing the end of history, the end of ideology, or whether we are just out of breath. The whole revolutionary situation of 1989 was nevertheless unique because its energy took the form of plurality and heterogeneity. The revolution was not a movement dedicated to the ideal of radical democracy so typical of modern politics and revolutionary changes. The revolution was a movement which expressed the need for *a radical version of liberalism.*

This liberalism can hardly be expressed in the common notions of natural rights or the modernist version of the social contract standing behind the legal and political principle of equality before the law. The liberal now must embrace the different, the heterogeneous and everything that has an irreducibly pluralistic character. The universal consensus is neither possible nor important in this condition. Plurality is not to be ordered as a catalogue of human rights and freedoms. The call for plurality, although it used the language of human rights, could not be framed in narrow, legal normative language. This call had a negative, pre-political and existential character. The legalist vocabulary of human rights turned out to be only a useful strategy for formulating this existential call for the conditions of anti-communist dissent and, later, revolution.

To secure legitimacy, the new political order paradoxically was required to secure its plurality, not its unity. The plurality which dominated the structures of the Civic Forum and other revolutionary organisations made it impossible to formulate any complex political programme in the language of consensus. Democratic legitimacy based on consensus represented only one of many legitimating strategies involved in these movements. A legalist strategy of the constitutional codification of the revolution and human rights also were present. This sort of legalism admits sources of normativity other than consensus and discourse ethics. The legalist revolutionary strategy is, however, inseparable from an existentialist position, which makes it impossible to state the problem of legitimacy of the revolutions and the post-revolutionary political situation into legalist language.

Plurality and unity, heterogeneity and homogeneity, singularity and generality, consensus and dissent, system and existential change; all are characteristic features of the 1989 velvet revolutions. Democratic consensus and systemic legality therefore become only particular legitimating strategies and cannot encompass the complexity of the revolutions and the new social and political situation. This complexity, however, also cannot be legitimated by its existentialist foundations. Singularity, from which every existentialist vocabulary is derived, cannot be translated into the systemic problem of legitimacy. *The 1989 revolutions dismantled the concept of one sovereign source of legitimacy.* They also went beyond the dualism of liberal democracy, in which individual freedoms and minority rights are given a legalist legitimacy and which is to protect them against all possible attacks from the majority political will enjoying democratic legitimacy. The pluralistic and heterogeneous revolutions in Central and Eastern Europe made the problem of the legitimacy of political domination and law has become even a bigger problem than ever before.

3 Legal Legitimacy and Legalist Fictions

The people's general will limited

The legitimacy of a democratic political system depends upon the fiction of the people being a political agent with one will which justifies positive political institutions and provides legal norms with general validity. Jean Jacques Rousseau's concept of the general will is then constitutive of democratic political regimes. It constitutes foundation of the political authority which is able to issue rules of behaviour for all citizens and claim for them a general binding force. The general will of the people is the legitimation fiction confronting the primary threat of all democracies, the abuse by a political majority of the minorities also existing in the given political community. The fiction of the people's general will is to constitute a homogeneous political condition. Highly questionably, this is done by ignoring the concept of the political minority.

The image of the people as a unified sovereign does not correspond to modern political reality. The modern mass societies with the parliamentary democracy do not have the people in the sense of a unified political agent. Instead of the homogeneous people and its will, these societies are subject to pressures from heterogeneous political interests. The problem of the general political will's formation has always been vital to and potentially fatal for the idea of democracy (Schmitt, 1985a: 28). In modern political history, the demand for political homogeneity also took the extremely dangerous idea of a nation subjected to the will of a political leader who must be powerful enough to overcome all potential threats arising from heterogeneity of purposes. Under various political and historical circumstances, as in Russia in 1917 or Germany in 1933, the demand for political homogeneity and strong leadership led to totalitarianism.

Some of the experiences of the contemporary liberal democracies show, however, that heterogeneity can have a strong stabilising effect and that the unity of a political community does not have to be determined by its homogeneity. Minority rights and a plurality of political interests may also establish the liberal democratic political system and the constitutional state. The constitutional principles of a free contest between different political parties and the representation of different political interests in constitutional bodies are necessary conditions of the rule of law system. Democracy need not be identified only with the fiction of the people's general will.

The legitimation of a political system by both democratic procedures and liberal principles must be formulated in the language of law, enforced by a law which obliges all political subjects. Political principles must be transformed into legal procedures. *The democratic fiction of the will of the people is diluted into the constitutive elements of modern legality.* Consequently, the question arises, whether the legitimacy of law is given exclusively by the character of the political institutions that legislate and apply legal rules.

Law legitimates and therefore stabilizes a political domination in all state societies, be they modern or traditional. Modern societies have developed a specific legal culture, which is usually defined in terms of generality, formal rationality, calculability and impersonality. The culture of legalism is both a technique of political power and manifestation of the modern ethic of individual responsibility and the modern political principle of equality of all citizens before the law/political authority (Shklar, 1964). This duality and relative social autonomy of modern legality raises many questions about the character of legitimacy. Is legality the source of legitimacy because its impersonal character makes the rule of law system the most effective way to reproduce political power in modern societies? On the other hand, does not legality legitimate political power because legality itself is founded on some ethical and political principles? If law legitimates political domination and authority, what is the source of law's own legitimacy? And if this source is finally ethical, how can those ethics be enforced in modern pluralistic societies except by means of law? So, in the end, is it not the case that legality is the basis of legitimacy because it is a powerful political technique for the enforcement of rules of human behaviour?

Analytical jurisprudence and the scientific legitimation of law

Analytical jurisprudence and legal positivism are products of modernity and specifically of the modernisation of legal systems. In forming the successful codifications of civil law in France (1804), Switzerland (1807) and Austria (1811) was a new school of legal theory which rejected the naturalist approach and sought to limit jurisprudence to the issue of validity and application of positive laws. The modern codifications had an enormous influence on the founding father of analytical jurisprudence, Jeremy Bentham, who proposed to modernise the English common law along similar lines to the continental legal systems in that it would rest on legal codes as the primary source of law (Bentham, 1983).

Modern legal positivism originally set itself the ambitious task of defining an autonomous paradigm for legal science. The positivist approach was to understand the legislation, functions, structures and reproduction of law independent of moral, economic and political theory and philosophy. Legal theory was to become the science of legal normativity by scientifically defining the nature and function of modern law. Legal positivism therefore arose as a grand attempt to give *a scientific legitimacy* to the law which need not refer to external moral and political elements. Instead of the democratic will of the people or universal moral principles, it is rationally and scientifically founded law that displays validity and can function as a logically coherent and hierarchical legitimate system. The strict separation of law from politics and morality also means a separation of scientifically established legal legitimacy from the politically and morally founded legitimacy of law. A legal theorist is an expert who maintains the functions of a legal system by the positivist methods. What is valid and binding in law is defined by this expert and not by a political community.

Legal positivism, like any other positivist theory, ultimately is a metaphysical project which defines the normative framework for law and the conditions of law's legitimacy. This project requires the creation of specific fictions which would make it possible to describe law scientifically as an autonomous, unified and self-contained system. The reality of law must be transformed into an ideal scientific construction in order to provide law with the scientific legitimacy.

The modernisation of law which called forth legal positivism and analytical jurisprudence involves two distinct developments; the growing autonomy of law and domination by law. The autonomy of law is the separation of the legal normative order from other social normative orders, primarily morality, politics, economics and social tradition. It is exactly this process which is examined and emphasised in the analytical jurisprudence of Jeremy Bentham and later John Austin. Both sought to establish law as a subject of scientific research, the structure and functions of which are independent of other social phenomena. This approach also explains their strong condemnation of natural law, which was seen only as a part of socially and historically limited morality.

Domination by positive law means that a modern political domination is impossible to define except in legal language. The famous statement of Alexis de Tocqueville that every tyrannical power requires a lawyer who must serve the tyrant contains only a partial truth (Bělohradský, 1988). Lawyers serve a tyrant by attempting to legitimate his/her rule in the language of law. It is, however, impossible to imagine liberal and democratic regimes formulating their power in non-legal language. Law becomes the sovereign instrument for defining any modern political power and will. Domination by law excludes all exercises of state power which could not find their support in law and go beyond a legal framework.

A system of positive law establishes itself in the process of social and systemic differentiation of modern society. Legal positivism is a reflection of this process (Luhmann, 1985: 281ff.). Consequently, modern positive law must look for its own source of legitimacy in itself and cease to understand legitimacy as a matter of political values and procedures superior to the legal system. Modern legal positivist science formulates *the problem of legitimacy as a matter of validity* and legitimation questions are marginalised within the legalist scholarship. The question of validity is more general than the fiction of a democratic general will of the people. The German philosopher of law Gustav Radbruch perceived legitimacy from just this perspective. According to him, the question of legitimacy is always a question of how law persists and remains law. Radbruch says that 'the juridical doctrine of validity turns into the principle of legitimacy, the postulate that each new legal order must have evolved from its predecessor in a legal way' (Radbruch, 1950a: 125).

The topic of legitimacy thus becomes entirely a legal matter. What is illegal automatically becomes illegitimate. Discontinuity and fracture between two legal orders means an illegitimate change of law because it is impossible to conceptualise such a change by means of the previous legal order. Revolution becomes a favourite jurisprudential example of the illegitimate change of law (see, for example, Kelsen, 1945: 117), in defiance of the fact that it is precisely the nature of revolutions to blame the old political regimes for having lost their legitimacy.

The difference between the political and legal positivist concept of legitimacy emerges here. It is a consequence of the paradigmatic change in modern legal science. Jurisprudence limits its focus to the field of positive law and deliberately excludes all non-legal elements outside the borders of legal discourse. Legitimacy, if it is to be examined by legal science at all, must be reduced to a matter of legal normativity and law's own inner laws and regularities. It is highly important to explain how modern positivist jurisprudence came to hold such a scientific perspective. In order to examine law as an independent normative order of modern society, it must *create fictions* about law's nature, origin and functions (Teubner, 1988: introduction). The fundamental function of these fictions is that they make it possible to speak about law as an autonomous and independent order of modern society. They make it possible to examine law independently of what are represented as the two external spheres of morality and politics. To create these *legitimation fictions of legality* is the crucial task of legal positivist theory.

It is plainly necessary that fictions play a crucial role in setting up the conditions of legitimate law, if legitimacy is to be regarded as only a technical question of the inner functions and structures of law. The role of jurisprudence in modern society in the process of the construction of the legitimate system of positive law takes on great importance. Jurisprudence seeks to explain how law functions in modern society (Castoriadis, 1997). Analyses of a system of positive law become the way to provide it with *scientific jurisprudential legitimation*. Legal theory is to express the inner demands of law and legality for rational legitimacy (Kerchove and Ost, 1994: 8).

Different kinds of legalist fictions

Historically, the first fiction significantly influencing modern legalist thinking is *the fiction of social contract* in the form designed by Thomas Hobbes in his *Leviathan.* Although it is inappropriate to call Hobbes a modern legal positivist, his works involve an extraordinarily strong emphasis on the role of positive law in the regulation of political institutions. The social contract is a fiction which explains the origin of political society and its positive laws, and which also sets up the principles of that society's legislation. However, Hobbes defines these principles 'naturally' in the language of natural law.

The idea of contract being the foundation of 'the eternal peace' among nations and within a nation is closely tied to the concept of civil society. The role civil society played in Adam Ferguson's thought has already been discussed. The contractual approach also pervades Immanuel Kant's political writings. According to Kant, the ideals of republicanism, civil society and freedom follow from the fiction of the political contract.

The argument that a contract between government and people is the primary condition of the acceptability of the political and legal order is deeply entrenched in modern legal theory and sociology. The founding fathers of sociology understood the contractual concept of society as a sign of modernity and analysed the growing importance of social relations based on contracts. Karl Marx examines contract as the basic fabric of social order in his *Capital* (1976). George Herbert Spencer adopts Henry Maine's legal historical scheme of social progress as a transition from status to contract (Spencer, 1969). According to Emile Durkheim, contract represents modern organic solidarity (Durkheim, 1964). Max Weber analyses purposive economic action carried out through contract as a principal expression of the rationalisation and disenchantment of modern society (Weber, 1978). According to Georg Simmel, relations between government and people have a reciprocal character and include a mutual obligation to subject the actions of both to the contracted rules (Simmel, 1950: 186-9). The concept of the rule of law itself is based on the notion that the relation between a legislator and citizens is ruled by a fictitious contract subjecting one's own behaviour to rules and securing the political values of certainty and foreseeability.

The social contract is unique because it combines moral and political prescriptive attitudes with modern scientific analytical method. The contractual model both constitutes the science of law and politics and formulates normative claims concerning law and politics. This typically double character is not found in the other legitimation fictions of legality and reconsidered only in the fiction of the just law.

....

The fiction of the political sovereign, to a large extent formulated by Hobbes, was elaborated by Bentham and later by Austin (Priban, 1997: ch. 2). It has a similar paradigmatic importance for modern legal and social science as the fiction of the social contract. The famous definition that 'law is the command of a sovereign' immediately evokes the response that nobody has ever seen a political sovereign acting in the way described by Bentham and Austin (for one of the critiques of the concept of the sovereign in legal and political philosophy see Duguit, 1970). However, the concept of a political sovereign is a theoretical construct and not a realistic description of a political system. It is therefore useless to criticise it for its inability to provide a 'realistic picture' of modern politics and law. In spite of the proclaimed realism of analytical jurisprudence, which is summed up in its metaphysical aspiration 'to describe the world as it is', the concept of a sovereign is a pure fiction. This fiction is to separate law from other fields of social reality and form a kind of modern scientific research focusing exclusively on legal phenomena.

According to Bentham and Austin, a political sovereign which unites a political community may rule independently of morals and values. The only criterion of sovereignty is the effectiveness of the political mechanism which is maximised by conforming to the order of a legal system. The modern image of politics and law as a kind of machine with a complicated inner structure and architecture, but also with a clearly defined centre causing its motion, finds one of its finest expressions here.

Bentham answers the question of who is the sovereign in a much more democratic spirit than John Austin. According to Bentham, a political sovereign is the people (Rosen, 1983). It is only democratically elected assemblies which can legitimately have the force necessary to protect the government against political criminals and bandits (Hart, 1983: 185). The political sovereign must have the form of a democratically elected body which represents the will of the people in the whole political community. The political sovereign is established by democratic procedures which provide important support to the sovereign's power by avoiding both anarchy and obsequious quietism. Anarchy means a danger that people will not respect laws, while quietism means a danger that people will think that they should always obey laws on moral grounds (Postema, 1986: 278-86).

According to Bentham, the political sovereign represents impersonal power and law is the sovereign technique for the exercise of such power. Unlike Bentham, Austin did not seek to identify political sovereign with political qualities of government such as democracy and the people. Rather, he simply assumes that the sovereign power of a given territory is the foundation of the existence of valid law in that territory. The sovereign's function is the same in all political systems. It is to unite political society into a totality of political subjects who obey the law.

The fiction of a political sovereign is to clarify the origin of and the reason for the validity and binding force of positive law. It requires political subjects who are addressees of the sovereign's commands. If the reason for legal validity is determined by law being the manifestation of a sovereign political will, it is then unnecessary to examine carefully the conditions under which an addressee of this will accepts commands in the form of law.

The Benthamite version of legalism pays little attention to the role of *belief* in the legitimacy of political domination and law as an issue in the legitimation of a political sovereign. It is enough that subjects behave with discipline and accept law because of their *habit of obedience*. The psychologically unsatisfactory argument of the habit of obedience is, according to analytical jurisprudence, an anthropological truism making it possible to found the validity and legitimacy of a law just on the fact that it is issued by a sovereign, which can enforce obedience by the threat of violence.

....

The fiction of the political sovereign has been subjected to many criticisms. One of the most persuasive can be found in the works of Hans Kelsen. Kelsen's main argument is that no law can look for the ground of its validity in the world of social and political facts such as political will, the habit of obedience and the effectiveness of sovereignty. Law must look for the ground of its own validity in the world of its own norms. The foundations of the law always must be legal normativity. In Kelsen's words, 'law regulates its own creation' (Kelsen, 1971: 278-9).

Kelsen severely criticises the sociological approach to law with its emphasis on the analysis of law as a social fact. According to Kelsen, there is no scientific justification for the sociological perspective advanced by Weber. It radically differs from the juristic perspective because it examines the condition of the validity of legal norms in its effect upon individual's actions and analyses the meaning of legal norms in terms of the meaning attributed to them by individuals (Kelsen, 1945: 175). The sociological perspective is unacceptable as scientific jurisprudence because law, in Kelsen's view, must not be examined through the famous *de iure/de facto* duality. Law must be examined in its normative unity and the only scientifically justifiable analysis of law must be concentrated, therefore, on law's normativity, on its *de iure* nature.

According to Kelsen's pure theory of law, law is law because it is law (for the critical analysis of Kelsen's understanding of law and its normativity see Hart, 1983: 287). The normative binding force of law cannot be derived from social facts. Law thus can never be reduced to the command of a political sovereign because such a command does not belong to the legal normative world. According to Kelsen, the democratic fiction that a parliament represents the people's general will and therefore can claim that its legislation is legitimate also is misleading (Kelsen, 1945: 292). It is not surprising that the political institutions of representative democracy claim to express the will of the people. What is disturbing for a pure theory of law is the possibility that an act of political volition could be the foundation of the body of law. The decision-making process of parliaments and any other political sovereigns are factual exercises of political power which establish particular legal normative orders. In contrast to this, Kelsen says that legal normativity itself is an *a priori* phenomenon which cannot be determined by political and social facts.

But what is the normative foundation of law? Kelsen comes up with his famous solution of the concept of *the basic norm*. This concept sharply separates, in the style of neo-Kantianism, the world of 'is' [Sein] from the world of 'ought' [Sollen] and refers the validity and effectiveness of every legal order to its normativity. Validity and effectiveness, according to the pure theory of law, has no sociological meaning and the sociology of law therefore cannot resolve the problems of legal validity and efectiveness. These problems can be resolved only within the pure theory of law which locates the very identity of a legal system in the concept of the basic norm (Raz, 1970: 100ff).

A basic norm is the ground of the existence and validity of all legal systems and the ultimate reason for the validity of specific legal norms. All legal norms in positive legal systems derive their existence from it. The basic norm is the answer to the question whether and under what conditions are legal statements concerning legal norms, duties and rights possible (Kelsen, 1945: 116-7). In this sense, the basic norm performs the role of the legitimation fiction of positive law and is a highly important and original concept in modern legal science. It is a uniquely pure attempt to supply positive law with scientific legitimacy.

Joseph Raz, however, even concludes that though the concept of the basic norm is intended to replace the concept of political sovereignty, there is no really important difference between the two concepts (Raz, 1970: 95). Even for Kelsen, law represents a specific order and organisation of power and behind all legal norms there *must* be an act of enforcement (or the concept of a legal system is absurd). This means that the sanctions and rules of positive law ultimately must derive their existence from an expression of the will of a political authority (Kelsen, 1945: 45, 121, 392).

The basic norm determines the validity of the positive law and enforcement which human political authority has at its disposal in modern society for the implementation of legal norms. Behind validity, there is no morality. The basic norm cannot be measured in terms of morals. Like Austin, Kelsen says that even when legal and moral norms occasionally overlap, it is impossible to speak about some minimum content of morality in law or the moral foundations of law, for even in these cases, morality becomes simply law because it is possible to enforce its rules by political violence (Kelsen, 1945: 410).

The basic norm is not a constitution in the sense of positive law. It is a transcendental logical foundation of law *constructed by legal logic*. It is not a positive legal norm (Kelsen, 1965: 1130, 1141). It is a theoretical fiction. Kelsen draws on Vaihinger's concept of philosophy 'as if' (Vaihinger, 1924) and says that the basic norm is a kind of fiction which helps to conceptualise the origin of the validity of legal norms (Stewart, 1980: 199-224). The basic norm is not a hypothesis which might be proved true. Instead, it is a fiction making it possible to establish a juridical discourse about the validity of norms and a relationship between the volitive act of a political authority and the normative expression of that act. The relationship between 'ought' [Sollen] and 'volition' [Wollen] is resolved by locating the ultimate meaning of the volitive act of the political authority in the concept of the basic norm.

The already complex nature of the basic norm becomes even more complicated when Kelsen is obliged to connect his theoretical construction to the volitive acts of the sovereign authority. If, regardless of Kelsen's stance, sanctions and enforcement *are* the substance of legal norms, it is necessary to analyse their binding force in relationship to the will of the authority standing behind such enforcement. Kelsen then retreats to the *fiction of a historically first lawgiver* who drafted a historically first constitution. The lawgiver can be a political assembly, or a tyrant. This lawgiver (as if) transforms the transcendent basic norm into the constitution which already and fully belongs to the sphere of positive law.

However, this fiction of the transformative lawgiver which translates the basic norm into the legal norms of a positive legal order has a damaging effect on the image of pure normativity which is to be the pure ground of the validity of all norms. Due to the factual act of volition of a political sovereign, pure normativity is somehow 'polluted'. Kelsen's sovereign *de iure* world becomes mixed with *de facto* elements of social and political power and he is unable to continue to give the normative the purely fictional character which allows it to be perceived only as an intellectual tool for the analysis of the nature of modern law.

Kelsen conceives of legitimacy as a problem of the continuation of the validity of legal norms and the legal order as a whole. A change of law is legitimate if it happens according to the inner rules of a legal order. The legitimacy of a norm means that this norm is valid *and effective* within a framework of law. Even Kelsen's principle of legitimacy, then, contains, together with the conditions of validity, *the principle of effectiveness* (Kelsen, 1945: 117, 119).

In the pure theory of law and modern legal positivism in general, *legitimacy is a matter of legality*. It is not a matter of some moral order or an act of political will. According to Kelsen, for Radbruch (in his pre-war, legal philosophical views) and others, legitimacy becomes a problem of succession of law's authority in situations when one legal order replaces another, or when new legal norms replace old legal norms. If this change occurs according to the legal rules and procedures which are built in the old legal order, it is considered legitimate. If this change happens irrespective of those rules, it is illegal and therefore illegitimate. Revolutions or state coups are typical examples of the illegitimate birth of a new legal order. In these historical situations, the original basic norm creating the old legal order is broken and it is necessary to create a new basic norm (Kelsen, 1945: 117-8). The basic norm is absolutely essential from the perspective of law's legitimacy. The limits of legitimacy of a legal order are the limits of coherence of the basic norm.

Prospective positivism and the return of ethics into legal positivist science

The function of all these legitimation fictions in legal positivism is clear - to define law as a completely independent phenomenon existing in modern society and set up the paradigm of modern legal science which would focus on such law. Legitimation fictions were to separate law from morality and, in the incredibly ambitious claim of the basic norm, normativity from facticity. *Legal science was to be the sovereign source of the legitimation of law.*

In spite of all these efforts, the rigid legalist approach failed. The statement 'law is law', originally intended as a liberal protection against the legal naturalist conservatism, became the worst nightmare and intellectual 'kitsch' of late Europe and its horrors of Gulags and Nazi extermination camps (Bělohradský, 1988). All fictions which legitimate law through purely legalist concepts seek to establish a pure juridical discourse and a legal theory freed from any other normative structures of modern society and from external judgements about law. However, any command of the political sovereign or any behaviour pattern can consequently become the content of a legal norm. Even a crime can become and achieve the force of law, as happened in the totalitarian systems. To put it mildly, the legitimation fictions of the political sovereign and the basic norm did not satisfactorily address this problem.

It is possible to discern in Bentham's work a concern about the possible consequences of defining law as the command of a political sovereign and a recognition of the need to address the political question of the sovereign's nature. It is as if Bentham was afraid of possible consequences of his own legal theory. This concern is barely present in Austin's concept of sovereignty. Habermas then is right to criticise the paradigmatic foundations of legal positivism for recognising only the existence of legal institutions without questioning the origin of the legitimacy of those institutions (Habermas, 1987b: 359-60).

Consequently, contemporary legal positivism has significantly changed the whole framework for consideration of the problems of the validity, effectiveness, and legitimacy of legal norms. Liberal democratic principles and their entrenchment in a legal system play an essential role in the works of Neil MacCormick, Ota Weinberger and other legal positivists. They also are essential for Raz's legal theory which takes its inspiration from critical examinations of Hart's and Kelsen's theories. While the problems of validity and effectiveness remain predominantly a 'legal' issue of coherence, enforcement and obedience, the broader problem of the legitimacy of law becomes a political issue of the democratic legislation and protection of human rights and freedoms. It also becomes a problem of the ethics of obedience of rules, which, as it raises questions of both law and morality, breaks down the typical legalist separation of law and morals. The validity and effectiveness of legal norms are different from their legitimacy. Legitimacy is determined by what is usually described as the principle of the rule of law. The main function of the rule of law is to subject the sovereign political power to legal procedures and to limit that power by imposing respect for a complete catalogue of civil and political rights (for this definition see, for instance, Neumann, 1986: 45).

This development in current legal positivism means that the whole paradigm retreats from the founding fictions that used to keep legal theoretical discourse together. Legal positivists now talk about the 'soft' version of positivism instead of the 'hard' version represented by Bentham's or Kelsen's theories (Campbell, 1996, ch. 1). It is significant that the current legal theoretical literature constantly oscillates between the problems of normative logic on the one side and political philosophy on the other. Neil MacCormick identifies what he calls 'the ethics of legalism' in modern legal systems (MacCormick, 1989: 184). Tom Campbell similarly elaborates a theory of 'ethical positivism' (Campbell, 1996), by which he means the complex of ethics common to both law and morality and can be derived from the logic of the creation and observance of rules of human conduct. This logic then forms an inherent part of the life of democratic political society. The topics, which cannot be grasped by the legalist approach, have thus been brought back into legal positivism. Franz Neumann's comment that the rule of law must always recall the transcendent ideal of freedom (Neumann, 1986: 256-7) has been given concrete shape in the legal positivist science of the last two or three decades.

Current legal positivist science has not brought anything interesting or new to the analysis of the problem of the legitimacy of law. It has replaced the original fiction of the sovereign or the basic norm with a kind of eclecticism which is to help legal science to overcome the impossibility of legitimating law and political domination exclusively on the basis of inner principles of legality. The democratic constitution of law-making bodies is taken as the automatic process of legitimation (Raz, 1979). The main problem this seems to leave is that of the legitimacy of judicial decision-making given the extent of discretion in the process of the application of law.[1]

Contemporary legal positivism's acknowledgement of the importance of judicial discretion stands it in opposition to the original positivist theories of Bentham and Austin, which assumed the subjection of judicial bodies to the sovereign parliament (Shiner, 1994: 41). Legal positivists recognise the presence of extra-legal elements in positive law, mainly the influence of moral political judgements, and can tolerate these provided that they do not infringe upon the basic consistency of legality.

Together with the acknowledgement of the role of moral political judgments in the process of judicial decision-making, legal positivism has had to come up with new attitudes to the legal normativity itself. Neil MacCormick thus says that every positive law involves duties of justice which belong to the sphere of morality. Law must regulate this sphere of morality, although it must not regulate and enforce morality as such (MacCormick, 1982: 35).

MacCormick's adoption of the concept of duties of justice from the moral theory of Adam Smith resembles very much what H.L.A. Hart described as the minimum content of natural law in positive law (Hart, 1994). In this context, MacCormick also speaks about the ethics of legalism and opposes it to legal moralism (MacCormick, 1989: 184). He refuses to accept any sort of the moral subordination of legality. However, MacCormick attributes a strong ethical significance to legalism for its subjection of government to the system of rules. Legalism diminishes the arbitrary use of political force and enhances the security of citizens and the predictability of the actions of government. Pragmatic technique here finds its ethical meaning.

MacCormick attributes to legalism a similar function to the one given it by Hobbes. According to him, the ethics of legality consists in its ability to prevent Leviathan from becoming an all-destructive Frankenstein. Legal reasoning is a specific, highly institutionalised and formalised type of moral reasoning. Behind both moral and legal forms of argumentation there

[1]There are a vast number of important legal theoretical books published in this field written by prominent legal philosophers, such as R. Posner (1990), R. Dworkin (1986), and D. Dyzenhaus (1991).

are normative structures of practical reason and reasoning (MacCormick, 1978: 272f).

MacCormick is perfectly well aware of all the deficiencies of legality and the chances of its political abuse and he still asserts that 'the independence or autonomy in the face of public action which bourgeois legality secures to people is a fundamental political and human good' (MacCormick, 1989: 191). Such legality can exist because we believe in it and in its concrete laws, and are convinced about the rightness of acting in accordance with legal rules. The legitimacy of law and the institutions of a legal system such as its courts derive from a larger political community and its definition of what is accepted as binding (MacCormick, 1978: 55f).

MacCormick takes the habit of obedience (as Bentham, Austin or Hart conceive it) as the foundation of legitimacy and understands it entirely in the sense of political sociology, as a consequence of the transformation of a political will into a general conviction about the rightness of legal norms and institutions. In MacCormick's legal theory, the Hobbesian relation between a will and reason, which is typical of the whole of modern legal and political science, is somewhat shifted back into the sphere of the will. MacCormick also recalls Hume's philosophy of normative scepticism in the statement that 'my belief that I ought to strive to be rational is not a belief which I can justify by reasoning' (MacCormick, 1978: 268). Rational arguments are absolutely essential, but the belief in rationality is a matter beyond the framework of rationality. MacCormick rejects the irrationalism and voluntarism of legal realists just as he rejects unreasonable trust in law as a rationally organised and practised system of rules. Law is understood as a normative order performed in a constant tension between will and belief on one side and rational argument on the other.

Following Hart, MacCormick develops the concept of legitimacy as effectiveness in the following way: instead of perceiving it as a part of the normative sphere of validity, he describes effectiveness as being based on *belief* about the binding force of legal norms which dominates in a political community. This is all closer to the will than to the reason. Far from being regarded as the matter of pure validity to which Kelsen sought to reduce (or elevate) it, the problem of legality and legitimacy returns to the world of collective political beliefs and moral judgments. It returns to exactly those spheres, which Kelsen sought to exclude from legal science through his fiction of the basic norm and his strong criticism of Weber's sociological theory.

Legal positivism therefore has developed a, somewhat delayed, *project of the extralegal legitimation of law and political domination*. This project is founded on the liberal theory of civil and political rights and freedoms and on the theory of the democratic rule of law. 'The iron cage' of modernity represented by the concept of legality as legal-rational domination, caused such disquiet that legal philosophers now seek to fill legality with the values and norms of liberal democratic politics, morality and practical reason. Nevertheless, at the same time, they pretend that the cage of legality functions perfectly and is a kind of morality itself. People only have to trust in it and justify it by practical reason. *The duality legitimacy/legality is thus impoverished and reduced to the duality morality/law or political principles/law*. Morality, certain political virtues, and the principles of practical reason must be incorporated into law.

The relationship between morality, practical reason and political virtue is complicated and controversial. Ronald Dworkin also rejects the classical moralist argument that legitimate coercive power has to be justified by moral reasons. According to him, a state becomes legitimate when its constitutional structure and practices have such a nature that citizens have a general obligation to observe its political decisions, which formulate concrete civil duties. Legitimacy is then acquired by practical reasoning within this general boundary. This, however, does not mean that the government could demand anything of its citizens and that citizens would have to observe all of its decisions irrespective of their content. The principle of general obedience is limited by the requirement that law conforms to the founding political ideal of *the integrity of political community*. This ideal must be pursued by a legal system. State and law become legitimate only when they support the political ideal of integrity (Dworkin, 1986: 191f). Legitimacy is a particular quality of a political community seeking integrity. In Dworkin's theory, practical reason finally must respect a particular version of political morality (although refusing moral arguments as foundations of politics) in order to secure the demand of the legitimacy of state and law. Law must express certain principles which are commonly designated as the rule of law. These principles must use their own legal language to formulate the general nature of political obligations and obedience and this makes it possible to integrate all citizens into the state.

Practical arguments for the legitimacy of the state and law finally cannot escape being affirmations of the moral version of the world, humanity and politics established in the modern concept of political universalism. The rule of law, David Dyzenhaus suggests, is a moral concept which must be entrenched in the liberal traditions of civil and political rights, an independent judiciary and democratic legislation by a parliament. It would appear, then, that Habermas' discourse theory, which mixes the liberal values with democratic techniques of government, could be reconciled with legal positivism and form an important part of the theory of the democratic and legitimate rule of law (Dyzenhaus, 1991: 267). According to Dyzenhaus, the legitimacy of law is a matter of the standards implicit in law which are revealed in adjudication (Dyzenhaus, 1994: 80-94). These standards, completely corresponding to Dworkin's views, are derived from liberal democratic political culture and the moral beliefs of this political community. Legalism, if it is filled with these moralist impulses, can be criticised and legitimated from inside.

Raz's legal theory of legitimacy, although it builds on the critique of moral normative apriorism in the form represented, for instance, by the theory and culture of human rights, comes to similar conclusions. Raz rejects legitimacy mediated by the concept of human rights and opposes to it the legitimacy by reasons given in practical rational argumentation (Raz, 1979: 12). Political authority is legitimate if its commands have the nature of exclusionary reasons (Raz, 1979: 27). Raz takes legitimacy into the exclusionary sphere of rational normative demands which have a *de iure* nature. These demands are not conditioned by effectiveness or *de facto* practised power.

Legitimacy is normative and its foundation is in practical reason. It coincides with moral authority when Raz says:

> No system is a system of law unless it includes a claim of legitimacy, of moral authority. That means that it claims that legal requirements are morally binding, that is that legal obligations are real (moral) obligations arising out of the law (Raz, 1984: 131).

Legitimacy finds itself ultimately outside the circular juridification of legality and is a matter of practical reason, political rationality and morality. Raz, Dworkin and other contemporary legal and political philosophers turn legitimacy into an exclusive matter of theory of practical reason and morality. The meaning of legitimacy is derived from a particular kind of moral philosophical speculation. The functioning of legitimate authority is determined by the normative claims of practical reason. *Legitimacy is a matter of scientific speculation* which finally sets up binding reasons for practical actions. This speculation and the arguments of practical reason founded the political morality of modern democratic and liberal political communities.

Because the concept of legitimacy here has no sociological meaning and it is therefore impossible to relate it to *de facto* existing social institutions, the definition of legitimacy must be *exclusive*. A political authority which does not derive its structures from the normativity of practical reason cannot be treated as legitimate. Legality must incorporate the normative claims of legitimacy into its structure. Legal philosophers demand that the formal rationality of legal rules and procedures must also include the substantive rationality of values and principles.

The positivist critique of legalism and its legitimation fictions of a-moral law can emphasise either the democratic or the liberal aspect. It can be either more normativist in the sense of supporting a priori *de iure* principles, or more realistic in the sense of respecting *de facto* existing institutions of the rule of law/law based state. The conditions of the legitimacy of law can be defined differently with respect to the relationship between human and political rationality and will. In all of these formulations, however, the legitimation of law must nevertheless befounded on the knowledge and ethics of the specific political community of the liberal democracies.

The basic norm as the fiction constituting legality must now be buried in order to save legality as a technique for legitimating the political domination existing in liberal democratic communities. When the principles of liberal democratic politics and practical reason are encoded into legality, it seems that legality can consequently provide political domination with legitimacy.

It must be declared that the rule of law and legality has the status of universal morality, or at least universal political virtue (Cotterrell, 1996: 463f.). Nevertheless, the reason, why Kelsen created his fiction, has never disappeared. It is as if current legal positivists want to ignore the problem of the existence of law in societies which are radically different from liberal democracies, though this is the very problem which formed legal positivism as an attempt to create an objective, value-free science of law. In modern legal positivism, the original legitimation fictions of legal positivism have been replaced by the paradigmatic inconsistency and moralism about legitimacy, which builds on liberal democratic foundations.

Scientific legitimation and the centralised models of legal science

The fictions of early modern legal positivism had a double function. The first function was to be the basis of the description of law, its normative structures, socio-political roles, and the logic of the creation and application of legal norms. The second function was to provide a legitimation of law in the language of legal science. Scientific arguments and intellectual constructs were to provide the prescriptive claims of positive law and secure the obedience of subjects of law. The seemingly value-free scientific language of legal theory was to explain the legitimacy of law in terms of the inner logic of the legal system and to exclude 'uncertain', illogical moments such as subjects' trust, beliefs and convictions concerning the rightness of their subjection and obedience to law. In modern legal theory, the legitimacy of law loses its transcendent metaphysical character. Scientific discussions are concerned only with the respective legitimations of different systems of positive law (Ward, 1992: 191).

Legal positivist theory could not defend this prescriptive and at the same time relativistic claim and, faced with the development of legal systems in 20th century, retreated from the idea of a-moral law that is legitimated exclusively in terms of the legal conditions of validity. Contemporary legal positivist theory abandoned the attempt to create a universal fiction of law and its paradigm is restricted to the analysis of the legal systems of western liberal democracies. Legal theory has lost its general character and has become a philosophy of the western liberal democratic rule of law.

A cultural and political contextualisation of legal science is, then, a consequence of this paradigmatic change. Nevertheless, behind this change there lies an ancient truism that the ultimate purposes of every positive law are rightness and justice. Legal positivism had to acknowledge the failure of its attempt to create an a-moral legitimation science of positive law. Rudolf Stammler's *de iure fiction of the just law* (*richtiges Recht*) (Stammler, 1925: 40f.) has been brought back into legal science to constitute a normative criterion for determining the proper function of the liberal democratic rule of law and its even-handed justice. Stammler's original neo-Kantian position and concept of the just law,[2] suggesting that law is just when it is guided by its own intrinsic values and distinct social and logical forms, has been transformed into the ethics of positivism, which then builds on more general ethics of social rules containing both 'the empires' of law and morality.

The fiction of the just law legitimates the existing system of positive law and operates within it in the form of the constitutive principles and procedures of the rule of law, for instance in the famous principle 'Treat like cases alike and different cases differently!'. The concept of the just law can also be detected in the famous 'Radbruch's formula', which helped the post-war German judiciary to distinguish between the justifiable and unjustifiable duties imposed by the Nazi positive law, and which is one of the most important contributions to the post-war development of the ethics of justice and positive law. This rule states that:

> Where the injustice of positive law reaches such measures that the legal certainty guaranteed by positive law no longer functions as the counter-balance of this injustice, unjust positive law must make way for justice (Radbruch, 1959: 33; this translation is taken from Minkkinen, 1999: 41).

The fiction of the just law is the product of an eclectic combination of the ethical claims of liberal democratic political communities and technical claims to establish sovereign political power on the principle of legality and even-handed justice. The positive legal system must be operating as an autonomous normative system, but all its operations are subject to the supervision and corrections of the 'supra-positive' law.

Behind the fiction of the just law as the basis of the legitimacy of a political and legal system there lies the idea that it is not only force but also a more general normative order and principles, which may give the law validity and an obligatory nature. The legitimacy of law cannot be derived from the conditions of validity defined by the system of law itself. It can be

[2]The problem here is that the English translation of *richtiges Recht* suggests its direct links to the notion of justice. The concept, however, is indicative of the idea of 'rightness' or 'correctness' referring to the intrinsic nature of positive law, not to a more general concept of justice. A more correct but less felicitous translation of the concept of 'the just law' would, therefore, be 'the right law'.

derived only from a comparison of the legal conditions of validity with the broader moral political context of law or with transcendental rules of 'correct' thinking.

The legal positivist concepts of legal legitimacy and their fictions reflect the modern image of society as a unit organised and managed from the centre. The centralised, hierarchical model of society was one of many aspects of modernity as a rational break with historically and geographically limited moral traditions. This model required universal validity on the ground of rational thinking, the ultimate stage of which should be science. Legal science attempts to base legitimation on the fictions of the political sovereign and basic norm were the product of scientific rational speculation and their function was to describe law as a united, centralised and hierarchical system. *The fictions were to establish the centre.*

This attempt to create scientific legitimacy in positive law failed and current legal positivism has revived the common concepts of morality and ethics. These concepts now are treated as an inherent part of the logic of positive law. This double character of legality and the operative role of the idea of justice in legal argumentation is analysed by Chaim Perelman in his interpretive legal theory (Perelman, 1963) which shows that the normative structures of legality operate both as an impersonal technique and an ethical claim.

In contemporary legal theory, the centralised and hierarchical structure of the problem of legitimacy still survives. Instead of the fictions of the political sovereign and the basic norm, legitimation discourse now discusses legal principles in their dual role of technique and ethics. Acceptance and application of these principles are conditions of the existence of the just law and subsequently the legitimacy of the system of positive law and political domination. Legal science, if it is to survive as a legitimation narrative about law and political domination, must incorporate ethics into its inner structures, where it must translate them into the language of legality.

The function of the fiction of the just law is clear: to reconcile ethical and legal discourse in the liberal democracies and keep law operating independently of the moral normative system. The internal unity of law, which was conceived by Kelsen as the basis of valid technique of social organisation, must become an ethical demand and respect the ethics of political community. This function, however, includes a strange and popular (especially among lawyers) idea that law is the main and ultimate integrative mechanism of modern society. Legality then legitimates modern political domination and integrates society, but only when it ceases to be 'the iron cage' and becomes also a reflection of the substantive morality and practical reason of society.

....

The dualistic conception of the legality as a technique and ethics is subject to many criticisms. Legal positivist fictions relate to both the descriptive and prescriptive aspects of the dualism. Their purpose is to establish a legal science which could analyse and describe the structures and functions of the system of positive law, its normativity and operations. However, these fictions also have an important integrative role because they determine the image of law as it ought to be.

Contemporary mainstream legal philosophy represents a grand attempt to legitimate the rule of law idea in the conditions of the liberal democratic political communities. Dworkin, for example, does not consider his theory to be general. According to him, his legal theory concentrates and analyses only one specific kind of legal system, the one which emerged in the modern liberal democracies. Legality is legitimate only when it corresponds to the principles of this democratic political regime and therefore enforces the catalogue of human rights. Such legality is an exclusively the property of one legal and political culture. All other legal systems cannot claim to be legal in the full sense of the word. The main task of legal philosophy and legal science is to provide this legality with a scientific explanation and scientific legitimacy.

This concept of legal legitimacy has always been castigated by the critical legal theory and some theoretical schools within the sociology of law. The critical legal theory questions law's self-legitimation by legal science. This is one of the main purposes of critical jurisprudence. For instance, according to Austin Sarat and Thomas R. Kearnes the ''critical story' calls into question law's legitimating narratives' (Sarat and Kearnes, 1991: 253). Critical legal theory depicts the conventional legal philosophy as just one of many legitimating narratives about law. Critical legal science must disclose the falsity of and the real power mechanisms behind this narrative.

Since the mid 80s, Peter Goodrich has been seeking to establish the theoretical foundations of the critique of legality along these lines. Like Sarat and Kearnes, Goodrich advances the argument that the general language of law, its formal structures and impersonality in reality, just blur social and political inequalities and injustices. Legality and the idea of formal justice before the law produce new injustices. Legality and liberal democratic ethics expressed through the law are nothing but a mask, for power and a particular strategy of social control.

According to Goodrich, legality has never been a unified discourse but has always contained a heterogeneity of vocabularies (Goodrich, 1990). The very nature of critical legal studies is that it rereads doctrinal scholarship and, by implication, rewrites the future of professional practice, from the epistemological standpoint of the other of legal knowledge. Critical legal science must think 'the difference of law' (Goodrich, 1995: 13). The task of critical jurisprudence is to develop a theory or doctrine which would offer an alternative to common legal positivism by expressing this difference of law and legality.

Critical jurisprudence attempts to establish a different type of legal knowledge, one which would reflect upon the legalist discourse from outside and subject it to a radical social and political critique. This reflexive attitude towards positive law and legal positivist theory is to expose the fundamental feature of modern legality to be its power to dominate political discourse through a seemingly general vocabulary. The modern image of legality helps to mythologise law and constitute the fictions which support the image of law as an exclusive product of technical rationality (Fitzpatrick, 1992).

According to Goodrich, there is a particular history and social meaning behind every fiction produced by modern legality. The metaphors of legalist language attempt to hide this particular nature, but, *in fact*, they are themselves products of that nature. Legality generates fictions which have the dual function of developing particular social and political strategies and of expressing in turn those strategies in the language of general concepts in order to claim their general acceptance.

According to critical legal scholars, law is politics in the disguise of normative universalism and image of an autonomously functioning system. This blurs the instability and contingency of our world. Law is to strengthen the image of stability and order. It appears therefore crucial to analyse these fictions of modern law and to point to the factual dependence of legal normative structures on the world of politics and many other non-legal structures.

These structures must have a legal form in order to correspond to the notion of the legitimate rule of law. Some critical legal theorists therefore see law as an 'intertext' in which are embedded non-legal elements such as the theological, moral, aesthetic or historical discursive formations, but suppressed by legal arguments (Douzinas and Warrington with McVeigh, 1991: 143). According to critical legal scholars, it is important to conduct a theoretical struggle against the ideology and political discourse of analytical jurisprudence. The modern concept of legality threatens to suppress the contingent and heterogeneous nature of law, suppressing the richness of law's images and differences. It is then considered very important to deconstruct the grammar of modern legality and make manifest the plurality of discourses hidden behind the seemingly homogeneous facade of law (Douzinas and Warrington with McVeigh, 1991: 145ff).

Critical jurisprudence uses deconstruction pragmatically in order to expose the 'veiled' face of law which is covered in the legalist discourse of legal theory. In contrast to the originally non-theoretical meaning of deconstruction, critical jurisprudence suggests that deconstruction is a theory which may be used to establish a counter-ideology which has the power to change the dominating paradigms of legal theory (Douzinas and Warrington with McVeigh, 1991: 146). Critical legal science takes upon itself the difficult political task of changing legal discourse and thus is obliged to come up with a new legitimating scheme. *Critical legal science defines the legal context as a political context.*

The efforts of sociologists of law to question modern legality have had similar consequences. Exemplary socio-legal criticisms of analytical jurisprudence and legalism are to be found in Eugen Ehrlich, who wanted to establish the sociological method as the most general method of legal science (Ehrlich, 1975). A similar treatment of jurisprudence also is present in Jean Carbonnier's sociology of law. Traditional jurisprudence deforms the reality of law and is a source of pathological law, not real normal law (Carbonnier, 1988: 20ff.; for an older view see, for example, Lévy-Bruhl, 1955). The sociology of law has, then, the crucial task of providing a truly scientific view and understanding of law.

Roger Cotterrell, one of the most important figures in contemporary British sociology of law, also believes that the role of the sociological interpretation of law is to disclose and demystify the legal doctrine, discourse and law's understanding of itself. The basic function of every scientific discipline is the advancement of knowledge. The sociology of law advances our knowledge about law's and legal doctrines' social foundations (Cotterrell, 1995: 49). Legal science and sociology, according to Cotterrell, are two disciplines, the intellectual confrontations of which stimulate the development of new knowledge about law. Sociological interpretation is an indispensable part of legal scholarship and the field of the sociology of law cannot be limited to a sub-field of sociology. Adequate knowledge about the nature of law and legal doctrine is impossible without the sociological study of law (Cotterrell, 1995: 71).

The sociology of law achieves the special status of providing a 'realistic' perspective on law and therefore the chance to disclose the true social nature of the power and ideological mechanisms lying behind the legal field. It helps us to overcome the ideological nature of legal scholarship. The role of sociological methodology is to understand law better and subsequently to contribute to the improvement of the real working of the law (Cotterrell, 1998). The 'realistic' sociology of law is contrasted to 'ideological' jurisprudence. The sociological perspective must consequently claim epistemological supremacy over pure or legalistic jurisprudence.

Adherents of the 'realistic' sociology of law use words such as 'must' and 'moral vision' when defining the paradigm of their discipline (Tamanaha, 1997). The sociological perspective has a privileged connection with the concept of truth. Sociology enjoys not only the status of a realistic science, but also of a moralist attitude which, by virtue of its own methodology, can reveal pathological elements in the life of society and thus contribute to the improvement of social reality. Within the context of the sociology of law, this social reality is the reality of positive law.

....

Critical legal theory and the sociology of law seek to make up a scientific framework or discourse which would theoretically prove the falsity of modern legality. The 'realistic' theory ought to replace legalism and its fictions. It is apparent, then, that critical legal theory and some schools of the sociology of law still constitute their paradigms on the distinction between truth and falsehood. The maintenance of this distinction has led to a call for a complex theory sufficiently sophisticated to challenge the false images of the legalist thinking and substitute for them the realistic perspective on law (Patterson, 1996: ch. 3). The attempt to describe the world 'as it is' and confirm the status of 'our' reality in a theoretical discourse still survives. Sarat, Goodrich, Douzinas and others remain, in a certain sense, traditionalists who still want to 'demystify' and unveil the false face of conventional legal philosophy and legality. They take conventional jurisprudence as a narrative masking the real, that is to say the violent, discriminatory and unequal, nature of modern law. *The narrative of critical jurisprudence, however, is then caught in the trap of the 'truth/falsity' discourse and the same problem of maintaining one exclusive vocabulary and scientific legitimacy.*

In critical legal theory, scientific legitimacy keeps its exclusive and dominating character. One theoretical discourse must rule because the status of our reality is derived from it. Even when deconstructing the falsity of legality, the illusion that we can say what the law really is and what should the right legal policy be like is still being reproduced.

The duality of descriptivity and prescriptivity common to legal positivism and legalist fictions is reproduced in critical legal theory and the sociology of law. Realism and scientific legitimacy remain untouched. The domination and exclusiveness of legalism, which are the first targets of critical legal science and the sociology of law, are given their new forms in these fields of legal studies. The hierarchical and asymmetrical model of legal science, favouring one discourse/system and subjecting other discourses/systems to it, remains untouched. Critical legal theory proclaims law to be a part of politics and explains the law's functioning by political concepts and strategies. On the other hand, the sociology of law starts from the realistic notion of one united common sense which is detectable by sociological methods and is to help us to construct a better and much more reflexive law. The sociological perspective, it is said, can represent such common sense and its normativity, pragmatics and value structure. Sociology can thus serve as a vehicle of moral criticism.

It would seem that the attempts of critical legal theory and sociology to criticise legalism by putting law in context and dismantling all possible hierarchical and asymmetrical models are themselves part of the scientific strategy which led to the construction of just such asymmetrical and hierarchical models (Nelken, 1998). A different (critical) reading of legality is different from the legalist reading and claims the status of the right reading. Under the surface of legal positivism and legality, something more fundamental is hidden, a true nature of law. This 'inner body of law' (Goodrich, 1990: 259) lives under the law and cannot speak in its natural pluralistic language. Critical theory must then remove law's surface and help the inner body to speak in public.

This approach is founded on the illusion that there may be an external view of law, which in turn corresponds to the modernist concept of science as a theoretical answer, which determines from the outside what law is and what it ought to be like. For critical jurisprudence, law is always 'Law' with a capital 'L', constantly blurring the real nature of political life and, fettering its subjects by dangerous fictions, and having the power to exclude unwanted genres from the public discourse.

Critical jurisprudence has to fight against this law and establish its own strategy of reading, writing and practising the law. Critical legal theorists, who are a part of an older tradition of legal realism, assume that the theoretical background of law is important even in a contingent and heterogeneous situation because it supplies the ammunition for political and ideological fights. Critical legal scholars assume that deconstructing legality and describing the law's otherness unveils the false and ideological nature of legality and also describes the true nature of law. This 'anti-foundationalist theory hope' looks for a different regime of reading the law, which would not only be different, but would also be politically right and theoretically correct.

This romanticising and resolute position is, however, paradoxically very close to the modern concept of science as the avant-garde instrument of practical change in the public life of modern society. There is always a danger that critical legal scholars and sociologists of law, when rejecting the concept of law's autonomy, will subject legality to other, political or social rules of reading, and so subsume the context of law under the claim that other/their regimes of reading the law have a more important and dominant role.

The project of delegitimation of legal institutions by political language has its roots in the belief that theoretical thinking has a very strong social power and that the role of law in contemporary society is absolutely crucial. *Law is taken too seriously and its limits are ignored.* Legality is finally translated into politics and, moreover, everything becomes politics. Law becomes everything and nothing at the same time in the discourse of critical jurisprudence. Although putting the emphasis on heterogeneity, critical legal theory finally constructs a strongly hierarchical model of legal discourse. It is as if the critical theory were only the dark side of analytical jurisprudence and could not be conceived without its legalism and positivism.

The sociological perspective also can assume the romantic mask of fighting for a better, more just law which will more adequately create a common space of social reality defined by common sense. The juxtaposition of the concept of common sense and expert legal knowledge does not involve only the truth/falsity distinction, but it also represents the need to define the foundations of our social reality, and specifically its hierarchy and asymmetrical nature.

Critical legal science and the sociology of law often castigate legal positivism for purporting to have drawn a false picture of law in its the discourse of legality and legal legitimacy. Nevertheless, this critique itself often represents a foundationalist model of *scientific* thinking and *legitimation* the primary task of which is to construct a 'realistic' picture of law beyond legality.

Scientific legitimation and its dissolution

Legal science offers many different definitions of law and legitimation strategies, when analysing contemporary legal systems. The German legal philosopher Adolf Reinach said that a legal theory was finally always a science of justice (Reinach, 1953). He correctly noted the general character of legal theoretical thinking to be that of an attempt to bring the ethical under scientific control by means of objective language of a legal science. Moral obligations are to have a scientific bias. In Reinach's statement legal modernity is given its pure form. Scientific definitions contain and express moral and political goals. The scientific mode of defining legality sets out the moral version of the world which is favoured by legal philosophers and theorists.

The statement that the final goal of legal theory is justice is only a different manifestation of the 'legitimacy by legality' demand. Legal science sets about defining justice by answering the banal question 'What is law?', to which there obviously is no satisfactory answer. All answers to it, even when they are couched in a highly sophisticated form of objective concepts and scientific definitions, mix up theses about what law and legality 'are' and what they 'ought to be' in order to make law and legality conform to the criteria of justice. *Legal theories always attempt to constitute legitimate legality*. Even the legal realists' critique of legalism is such an attempt, although it is stated as a profound critique of legal paradigm.

Legalist attempts to draw a clear distinction between 'is' [Sein] and 'ought' [Sollen] in order to build legal science as a science of the 'ought' have finally ended up in the reunification of both worlds within the scientific discourse of soft legal positivism. Legalism has been able to survive as a science only by contradicting to its own original demands for a sharp separation of law and morals. *Pure legal science is founded in a 'dirty' ethical search for justice and legitimate law.*

It is no surprise that legal science can never be consistently stated in the terms of the pure discourse which was the primary goal of the founding fathers of modern legal positivism. Legal theory translates the real problem of the legitimacy of political domination and law in modern society into positive scientific language. For modern political systems, the seemingly impersonal and formal rational foundations of legality seemed to be the only way to secure political integration and legitimacy. Searching for definitions of legality, legal theory in fact elaborates a set of classifications which are to describe modern legal systems, but which also justify and legitimate them.

The typical solution of the problem of legitimacy in modern society depends on connecting science and legality. Scientific knowledge establishes its own inner grounds of legitimacy and, subsequently, these grounds become the grounds of the legitimacy of legality and political order. The impossibility of a pure legal theory able to ground its fictions is an example of how legal science itself 'suffers' from the disunity of its own foundations, and therefore cannot offer a sovereign, 'grand narrative'[3] to contemporary societies. The growing plurality of definitions, theoretical constructions and fictions in legal theory reflects the growing plurality of legitimations and the impossibility of giving a simple answer to the question of legitimacy.

Any vocabulary constituted on such distinctions as truth/falsity or fact/fiction turns out to be profoundly insufficient to the understanding of

---

[3]The term 'grand narrative' has been introduced into political philosophy and sociology by Jean-Francois Lyotard (1984).

the current problem of the legitimacy and legitimation of law. Legal science constantly produces new definitions of and scientific legitimating narratives about law and legality, although it can never conform to the universalistic demands of purportedly scientific definition. Conversely, the growing plurality of legal theories is evidence of the failure to construct the universal legitimacy of law by the employment of scientific discourse of positivist legal philosophy.

Faced with this plurality of legitimations within the scientific discourse itself, it is not much use to ask what is truth and what is false when one wants to analyse and legitimate law. The plurality of the attempts to make up and constitute legitimation schemes and narratives about law expressed in the different theories is what is interesting in itself. It is not important whether those narratives about legality are true or false. The most important fact is that there is an obvious need in contemporary societies and science to provide the constructs which are to legitimate legality and political orders.

Legalist fictions have an entirely *functional meaning* because they attempt to understand, explain and accept law in systematic structures and language which often are incomprehensible. At the scientific level, these fictions function in a very similar way to the various 'lay' interpretations of law which are to be found in everyday reality and help people to make their behaviour conform to the rules and regulations of positive law.

The purpose of legalist fictions is to provide a general picture and explanation of law and therefore to generate its general acceptance and consequently its better functioning. In other words, legalist fictions are to support and prove the founding thesis of a modern state and society that 'law is legitimate violence which everybody is obliged to accept'.

The legitimating fictions of legalism and legal science in general have failed to provide modern law and legality with a scientific legitimacy. This is the reason why contemporary legal positivism has given up the pursuit of a purely scientific framework which would be able both to describe structures and functions of all existing and past legal systems and legitimate the modern concept of legality. The scientific legitimacy given to the liberal democratic system of law in the works of Dworkin or Raz represents only a small fragment of the original legal positivist project. The 'realism' of the critical jurisprudence and the sociology of law also cannot offer a generally valid legitimation framework and the main value of this 'realistic' view is that it discloses the merely relative validity and the external limits of the current discourse of legal science. Legal science only reproduces a growing social, ideological and cultural plurality.

4 Postcommunist Legitimations and Constitutional Justice

Legalist revolutions?

The 1989 revolutions against communism dissolved the modern fiction of the sovereign people, but they did not question that it was necessary for the revolutions and the new regimes to have democratic legitimacy. The people ceased to be a historical representative of the common political will and turned rather into a mere label for a politics of plurality and difference based on individual and collective rights and freedoms. This politics has deep existential aspects. For reasons set out more fully in the second chapter, it was impossible for the revolutions and the new regimes to formulate one strategy and vocabulary which could operate as a sovereign legitimation framework.

From the perspective of legitimation strategies of the 1989 revolutions are very ambiguous, despite the fact that their second characteristic feature, beside democratic legitimation, was use of the vocabulary of individual and collective human rights and freedoms. It involves a legalist attitude towards the rule of law and constitutional protection of those rights and freedoms. *The legalist legitimation* of human rights and freedoms and the democratic rule of law were a very important, but not the only legitimation framework used in the revolutions.

The ethics of legalism derived from contemporary legal positivism were given a distinct form in the legalist concept of the revolutions. The principle of the rule of law, so strongly enunciated in all revolutions against communism, has primarily a deeply ethical meaning. It is treated as a political and revolutionary virtue which must be heavily defended. *The ethics of legalism and the fiction of the just law have a very strong persuasiveness and legitimating force.* This force often is more important than the force of democratic legitimation and can operate quite independently of it.

The legalist legitimation framework was especially significant in the two countries in which the revolutionary changes started early and were continually developed during the round table talks. In Poland and Hungary, the communist government and the opposition negotiated a series of gradual political and legal changes. It was necessary to formulate rules and procedures for such a complicated process and therefore, *the fiction of the legal revolution*, a revolution limited by the existing communist constitutional and legal framework, emerged. Its main purpose was to help to dismantle the communist system and to establish the liberal democratic rule of law by peaceful means. The constitution of this fiction was supported by all parties to the round table talks. At one conference in the middle of 1989, the Hungarian communist minister of justice and legal scholar Kálmán Kulcsár set out the three key issues of the Hungarian political transformation. They were: the rule of law, constitutionalism, and human rights (Casper, 1991: 442).

The legalist attitude towards the revolutionary changes in Hungary led to the basic persistence of the 1949 communist constitution, though it was, of course, substantially changed. The provisions establishing the one political party system and the principles of communist power were replaced by provisions protecting human rights and the principles of the democratic rule of law. The use of the old constitution to set out the new political conditions represented something of a 'squaring the circle' (Arato, 1993: 674).

The rule of law was established, but the way it was done was ruled by the fiction 'as if' this system already existed during the time when the communists were negotiating with the opposition in the round table talks. This fiction also had a concrete impact on the new liberal democratic legal and political system. The legalist strategy of the revolution made it, for instance, impossible to deal with the communist past in a more radical political way. The Hungarian constitutional court held that the Zetényi and Takács law of 1992, intended to prosecute some communist political crimes, was unconstitutional. The court declared the law void on the ground that it would amount to retroactive justice and therefore to the infringement of one of the constitutive principles of the rule of law, the principle of legal security (decision of the Constitutional Court of Hungary n. 11 of 1992, III.5. AB).

Poland had a similar legalist concept of the revolution. The communist constitution of 1952 remained in force but was gradually brought into conformity with the new political and legal conditions (the fundamental constitutional changes happened in 1993 and then in 1997). The principle of the rule of law led to the development of the self-limiting revolution. To have 'a democratic revolution' invoked subjecting the revolution to a rigorous legal framework and avoiding the lawlessness of, for instance, retroactive legislation and legal discontinuity (Brzezinski and Garlicki, 1995: 32). Although the Polish Constitutional Tribunal did not completely reject the possibility of departing from the principle *lex retro non agit*, when prosecuting the political crimes of Stalinism, it held that this possibility could arise only in very exceptional legal situations, which could be given absolutely clear legal definition (Judgment S 6/91, 25 September 1991, Orzecynictwo Tryb. Konst. 290, 294).

The legalist legitimation strategy was present from the very beginning of the revolutionary changes even in those countries in which the round table talks had to be brought about more by revolutionary agitation in the streets and squares than by a carefully planned process of political changes within a stable procedural framework. In Czechoslovakia, one of the first revolutionary demands was to abolish those provisions in the communist federal constitution which established the leading role of the Communist party. In December 1989, the Civic Forum produced its own draft of the new democratic constitution for the Czechoslovak federal state. One of the most valuable, but unfortunately only rare, successful outcomes of the constitutional transformation of the Czechoslovak federation after 1989 was the enactment of the Charter of Fundamental Rights and Freedoms in 1991.

In all the post-communist countries, issues such as the rule of law, the relationship between legitimacy and legality, and retroactive justice in the post-revolutionary laws were largely determined by legal and political discussions, and the resulting legislation which took place in the first half of the 90s. In Czechoslovakia and, later, in the Czech Republic, discussions about the legality and legitimacy of the communist regime played a very important role and influenced, for example, the lustration law forbidding the employment of some communist party officials and members of secret police in certain positions within the state administration. Another example of the impact of those discussions on the legislation were the laws for the restitution of property.

How could the past communist system be criticised and condemned in legal or legalistic terms? It had had its own constitution, legislation, laws and judiciary. Was it subject to the rule of law (a law based state/*Rechtsstaat*)?[1] If it had not been subject to the rule of law, why did the new liberal democratic regime adopt a substantial part of its laws? These are questions which influenced the political language of postcommunist societies in the first period after the revolution.

The question whether the communist regime was legal and legitimate was the subject of so many public debates that it was even comically raised in a play given by the National Theatre in Prague.[2] The theoretical and practical importance of the relationship between legitimacy and legality increases enormously during episodes of sudden political change and the reconstruction of legal systems. It is tempting to say that against the background of the 1989 revolutionary changes in the former Soviet bloc countries a revision and possibly a new formulation of the whole question of the legitimacy of law and political domination can be achieved.

It was an easily recognisable fact that, despite the survival of certain constitutional and legal documents of the former communist regime in the new political and legal conditions, there was a substantial difference between the principle of socialist legality and the liberal democratic rule of law. The above mentioned continuity of the Hungarian constitution from 1948 was entirely formal because a vast majority of its original provisions were subjected to fundamental change during 1989 and 1990 (Elster, 1991: 462-3). The Polish communist constitution from 1952 was a similar example of how the original legal text was completely redrafted and rewritten during that time. The Polish Constitution adopted in 1997 has almost nothing in common with the text of 1952. After 1989 in Czechoslovakia, the old communist federal constitution significantly contributed to a crisis of federalism, which led to the splitting of the country in 1992.

Taking into account the potential arbitrariness of socialist legality and the permanent threat of intervention by the communist party in judicial decision-making, it is hardly surprising that the rule of law became one of

---

[1]The concept of the law-based state may seem quite unusual to English readers, but it is so far the most common translation of the German term *Rechtsstaat* and its equivalents in other European languages. Therefore, in this chapter concerning mostly the problems of post-communist constitutional systems and justice, I will use the term law-based state where I mean *Rechtsstaat* and English readers would expect the concept of the rule of law.

[2]It is the play *Strange Birds (Podivní ptáci)* by the distinguished Czech playwright and film director Antonín Máša. This play was one of first critical reflections on the Czech postrevolutionary situation (Máša, 1996).

the most important revolutionary demands even in those countries, which, instead of having long round table talks, experienced sudden revolutionary change. The revolutionary vocabulary in Czechoslovakia and East Germany contained, besides its other features, a legal positivist vocabulary demanding the re-establishment of legality, due process of law, and generally binding impartial procedures.

Legal positivism and a formal legalist approach had a strong critical force because those qualities of law, such as the regularity, foreseeability, security, iterability, or integrity, which contemporary legal positivists claim to be the ethics of legalism, turned out truly to be important values protecting individual autonomy and security. These qualities of law are efficient tools for criticising a political regime which does not hesitate to promote to the judiciary according to momentary political circumtances and which legislates, not by parliamentary rules, but by the secret rules of the Central Committee of the Party.

The famous slogan of legal positivists 'Justice according to law!' can really have a strong critical meaning when confronting the communist power which uses 'quasi-natural law' arguments. The arbitrary, repressive and discriminatory nature of this power was often ideologically explained by reference to the principle of the historical role of the working class, which was to abolish economic exploitation and introduce ultimate historical and social justice. The communist system was also backed by the principle of the subjection of the judicial power to the 'objective' interests of the socialist regime, as formulated by the Communist Party, or rather by its Central Committee and the repressive forces of secret police (for further information see Pelikán, 1971). As Otto Ulč says of this system of justice, one of its key concepts was 'classness', and this, according to Viktor Knapp, a key figure in Czechoslovak communist jurisprudence, was 'a brilliant discovery of legal science!' (Knapp, 1959: 29). Ulč describes his own experience and doubts about the concepts of socialist legality and condemns its arbitrariness:

> Nothing was more harmful to the pursuit of justice than the insistence on the implementation of the omnipresent enigma termed as 'classness'. ... in Marxist terms the concept of 'blind justice' and 'equality for all' is an idealistic delusion. Even after the successful proletarian revolution, the laws and the courts remain the instument of the new ruling class designed to liquidate the political, economic, and ideological remnants of capitalism. ... We felt, rather, that the whole class-concept 'discovery' was irrational, ambiguous and

> arbitrary. No one has ever been able - or willing - to define a class enemy (Ulč, 1972: 30-1).

Set against this characteristic arbitrariness and holistic nature of socialist legality, the liberal concepts of human rights, civil freedoms and the democratic rule of law represented a strong political demand which was to be achieved through revolutionary action and subsequent social, constitutional and legal transformation.

Together with the Charter of Fundamental Rights and Freedoms and some other constitutional documents, the immediate outcome of a legalist strategy and the calls for the rule of law was the incorporation of international human rights treaties into the Czechoslovak constitutional and legal system. Article 10 of the Czech Constitution, adopted on 16 December 1992 and brought into force on the first of January 1993 with the split of the Czechoslovak Federal Republic, provides that:

> International treaties concerning human rights and fundamental freedoms, which have been ratified and promulgated and by which the Czech Republic is bound, are directly applicable and take precedence over an act of Parliament.

This principle means that international documents on human rights have the binding force of constitutional laws and all legal documents must conform to their provisions and regulations.

As well as this incorporation of international treaties concerning human rights and fundamental freedoms into the constitutional system of the Czech Republic, there was a need to formulate the principle of the people's political sovereignty in a new way different from the communist constitutional system. The Constitution of the Czech Republic mentions the principle of the sovereignty of the people in Article 2:

> The people are the source of all state authority; they exercise it through the organs of legislative, executive and judicial power (article 2, section 1) ... State authority serves all citizens, and may be exercised only in cases, within the limits and in the manner provided for by the law (article 2, section 3).

These provisions have to be read carefully and interpreted within the context of the preamble to the Czech Constitution which emphasises the values of civil society. The legislative intention of Article 2 was to identify the people with the citizens of the republic, that is to say, with citizens of different political opinions, social traditions, and historical and cultural backgrounds. The plurality of civil society is implicitly contrasted with the ethnic national concept of political sovereignty and plays an important symbolic role in the whole process of the transformation of post-communist societies. The ethical revolutionary demands of plurality and civil freedoms have found their constitutional and legal form.

The incorporation of natural rights and ethical discourse into the language of the Constitution of the Czech Republic and the Charter of Fundamental Rights and Freedoms, which also were part of the legal and constitutional reconstruction after 1989, is a much more subversive strategy from the positive lawyers' perspective. The constitution-makers were deeply convinced by the experience of the past that not every law is the law. Recent history has proven that it was not sufficient to conform to the legalist formal notion of law. Instead, legal normativity must primarily conform to the normativity of democratic liberal political morality. It was as if the Czech constitution-makers wanted to codify exactly what was described as the fiction of the just law, legitimating the system of positive law and legislation in liberal democratic societies (Přibáň, 1995).

One product of this codification of the just law is the preamble of the Charter, which explicitly mentions the inviolability of the 'natural rights of man'. However, article no.85 of the Czech Constitution, prescribing the oath of a judge of the Constitutional Court to protect 'the inviolability of natural human rights and of the rights of citizens', is even more important. Unlike the Charter's preamble, which has the function only of providing guidelines for the interpretation of the individual provisions of the legal text, the judge's oath obliges him/her to follow certain extra-legalist principles and incorporate them into the system of the Court's decision-making when necessary.

Post-communism as a process of re-modernisation

The starting point of the Velvet Revolution in 1989 was recognition of the democratic deficit of communist political discourse. The totalitarian system excluded any political discussion which was not of a ritualistic character and could not be controlled by the of political power. The post-revolutionary developments were subsequently characterised by an outpouring of political rhetoric in which all social issues were subjected to political analysis. Citizens and new democratic institutions sought to understand and define the emerging political and social conditions and consequently produced this overflow.

For several reasons, totalitarianism means the end of politics in the sense of a free public exchange of citizens' opinions and interests. The first reason is the disappearance of the distinction between the private and the public which defines limits on political power. Totalitarian power does not recognise any limits and expands according to its immediate needs and strategic interests.

The second reason is the subjection of the formerly sovereign political institutions of the modern state to the sovereign power of the communist party. Instead of state power being organised as a balance between different political forces, the state in a totalitarian society is completely subjected to the central power of the Party. Party positions are more important than positions within the state hierarchy, Party instructions are more important than laws and adjudication.

The third reason is the exclusion of all political programmes and ideologies not defined by the Party. All political opinions disqualified after ideological scrutiny by the Party are treated as extremist. Consequently, the Party itself is permanently fighting against many different kinds of 'deviance' within its own structures.

In totalitarian political systems, politics as a public space does not exist, because the state generates instability rather than stability for its citizens. State sovereignty is 'privatised' by the Party which constrains political communication within exclusive ideological limits. Politics thus, paradoxical as it may seem, disappears when everything must be subjected to one sovereign political vocabulary.

Post-communist societies are thus engaged in what may be described as the renewal of politics. The main objective of the first period of post-revolutionary transformation is the dilution of the sovereign power of the Communist Party into the common model of the constitutional separation of powers, the definition of strict rules and limits on those powers, and the renewal of political debate. After this transformation, extremists are defined not by their difference from the exclusive ideology, but rather by the extent of violence and hatred involved in their political programmes.

The whole process of transformation must be understood as a process of modernisation. This may seem rather strange to say in the Czech case, because Czech society was engaged in rebuilding political and constitutional institutions which had existed before the Second World War. After 50 years, Czech society has returned to liberal democratic constitutionalism, a market economy and civil society traditions. This process is not a simple re-make of history. It is a complicated attempt to reconstruct conditions which the generations living today, with the exception of the oldest, have never directly experienced. It is for this reason that we should speak of the process of re-modernisation, the primary goal of which is the establishment of the institutional framework of a modern society.

As well as the establishment of liberal democratic institutions, a market economy, and the adoption of many new private and public laws, this reconstruction involves a more general reflection on the nature of this 'construction time' itself. Society and its different institutions constantly reflect upon their own transformation and seek to describe, understand and consequently influence it. This reflexivity is manifested in citizens' preoccupation with politics as a natural reaction to the processes of social change. It is typical of post-communist societies to attribute clear political causes to all social problems. The perceived importance of political institutions and their transformation is the corollary of the feeling of insecurity and political anomie during that transformation.

In this re-modernisation of Czech society, the Constitutional Court plays an enormous role. Its judgments do not only interpret and apply the rules of the new Czech Constitution, but they also seek to specify in normative terms the nature of the new political regime itself. The judgments of the Constitutional Court must be understood as autonomous, political-moral, 'legislative' attempts to draw a plan for liberal-democratic politics in post-communist Czech society. The moralist and political vocabulary of the Court's judgments goes beyond the usual limits of moral and political arguments employed by constitutional courts in established liberal democracies. For the Court, the use of this vocabulary often is not only a supplement to legal reasoning. The Court's decisions include extensive passages concerning the nature of democratic legitimacy and, surprisingly, attack the concept of formal rational legality, a concept which one might have thought it would regard as appropriate for its own legitimation.

In an examination of the functions of the Czech Constitutional Court, I want to test the thesis that the process of post-revolutionary transformation brings about a polarity in the function of constitutional justice. Unlike law-based state systems in established liberal democracies, in which the courts use moral and political arguments to supplement the principle of formal legality, the Czech Constitutional Court even acts as a fundamental critic of formal rational legality in order to define and 'legislate' the space of democratic politics and morality. This *political hypertrophy* of constitutional justice is typical of the period in which a new legal system does not yet operate as an autonomous system, but in which it is no longer subject to the one party political system characteristic of a totalitarian society.

Constitutional justice in post-communist countries

In Poland, the Constitutional Tribunal was set up before the fall of the communist regime in 1985. Its role was expanded by the constitutional changes of October 1992. The image of the law-based state is inseparable from the adjudication by the Constitutional Tribunal and its involvement in the country's political disputes (Brzezinski and Garlicki, 1995; Brzezinski, 1993: 42). Even more active involvement in political life can be seen in the work of the Hungarian Constitutional Court, which was established in 1990 (Sajo, 1999). The role of the Constitutional Court of Slovakia between 1994 and 1998 was uniquely important, even by post-communist standards. In this period, Prime Minister Vladimír Mečiar and his political allies broke many liberal democratic principles. In the end, the Court turned out to be the last constitutional institution trying to protect the system against these flagrant abuses of political power (Bútora, 1997). Disputes between the Russian Constitutional Court and the presidential power, although of a different origin and nature, were similarly confrontational.

These facts should not be very surprising. In European continental legal culture, constitutional courts defy the principle that statutory law is the only and ultimate source of law. All the European post-communist countries belong to this culture. The constitutional courts consequently have developed a system of constitutional law using precedents as a source of law. The political role of constitutional justice has grown immensely and this causes a number of legal and political conflicts in these countries. This expanded role and the growth of constitutional precedents has been rejected by some politicians who are members of the legislature or executive. They are resisted even by the lower courts and the supreme courts, because adjudication becomes much more complicated (see, for instance, the judgment of the Constitutional Court of the Czech Republic, n.275/96 III. ÚS).

The German legal system established after 1945 developed a constitutional culture involving precedents as a source of law. It was held that the sovereignty of statutory law was to be limited, and it must coexist with reasoning founded on human rights arguments (for the importance of human rights, see Grimm, 1994: 277). The German Constitutional Court attacked the formalist application of legal and constitutional rules and favoured broader arguments based on values, the principle of justice and fundamental human rights, for example, in the famous case *Lueth* and the case of the former border guards of the German Democratic Republic.[3]

In German legal theory, the Constitutional Court has an important role in the creation of legal norms and constitutionalism. It is important to the constitutional system that the Court does not have the simply passive function of applying constitutional norms. It participates in the making of the whole constitutional system and, within the limits of the written constitutional rules, determines the normative framework of the law-based state. The German legal theorist Ulrich Preuss acknowledges this special role of the German Constitutional Court and calls for the Court to exercise *self-restraint* (Preuss, 1964). Because it is technically impossible to establish limits on the Court's interpretation of the Constitution, it is necessary to trust the Court not to break certain abstract principles of the constitutional law-based state.

The involvement of the Court in resolving political conflicts and its direct participation in the normative building of the constitutional order of the law-based state is, therefore, neither surprising nor specific to post-communist countries during their transformation from totalitarianism into liberal democratic regimes. In these countries, constitutional judges are aware of the fact that they can act like Dworkin's Hercules and in fact quite often make use of the opportunity. But in confrontational and unstable situations, such as the 1993 conflict between the Russian Constitutional Court and President Yeltsin, this Herculean attempt to enter directly into the field of politics can badly damage the whole constitutional separation of powers (Hausmaniger, 1995: 349). However, severe political

[3]The Constitutional Court's decision in the case of the former members of a border guard was published in Karlsruhe, 12 November 1996: Order of 26 October 1996 - 2BvR 1851/94, 2BvR 1853/94, 2BvR 1875/94 and 2BvR 1852/94.

conflicts emerging from judgments of a constitutional court can occur even in relatively stable conditions, for instance in the decision of the Polish Constitutional Court on abortion.

Nevertheless, in post-communist countries, constitutional judges often see fit to do even more than act like Hercules. They are confronted with the temptation to step out of the playground of the constitutional process and enter directly into the battlefield of political conflict. They do not confine themselves to the field of the legal reflection on political problems. They directly employ purely political arguments (as well as constitutional ones), when seeking to define the political system as such. It is precisely this judicial activity which makes the decision-making process in the post-communist constitutional courts unique. Post-communist legal systems are at present not sufficiently structured to make it unnecessary for the constitutional courts to move freely from legal discourse into political or moral discourse. Many examples of this may be found in the judgments of the Czech Constitutional Court, which I examine in the remainder of this chapter.

All post-communist societies had to endure a phase, common to revolutions, in which the old power is fading away and the new power is coming in. In this situation, it is important to construct certain legitimation strategies for and fictions of the transition. The legalist fiction of the just law has thus a much more legalist form in those countries in which the whole process of revolutionary transformation emerged gradually through the round table talks. In those countries in which the round table talks had merely a more or less symbolic function and the revolutionary transformation was happening under the pressure of crowds in the streets, there seems to exist a high level of uncertainty about the nature and outcomes of the revolution. The pressing need for a moral and political interpretation of the revolution which can legitimate the revolutionary changes and achievements, is a consequence of this uncertainty.

In countries such as the Czech Republic, the fiction of the just law has a decidedly moralist character and the legitimation of the law based state occurs primarily as a process of the moral and political legitimation of the new emerging legal system. The following parts of this chapter will analyse the arguments about the legitimation of the law based state which were employed by the Constitutional Court of the Czech Republic.

The moral authority of the legislative body

The very first decision of the Constitutional Court of the Czech Republic had extremely important constitutional and political significance. It concerned the *Act on the Lawlessness of the Communist Regime and the Resistance Against It*, the content of which was politically controversial and caused a number of disputes (The Act n. 198/1993 of the Collection of Laws of the Czech Republic). This Act was intended to put an end to the prolonged discussion, dating back to the Velvet Revolution in 1989, about how to deal with the communist past and the consequences of communist government. Like other post-communist countries, Czech society was looking for an opportunity to judge its own past.

Some politicians proposed to use the standard criminal tribunal to try political crimes and crimes against humanity. Others favoured placing the top officials of the communist regime before a moral version of the Nuremberg Trial, one which could pass only moral judgment and not penal sanction. Both proposals sought to put the past communist regime on trial, be it under the criminal law or with only moral consequences.

In this respect, it is interesting to see that the 'truth commission', so popular and influential in South Africa and some Latin American countries, was not adopted in the post-communist countries. The transition from communist dictatorship to democracy occurred without any official form of moral judgment or quasi-judicial procedure at all. Under these circumstances, when victims of the communist repression did not receive adequate moral or legal satisfaction, the Czech parliament decided to produce its own legislation. From the very first moment of its enactment, the *Act on Lawlessness of the Communist Regime and the Resistance Against It*, caused much controversy, particularly as its language was quite unclear. Communist party members of Parliament were especially severe in their protests against the law.[4] It was communist members of Parliament who finally initiated the constitutional petition which led the Constitutional Court to consider the matter. The Court's judgment (n. 19/93Pl.US) did not concentrate only on the concrete constitutional complaints raised by the 41 members of Parliament. Its reasoning included a very detailed analysis of

---

[4]It is important to know that the Communist Party of Bohemia and Moravia [KSCM], unlike most communist parties after 1989, refused to transform itself into a social democratic left party and remained a hard core Stalinist political force.

the legitimation background of liberal democratic power and the law-based state.

The authors of the petition attacked the Act as a whole and asked the Constitutional Court to declare it unconstitutional and void. They claimed the second section of the Act to be unconstitutional because it described the communist regime as illegitimate (para. 1 of the judgment's part concerning objections to section 1 to 4 of the Act n. 198/93Sb). The petitioners emphasised that the new liberal regime incorporated the legal order of the former communist regime and adopted the international legal obligations of communist Czechoslovakia, that is to say, that it accepted the legitimacy of the communist regime and its laws. The petitioners also targeted the second paragraph of the first section of the Act which recognised the joint responsibility of those who actively supported the communist regime for the political crimes committed by that regime. In contrast to the following section of the Act, which declared the communist regime criminal and illegitimate and expressed moral recognition of its victims, the concept of responsibility in the disputed paragraph, according to the petitioners, was leading to criminal liability (see para. 5 of the judgment's part concerning objections to section 1 to 4 of the Act n. 198/93Sb).

The Court had to resolve the technical relationship between the criminal law concept of responsibility and the responsibility for political crimes orchestrated by the communist regime referred to in the Act. The judgment distinguishes between the concept of responsibility in the criminal legal sense, which requires all the substantive elements of a given criminal act to be established, and responsibility as it appears in sections 1 to 4 of the Act. This latter responsibility, according to the Court, signifies only the moral responsibility of individuals who actively participated in the repressive political system. The Act is described as a general statute and its norms as declaratory norms without imperative, legally binding force (see para. 8 of the judgment's part concerning objections to section 1 to 4 of the Act n. 198/93Sb).

According to the Court, Parliament may adopt such norms at any time and it is, therefore, necessary to distinguish between two senses in which Parliament may function as a legislator, the imperative and the declaratory, in the latter of which it does not intend to introduce legal obligations by its enactments, but to express political ideas and moral judgments. The Court gave Parliament the power to act as a supreme legislative body not only in a purely legal sense, but also in terms of moral authority. It gave Parliament the power to generate, through legislative acts, the moral legitimacy of a political regime.

The Constitutional Court believes that Parliament has a function of moral authority that may seem to correspond to the common practice of legislatures. For instance, the Polish Sejm's resolution on lustrations of 28 May 1992, which urged the minister of interior to provide information on secret police agents inside the legislative, administrative and judicial bodies, caused a huge constitutional and political crisis and finally led to the resignation of the government (Osiatynski, 1992). Legal theoretical doubts about the imperative character of parliamentary resolutions, especially in relation to legislative parliamentary acts, were raised in the Polish Constitutional Tribunal, which declared the resolution on lustrations unconstitutional and void.

In the Czech Republic, behind the view that the Parliament can express its political opinions and moral judgments through legislation, lay the Constitutional Court's acute concern about the extent of the legitimacy of the new political regime in the public mind. The Court ruled, therefore, that it was possible to legislate of morality and political beliefs, although the judges must have been aware that when exercising this function Parliament was operating with exactly opposite effect to its exercise of its legal legislative function. While parliamentary legal legislation operates to subject the state-organised society to certain norms and to integrate it, parliamentary moral legislation produces a differentiation of a political society.

No moral judgment or political belief can achieve supreme and universal binding force in modern society. When Parliament acts as a body representing the sovereign political will of the people, its function is to strengthen this fiction of the general will of the people. It is expected to adopt legal norms, which by their general nature, regulate social life. When, on the other hand, Parliament expresses moral or political judgments, it must naturally exclude, or at least ignore other political or moral judgments incompatible with its own. As moral legislator, it acts against its own fundamental fiction of the general will because morally and politically inconsistent judgments are excluded from Parliament's will and achieve the status of unacceptable or even extremist beliefs.

The Constitutional Court was able to take into account the problematic character of the moral legislative activities of Parliament when considering the introductory declaration of Act n.198/93Sb. This states that Parliament will use the Act as its point of departure in its future activities. To the objection of the petitioners that the legislative sovereignty of Parliament is restricted, the Court ruled:

> This declaration is an expression of political will of a programmatic character, a will established at a certain time and with a certain line-up of forces in Parliament, a fact which may not be interpreted inconsistently with the right of Parliament, in the area and within the bounds of its competence, to adjust the matter differently at another time, nor inconsistently with the principle of the free exchange of views on the floor of Parliament (see para. 18 of the judgment's part concerning objections to section 1 to 4 of the Act n. 198/93Sb).

In the light of this reasoning, which certainly has its place within the system of parliamentary power in the democratic law-based state, the Court should have answered the question whether all Parliament's moral and political argumentation is also subject to this change and whether the moral political principles of a liberal democratic regime and the rule of law are only the results of the momentary distribution of political forces in Parliament.

The Court seems here to express a common and hardly questionable proposition about parliamentarianism. It would, however, consequently be obliged to conclude that the moral legislative activity of Parliament is also only the contingent result of particular political forces and expresses only the limited conviction of majority members of Parliament in the field of politics and morality. The Court, however, obviously did not favour this conclusion and supported Parliament's moral judgment. A moral judgment about the nature of communist totalitarianism should not be just a momentary result of Parliament's majority will. It should also be a moral pillar of a liberal democratic regime and a law-based state. From the perspective of liberal democracy and its law, this moral judgment, so carefully specified and applied in the Constitutional Court's judgment, has fundamental and transcendent meaning.

When applied to the communist regime and its ideology, we do not mind this kind of moral legislative function so much. We may not find the exclusion of communist morality and political beliefs so painful. Nevertheless, there are other morally controversial cases in which Parliament, in its role of supreme moral authority, may act in a highly objectionable way. It may cause a lot of moral and political confrontations and ultimately lose just the kind of moral legitimacy in society which it seeks to achieve by its moral legislation.

The bizarre role of moral legislator which the Court explicitly ascribed to Parliament in its judgment, is founded on the hierarchical and centralist model of modern political society in which the people delegate their power to a representative body. This body becomes *de facto* the political sovereign. But this centralist model originally implied the liberal idea that the political sovereign should make law and never get involved in matters of morality, which belong to citizens' private sphere (Bentham, 1983: ch. 3, art. 1). When the Czech Constitutional Court ruled that the political sovereign could also act as a moral authority in order to support the legitimacy of the liberal democratic political regime and the law-based state, it did so because it feared that the framework of the new political regime of post-communist Czech society was insufficiently stable. It was, therefore, appropriate for constitutional institutions such as Parliament to contribute to the development of a liberal democratic vocabulary and of moral beliefs corresponding to democratic principles of government. The Court did not find it immoral that the Czech Parliament should tell its citizens what they should think as free agents of the democratic system. On the contrary, it gave Parliament the power to operate as a moral authority in the future.

The Court's definition of democratic politics

The Court's moral and political interpretation of the concept of responsibility had a strong pragmatic basis. The Court wanted to demonstrate the constitutionality of the *Act on Lawlessness of the Communist Regime and Resistance Against It,* but it did not want to create a state of legal instability by recognising the possible criminal legal consequences of individual provisions of the Act. To declare the Act void and unconstitutional would be regarded by the majority of citizens as an unacceptable way of dealing with the communist past. On the other hand, to open up the possibility of criminal prosecution under the Act would involve an unacceptable infringement of the principles of a law-based state.[5]

This interpretation was the starting point for the Court to engage in its own extensive discussion of the nature of the law-based state, performing the same political and moral legislative role itself which it ascribed to Parliament. To the objection that it was unconstitutional to call the communist regime from 1948-1989 illegitimate, the Constitutional Court responded with a detailed analysis of the principles of a law-based state (compare para. 21 of the judgment's part concerning objections to section 1 to 4 of the Act n. 198/93Sb). The Court correctly refused to perceive the problem of legitimacy in a narrow sense, as a problem of the continuity of the legal system. It refused to call the communist system legitimate simply because the new liberal regime incorporated its laws and acknowledged its international legal obligations. From a theoretical legal viewpoint, it is interesting to see that the communist petitioners completely accommodated the legalist concept of legitimacy we have seen in Hans Kelsen's pure theory of law (see the analysis of Kelsen's jurisprudence in chapter 3 of this book). According to them, all acts bearing a legal form are legitimate. The petitioners were mainly concerned to prove the existence of legal continuity after 1989 and thus to blur the sharp political discontinuity between the past and the current conditions born out of the Velvet Revolution.

The Court refused to understand the legitimacy as a mere technical function of legality and concentrated on the wider moral political context. According to its judgment, the new Czech Constitution adopted in December 1992 is not value-neutral and therefore does not regard the principle of legality only as a kind of technique independent of more general values. The Constitution incorporates the leading ideas and values of democratic political society and subjects legality to them (see para. 24 of the judgment's part concerning objections to section 1 to 4 of the Act n. 198/93Sb).

According to the Court's judgment, the constitutional law-based state must have democratic legitimacy, not only legal legitimacy in its formal sense. The legitimacy of the political regime is derived from the democratic political principles, the observance of which characterises all

[5]It is necessary to emphasise that the Court refused to conceive the concept of responsibility in terms of criminal law. Nevertheless, the Court also stated that individual acts criminal and punishable according to laws in force at that time, must still be prosecuted.

law-based states and the principle of legality itself. The people bear *constitutive* power, while law is the product of *constituted* and institutionalised internal state power (see para. 29 of the judgment's part concerning objections to section 1 to 4 of the Act n. 198/93Sb). This constituted power, moreover, must not be concentrated in one institution but must be established according to the traditional principle of the separation of powers. (The Court speaks about other values constituting a democratic law-based state, but its analysis is principally focused on the principle of the people's sovereignty and the majority will manifested by constitutional bodies.)

The legitimacy of the law-based state depends upon its democratic nature. It must have democratic elections, its constitutional bodies must make decisions according to the majority will and all laws must have a double democratic background; they must be adopted by democratic parliamentary procedures and those who adopt them (members of Parliament) must be democratically elected. Legality is subject to the legitimation framework of democratic procedures.

....

The Constitutional Court of the Czech Republic returned to the problem of democratic legitimacy in another controversial case in 1994. This concerned the legal validity of President Beneš' decrees on the basis of which the Czechoslovak state confiscated property of the Sudeten Germans and expelled them from the country after the Second World War in 1945. This case was politically delicate because it concerned the possibility of the restitution of this property to the Sudeten Germans by the Czech Republic. The post-war expulsion of Germans from Czechoslovakia and Poland and the issue of their compensation was a problem in international politics at that time because the German conservative government, and particularly Bavarian right wing politicians, applied constant political pressure for restitution on its neighbour states.

The petition sought the annulment of Presidential Decree n.108/1945Sb., on the Confiscation of Enemy Property and the Funds of National Renewal on the grounds of its unconstitutionality and unlawfulness. It described the decree as an act of political and revolutionary violence, incompatible with the contemporary principles of the law-based state which now bound the Czech Republic. The petitioner demanded the annulment of the decree *ab initio,* on the grounds of its undemocratic character and inhuman substance and for its inconsistency with the Czech constitutional order and international treaties on human rights (see the Court's judgment, n. 14/94Pl.US, para. 1 of the reasoning).

The Court began its judgment by noting the consistency of the decree with the fundamental principles of the law-based state. It then considered whether it may have been legitimate for President Beneš to decree such laws. In this context, the Court emphasised the contrast with the nature of the Nazi political regime, the legal system of which was subject to totalitarian power and served German nationalist and racist interests. The Nuremberg laws from 1935 were taken as examples. In contrast to the German Nazi legislation, the Court referred to the Czechoslovak Constitution of 1920, which defined the democratic and civic character of the Czechoslovak state and subjected its constitutional institutions to democratic legitimacy. In this judgment, the principle of democratic legitimacy is again explicitly superior to the principle of formal legal legitimacy.

The principle of democratic legitimacy was also mentioned in connection with the incorporation of the President's decrees into the post-war Czechoslovak legal order, when these acts were approved by the Provisional National Assembly in its Act n.12/1946Sb (para. 7 of the reasoning). The Court conceived the problem of legitimacy in a way very similar to its approach in its judgment concerning the *Act on Lawlessness of the Communist Regime and Resistance Against It*. A democratic political regime is contrasted with a totalitarian regime, this time the Nazi political regime.

While in democratic pre-war Czechoslovakia the people accepted the law-based state on the ground of general consensus, the Nazi totalitarian state enacted its law by violence and terror. According to the Court, consensus as the concrete expression of the democratic principle of the people's will is a source of legitimation.

The Court continued to define a democratic regime on the basis of citizenship and contrasted the democratic-republican principle of citizenship with the nationalist concept of citizenship as a community of blood and race (para. 22 of the reasoning). The conflict between democracy and totalitarianism is depicted as a conflict between republican and racist values. According to the Court, even during the critical years of occupation and war Czechoslovak citizens of German nationality had been able to make a choice whether they wanted either to defend actively democratic values and participate in the resistance against totalitarian occupation power or to join the masses supporting the Nazi regime on the ground of ethnicity and race.

The concept of *guilt* is separated from the concept of *responsibility*. Unlike criminal guilt, responsibility is much more a matter of social and historical values. Responsibility is perceived as a civic virtue of a human being living in a democratic society which is essential to such a society. It is a matter for the individual's conscience. In the Nazi totalitarian regime, responsibility is transferred to the power elite, although this elite in fact behaves without any sense of responsibility (para. 25 of the reasoning). No democratic regime can survive without responsible citizens. This legal construct constitutes another condition of democratic legitimacy, the loyalty of citizens to the democratic state and its values. It is impossible to imagine any functioning democratic power and decision-making without this loyalty.

The concept of loyalty, employed and analysed by the Czech Constitutional Court, is similar to the concept of guilt developed by the German philosopher Karl Jaspers. Jaspers distinguishes between criminal and political guilt in order to show that the German nation as a political entity is guilty of what happened during the Nazi period and especially the Holocaust policy (Jaspers, 1987). The Czech Constitutional Court tried to prove that, although not guilty in the sense of being criminal, the citizens of pre-war Czechoslovakia of German ethnicity have a political responsibility for the break-up of the liberal democratic system. Moreover, the Court drew a concrete political consequence from the political guilt of ethnic Germans living in Czechoslovakia before 1945, using this to justify the political decision to deport them to Germany after the war.

....

In these decisions, the Constitutional Court sought to establish the legitimacy of democracy by contrasting democracy to totalitarianism, in the first case with communism, in the second with Nazism. This creates some difficulties. The Court must explain why democracy is better than totalitarianism. To do so it must use moral language, but this 'throws' the Court's reasoning out of the 'legal orbit' specified by the Czech Constitution. The more the Court uses moral language and arguments, the more it is detached from this orbit. Instead of being confined to the Constitution and laws, judicial reasoning enters the language of the political and moral worlds again. By proceeding in this way, the Constitutional Court conducts itself not as an institution for legal constitutional communication, but as an institution using the language of politics and morality to attempt to determine the limits of moral and political communication. But once an institution primarily defined by a constitutional law enters a referential framework in which legal rules are not important, it cannot then rely on their legal force when it seeks to establish their validity.

The Court employed a powerful but nevertheless controversial definition of legitimacy when it stated that the decisive condition of legitimacy was respect for the principle of the sovereignty of the people and the democratic procedures of decision-making according to the majority will. The fiction of the general will of the people is the constitutive power of democracy which functions as the foundation of the constituted political bodies. The difference between the constitutive and constituted power is the basis of the democratic rule of law. However, the distinction between guilt and responsibility, present in the Court's judgment on the Decree of the President n.108/1945Sb., shows that democratic or any other legitimacy must in fact operate in a 'land of shifting sands'. Loyalty is impossible to codify, define or describe in normative legal terms. Nevertheless, when loyalty ceases, a political regime collapses.

When the Court ascribes the authority of moral legislator to Parliament and seeks to act as a moral or political authority itself, it is obliged to define the content of such loyalty. It is to say that the Constitutional Court places itself in a position where it feels obliged to give an opinion on the proper content of a political belief. Those subject to the law and political order must have that belief. The Constitutional Court (and the Czech Parliament) wanted in fact to give solid foundations to liberal democratic morality and to convince people to believe that liberal democratic politics were 'the right thing'.

Critique of the principle of formal legality

The attempt to define the legitimacy of the law-based state in purely democratic terms has enormous importance, in spite of all the contradictions it involves. This attempt represents an important reflection on the political system of liberal democracies by the principal constitutional institutions. However, it is important to remember that the reasoning of the Constitutional Court exceeds the boundaries of the constitutional legal context. It belongs rather to the moral political context, which can never have a direct impact on the normative structures of law. Besides addressing the problem of democratic legitimacy, the Constitutional Court has given its attention to another perennial issue in legal and political philosophy, namely, the critique of the formalist concept of legality and legalist scholarship.

In its judgment concerning the *Act on the Lawlessness of the Communist Regime and Resistance Against It*, the Court criticised the positivist, seemingly value-free concept of legality and the law-based state, which determines the whole of modern legal thinking and which influenced the Czechoslovak Constitution of 1920 (See the Court's judgment, n. 19/93Pl.US, para. 25 in the part concerning objections to section 1 to 4 of the Act n. 198/93Sb). The Court challenged the concept of the law-based state as an institution which operates through general rules and procedures from which are eliminated individual moral judgments and social values. The restrictive concept of the law-based state as an impersonal technique of any government (von Mohl, 1844) proved to be inadequate and the principle 'law is law because it is law' turned out to be powerless in the face of brutal injustices.

The Court came to the conclusion that the legalistic concept of political legitimacy is insufficient and that it even opens the way for a legal transition from democracy to political totalitarianism. Germany in 1933 and Czechoslovakia in 1948 may serve as historical examples of how criminals can come to power legally and install violent political regimes.

The Court's judgment articulates the view that we should never expect law automatically to be just law, and goes beyond the limits of legality and legal procedures when it states:

> Our new Constitution is not founded on neutrality with regard to values, it is not simply a mere demarcation of institutions and processes, rather it incorporates

> into its text also certain governing ideas, expressing the fundamental, inviolable values of a democratic society. The Czech Constitution accepts and respects the principle of legality as a part of the overall basic conception of a law-based state; positive law does not, however, bind it merely to formal legality, rather the interpretation and application of legal norms are subordinated to their substantive purpose, law is qualified by respect for the basic enacted values of a democratic society and also measures the application of legal norms by these values (para. 25).

In contrast to the traditional value-free concept of the law-based state, the Court talks about the concept of the 'constitutional state'. This constitutional state is not built only on *formal* rational legality, but derives *substantive* rational legitimacy from the democratic principle of the sovereignty of the people. It is ultimately only a democratic regime, which can claim legitimacy as a law-based state. By holding this, the Court is refusing to acknowledge that legality itself is sufficient for legitimacy. The Court even maintains that formal rational legality may be a tool for undemocratic regimes, enabling them more coherently to formulate and more efficiently to execute their ideological and repressive goals. The complex view of the Constitutional Court on the relationship between formal legality and legitimacy is formulated in the following terms:

> The legitimacy of a political regime cannot rest solely upon the formal legal component because the values and principles upon which a regime is built are not just of a legal, but first of all of a political nature. Those principles of the Czech Constitution, such as the sovereignty of the People, representative democracy, and the law-based state, are principles of the political organization of society, which are not entirely normatively definable. Positive law proceeds from them, however normative regulation does not make up the full contents of these principles - something apart from it remains (para. 29).

The Constitutional Court perceives formal legality merely as a technique for the exercise of political power, and refuses to recognise that a system of political domination is legitimate just because it employs formal legal procedures. However, the Court also comes to the conclusion that before

1989 'legal norms were fictional'[6] and could be manipulated at any time in favour of the momentary political interests of the Communist Party.

It is as if the Court wanted to analyse the frightening phenomenon of 'the banal evil of totalitarianism'. Communist law-makers and those applying communist laws, which often had a criminal nature, were defending themselves with the famous argument: 'I was just carrying out the orders of the Party'. Adolf Eichmann's spectre of banality was also operating in communist regimes.[7] However, the Court's reasoning seems to ignore a distinction between the arbitrary and formally legal aspects of the communist regime. After its strong criticism of the formal rational concept of legality which was attributed to the communist regime, the Court paradoxically speaks about the poor condition of legality in the communist regime (para. 16 of the part concerning objections to section 5 of the Act n. 198/93Sb).

The Court's judgment necessarily leads to the conclusion that there are *two concepts of legality*; the first one is real and right, while the second is a mask for arbitrary use of political power and violence. Its position here surely suffers from logical inconsistency, when one concept, without any explanation, is given two opposite meanings.

I believe that this inconsistency is caused by the Court's attempt to identify legitimacy with the subjection of formal legal procedures to the substantive principles of democratic legitimacy and the values of democratic political society. These principles are specified as the people's sovereignty and representative democracy, and the law-based state, with its formal rational legality, must be subject to them. Legality then becomes a concept with an extraordinary width and its meaning differs according to the nature of the different contexts in which it is used.

The Court, however, says very little about the detail of the moral and political values which inform its judgment on *The Act on the Lawlessness*

---

[6]See para. 5 of the part concerning objections to section 5 of the Act n.198/93Sb. The term 'fictional' is used in the sense of 'fake', here. This usage is entirely opposite to the meaning of the concept of 'fictions' developed in this book.

[7]The Court pointed to this fact when it quoted from the testimony of Ladislav Kopřiva, the Minister of State Security in 1950-1951, concerning the political trials and executions of the early 50s. His defense was: 'I was just carrying out the orders of the Party. It is, after all, absolutely clear that I could not have arrested ministers and the General Secretary of the Party on my own initiative. However, if I had not carried out this order, I could have been convicted together with the others'. Quoted from the Court's judgment 19/93 Pl US, para. 9 of the part concerning objections to section 5 of the Act n. 198/93Sb.

of the Communist Regime and Resistance Against It. This is particularly odd as the Czech Constitution gives a constitutional judge the power to make use of extralegal reasons. However, the Court's judgment concerning the Beneš Decree does include some explanation of the role of moral and political values in a democratic, law-based state. This judgment considers the democratic legitimacy of the governmental system to be prior to formal legal requirements. The judgment mentions the system of liberal democratic values which informed the Czechoslovak Constitution of 1920,[8] a system in conformity with the international legal order and containing a catalogue of human rights and freedoms.

The Beneš Decree is depicted as a legal act which was a product of the democratic constitutional order of pre-war democratic Czechoslovakia, the order violently destroyed by the Nazi German occupation. According to the Court, the Beneš decrees manifest the legal continuity of post-war Czechoslovakia with the pre-war democratic constitutional order. Their passage was, moreover, based on the principle of democratic legitimacy and corresponded to the common practice of other European countries occupied by Nazi Germany.

The constitutionality and democratic character of pre-war Czechoslovakia is contrasted with the racist and totalitarian political regime of Nazi Germany. The Court's judgment distinguishes between the formal concept of legality, expressed in the principle 'law is law', and the substantive concept of legality deriving its legitimacy from democratic lawmaking and the separation of state powers. Democratic legitimacy is supplemented by an indispensable catalogue of human rights and freedoms which also determines the nature of the democratic law-based state.

The judgment, however, interprets this catalogue and implicitly all moral political values as a part of the democratic regime, because all these rights and freedoms follow from the civic principle of the democratic formation of political society and state power. Minority rights, for instance, are perceived as the fulfilment of the democratic ideas of formal equality before the law and substantive political and social equality. The Court takes the liberal aspect of the law-based state as a part of its more general democratic aspect. *What is liberal must be derived from what is*

---

[8]This reading of the Czechoslovak Constitution of 1920 contradicts the Court's criticisms of the same constitution for being formalist and influenced by a value-free concept of legality. See supra pp. 111-2.

democratic. The catalogue of civil rights and freedoms serves the democratic principles of the law-based state.

This subjection of the values of the law-based state, which are the foundations of human rights and freedoms, to democratic discourse involves more than a rejection of the formal concept of legality. It is another reflection of the centralised and hierarchical model of legitimation we have seen was employed by the Court. This model takes the people's sovereignty as its central point and the whole political reality, including moral values, law-making and the application of laws, is only a derivation from this leading principle. Human rights and freedoms have their political value only because they support the democratic political environment and, first of all, the principle of equality in its formal and substantive sense.

Democratic politics and the morality accompanying it determine the conditions of legitimacy of a political regime. Law is a part of it. However, it is nothing but a tool for expressing the democratic principles of the sovereignty of the people and democracy.

The constitutional court - legislator or interpreter?

I am not primarily interested in the juridical aspects of the reasoning of the Constitutional Court. I will not therefore analyse the problem of the compatibility of its broad political and moral reasoning with the constitutional principles of the Czech Republic. I will not examine to what extent the Constitutional Court's discretion is compatible with the system of checks and balances in the Czech Republic.

The most interesting fact is that, in the above mentioned judgments, the Constitutional Court leaves the legal context and deliberately enters the field of politics and morality. It attempts to operate here as one of the actors defining the political culture and morality of the new political regime. It did not use moral and political arguments only to support its decisions. It sought to fashion the moral and political context of the Czech society. It sought to participate in the development of the normative structure of those contexts.

In other words, the constitutional Court left the self-referential framework of modern positive law, within which it should confine itself to clarifying the legal and constitutional context of society, and attempted to define the moral and political conditions of legitimacy for a democratic law-based state. From the perspective of interpretive technique, the Court wanted to give effect to the intention of Parliament in passing the *The Act on the Lawlessness of the Communist Regime and Resistance Against It* (on the intentionalist legal theory and its techniques see Marmor, 1992). In the judgment on the Beneš Decree, the Court used primarily an analysis of the international legal and political context.

The problem of legitimacy, so fundamental to both decisions, does not, however, have a legal character and steps outside the framework of the constitutional and legal system. Both judgments thus become very important documents, the purpose of which is to provide a theoretical explanation of the institutionalisation of a liberal democratic law-based state. This theoretical goal must include an explanation 'both of the law which begins by inscribing itself there and of the right which authorizes it' (Derrida, 1996: 4). The Constitutional Court left the orbit of inscribed law, the Constitution, in order to address the second issue of the right authorising the law. This right is at the core of the legitimacy problem. It can hardly be restricted to legal or constitutional discourse, because the origin of law is ultimately never a matter for the law itself (Derrida, 1992: 14, 38).

The Court's activity is complicated by the fact that it wants to provide 'the right for the law' in the political environment, where this problem is heavily contested and produces many conflicts. These constitutional judgments attempt then to provide such a right and support it by the weight of the Court's authority. The support of a particular legitimation discourse by constitutional authority nevertheless brings many problems and doubts about the legal and political appropriateness of such support.

The Court's interpretation of 'the right to make the law' is built on the rather conservative sociological distinction between effectiveness and legitimacy, which takes effectiveness as primarily instrumental and legitimacy as evaluative (see, for example, Lipset, 1981). The Court criticised formal rational legality for its instrumental character and ignorance of values, which can allow undemocratic regimes to abuse it. According to the Court, the formal concept of legality is only an instrument of power, the legitimacy of which is very unclear and depends upon its political environment. Impersonal, rational and value free legality cannot themselves legitimate a political order. Legality itself must be legitimated by its subjection to the principles and values of democratic politics and morality. The problem of a legitimate law-based state becomes the problem of establishing values and principles which must be indisputable and therefore can claim a universal character. This, however, means that everything outside these principles becomes illegitimate.

In criticising the formal rational concept of legitimacy, the Court ignores two important facts. The first is the formal legal legitimacy of the Court itself. Without formal rational legality, it would be impossible to establish the Court! What is legitimate must be formulated in the language of law. The Court does not seem to take into account that legitimacy, together with moral judgments, involves the problem of validity and obedience. Some decisions are enacted and become legitimate although we may morally and politically disagree with them (MacCormick, 1978: 62).

The second fact is even more important. The Court ignores the idea that legitimacy is finally always 'a belief in legality' (Rheinstein, 1954: 8). This means that, in spite of many different ways of formalising and bureaucratising the legitimacy of a political community in rules and rational principles, it is finally the belief of members of this community in certain institutions, rules and procedures, which leads to their acceptance. The legitimacy of all political and legal institutions, including the legitimacy of a democratic law-based state, is ultimately subject to the beliefs of the political community. It does not mean that the political community must express itself actively in some form of social consensus. It only involves the simple fact that certain decisions are accepted by this community as legitimate (MacCormick, 1978: 55).

This belief in legitimacy then means that it is impossible to define *a priori* what is legitimate and what is illegitimate. The Court wanted to resolve the problem of legitimacy by avoiding seeing it in terms of the social acceptance of legal rules. Instead it wanted to define or 'legislate' the sole and exclusive legitimacy of law as that derived from democratic principles of constitutional power.

……………………………………

Within post-communist Czech society, the Court was acting as a moral legislator, seeking to achieve the impossible and resolve the problem of legitimacy by some form of substantive democratic morality. The Court has defined the limits of the political context of Czech society and tacitly assumed that all opinions outside this morality are illegitimate. From a sociological perspective, this attempt reduces the enormous political anomie existing in all post-revolutionary societies. It seeks to understand existing conditions and to create a stable framework for democratic political communication. The Constitutional Court has used its legal authority to enter the political and moral sphere. It wanted to re-shape those contexts. However, it cannot use its legal power in this effort and the persuasiveness of its arguments is subject to the rules of political contest.

The arguments of the Constitutional Court regarding the legitimacy of the law-based state are also special because they do not 'legislate' anything new. They 'legislate' for the moral and political environment which exists and functions in liberal democratic, law-based states. The Court does not invent some new legitimation framework. It simply summarises and interprets existing law-based states and attaches to them ultimate normative power. What looks like a kind of 'legislation' inside Czech society is nothing but another moral political interpretation of western law-based state systems. The Constitutional Court thus acts in *the double role of legislator* (inside its own system) *and interpreter* (in respect of the environment of post-communist society).

The Court's definition of politics and the limits of a legitimate legal system cannot be given validity in legal terms. The Court's definition of legitimate law does not affect the inner structures of the system of law and legality. It belongs to politics and morality. The Court cannot therefore demand legal validity for its own normative legitimation reasonings. They may contain the authoritative language of a legal text, but in fact they have only the power of moral persuasiveness. They are only one of many contributions to the process of establishing free and democratic debate. They become a product of what they want to define; free and democratic politics. The Court's legitimation judgments are unique just because they are futile attempts to define what is impossible to define in open democratic societies. It always comes *ex post.*

The fiction of the just law and the environment of legality

The Constitutional Court's references to the natural rights of man or its attempts to define liberal democratic morals and politics were motivated by the Court's recognition of difficulty of the complexity of the political, constitutional and social transformation of the Czech Republic and other post-communist societies at the beginning of the 90s. The Court assumed that the mere incorporation of international legal documents and the new constitutional legislation were not sufficient for the protection of human rights and civil freedoms and for the legitimation of the new liberal political system. The laws, though not being taken completely sceptically, were thought to be just a part of the legitimate legal and political order. It seemed therefore necessary to look for a more general and universal legitimation strategy. For legal positivists and many public lawyers, all those extra-legalist legislations and judicial decisions represent a dangerous and unwanted element because they can undermine the whole logical and semantic structure of the individual provisions of the constitutional laws. In this sense, the language of the Czech constitution-makers and constitutional judges represents a sort of dirt in the analytically clean language of the law, going well beyond the rule-based ethic of legalism. But this natural rights vocabulary was not just a Freudian 'slip of tongue'. It deeply influenced the whole constitutional system and the decision-making of the Constitutional Court of the Czech Republic.

Positive legal procedures and rules obviously constitute an important condition of modern political liberal domination. They can be the basis of a fight against communist ideology and its dangerous language of the ultimate natural law of one social class. The double legitimation strategy of the natural rights of man and positive law codification of the liberal democratic system in the new constitutional and legal system of the Czech Republic, nevertheless indicates that positive legal rules and procedures can hardly be the only source of a legitimate liberal political and legal system. The legitimate law and political domination are also determined by extra-legal arguments and vocabularies.

In other words, the formal concept of legality and legal procedures cannot generate all the conditions of legitimacy themselves. This legitimacy depends also on the environment of the system of positive law. The character of Czech constitutional documents from the first half of the 90s manifests a limited legitimating power of the language of legality and a necessity to retreat to legitimating strategies which, from the perspective of positive law, are exterior and 'suspicious'.

The legitimation fiction of the just law is one of many examples of re-modernisation in the former communist countries. Its purpose is to define a common space for the new, emerging, political society. This fiction is ambivalent and can have either a more legalist form, or, as in the judgments of the Czech Constitutional Court, a more moralist form.

The moralist formulation of the fiction of the just law nevertheless raises the question of the universal validity of law again. The classical liberal theory of law sought to solve the problem by declaring the law a morally neutral order, the legitimacy and universal validity of which are secured exactly by its a-moral nature. Moralism in the fiction of the just law is, then, a reaction to the failure of formal legality to provide political orders with legitimacy. However, this moralist version of the just law fiction ends up in the absurd situation in which the historically specific institution of liberal democratic political morality is required to declare itself to be the universal moral foundation of any legitimate legal system.

While legalism attempts to neutralise the particular moral convictions of individuals in modern society, the moralism hidden in the fiction of the just law is, on the other hand, to provide a particular morality with general legitimacy. However, if legalism has failed to create the legitimate order of modern political society, it would be wrong to expect any moral order to do the job. The problem is not whether to choose the moralist or the legalist vocabulary, or whether to use any mixture of them. The problem is that, in current social and political conditions, no vocabulary can claim general validity as such (Douzinas, Goodrich and Hachamovitch, 1994: 24ff).

Against the background of the analysis of the Constitutional Court's decisions, it turnes out to be unlikely that the work of legitimation might be carried out by some more general and sovereign language of political morality. The problem of legal legitimacy cannot be resolved by simply modifying the legalist legitimation and accepting the legitimating sovereignty of democratic procedures and values. The 1989 revolutionary changes and subsequent transformations of post-communist countries proved that legitimacy is not only a matter of either formal and technical legality, or liberal democratic principles and values. Nevertheless, the very existence of the need for extra-legal legitimations which follows from the inability of legal language to provide universal legitimation framework leads us to the problem of the relationship between the legal system and its social environment.

5 The Legal System and its Environment: The Conditions of the Process of Legitimation

Legitimacy as belief

A common understanding of the problems of the legitimacy traces then to a tension entrenched in the concept of legality. It is both a technique for the organisation of modern societies and an expression of the political ethics of those societies. The rule of law [*Rechtsstaat*], if it is to be called the rule of law at all, must be an effective mechanism of political enforcement, but its character also must be democratic and liberal. Liberal ethics, in the legal language of the catalogue of human and civil rights and freedoms, make up the external normative framework of legality. Legality can achieve its legitimacy only if it adopts this ethical framework. Legality becomes legitimate when it expresses a particular ethical version of the political world. Legality also must observe the principles of democratic decision-making. This necessity was reflected and indeed overemphasised in the judgements of the Constitutional Court of the Czech Republic, which we have examined. Democratic legitimacy is a necessary condition of the rule of law. Without the fiction of the democratic sovereignty and the will of the people, the vast majority of contemporary states and political societies could hardly contemplate their own political survival.

The sovereignty of the people and the concept of basic human rights determine the legitimation scheme of the current rule of law. Democratic legitimacy is primarily a matter of political virtues and moral values. Its technical aspect, which is obviously vital to the reproduction of political society, has only a limited importance for the problem of legitimacy. Nevertheless, it is impossible to draw a clear dividing line between the world of values, reflected in the problem of legitimacy, and the world of technique, represented by the criterion of effectiveness. Technique is the internal aspect of legitimacy. It cannot be separated from the problem of legitimacy. The modern concept of legality originally had a strong technical meaning. Legal legitimacy meant a state which worked out formal, general and impersonal legal techniques for the purpose of organising, disciplining and subjecting its own citizens. Many different political regimes adopted the concept of formal legality and the liberal democratic ones themselves use it as the means of translating its political and ethical principles into effective imperatives. In spite of the different meanings of the concept of legal legitimacy, it turns out that all notions concerning the legitimacy of legality must reflect one of the most important problems of legal theory and practice, the problem of the enforcement and acceptance of law.

To ignore this double character of the problem of legitimacy would be to misunderstand its internal dynamic and structure. In modern societies, legality originally dominated the relationship of legality and legitimacy. To the sociological, political and jurisprudential question: 'Which political domination and order can claim legitimacy in the modern society?' was given the answer: 'A political domination is legitimate because it is entirely defined in legal terms.' However, *the problem of legal legitimacy* is almost immediately turned upside down and *becomes the problem of legitimate legality.* Instead of legality perceived as an instrument for the legitimation of the political order, the problem is referred back to the structures of legality itself, to its own normative background and social effectiveness. It is legality itself that is subject to the test of legitimacy. Today, the result of this practical test, during the course of which humankind has had to endure the different forms of totalitarian and authoritarian political regimes, are the seemingly stable normative foundations of the legitimate rule of law. These foundations are defined by democratic procedures and liberal ethics 'legalised' in the concept of basic human rights and freedoms.

According to its adherents, legality founded on liberal democracy can claim to be enforceable and all citizens must obey it. *Legality is legitimate and acceptable because it is liberal and democratic.* The state's monopoly of violence is legitimate in modern political societies, if that state is democratic and if it confines itself within liberal limits. This answer may satisfy a political or legal philosopher who speculates about right law or good legislation. It can, however, hardly satisfy a legal sociologist who must always analyse the factual processes of the law's enforcement and social acceptance. The legitimacy and acceptance of law and political domination cannot be reduced to *a priori* valid but merely theoretical arguments. Max Weber always described the form of political domination typical of modern society as legal-rational and conceived legality to be an essential impersonal technique of the organisation of modern political society by means of general and rational rules (Cotterrell, 1983: 81). Nevertheless, Weber never reduced the problem of legitimacy to these legal procedures and rules. According to him, legitimacy, be it charismatic, traditional or legal, always also requires *a belief* (*Glaube*) on the side of those who are to be subjected to this political domination (*Herrschaft*) (Weber, 1978).

It is in Weber that the basic problem of legitimacy in modern societies is given its clearest statement as the tension between the impersonal and rational order of procedures and rules on one side and the belief in this order on the other side. Neither the theory of communicative reason, nor the social theory of autopoietic systems, which comes with a broad definition of procedures as rules or modes of social communication, can avoid or resolve this tension. This tension may be formulated as *the tension between the universality of rules and procedures of systemic rationality and the contingency of the belief in these rules and procedures.*

Such tension is present for instance in the legal theory of Carl Schmitt, who understood it as an unbearable aspect of modernity threatening the stability and unity of the state. Schmitt's concept of the enemy, which is central to his political works, is just a reflection of the contingency of the belief of modern people in the legitimacy of their political order. According to Schmitt, legality as defined by Weber, was too weak and corresponded too much to the liberal values of an open and free discussion. At the beginning of 20th century, these values turned out to be old fashioned and useless in the face of the tendencies leading towards the totalitarian state (Schmitt, 1985). Instead of a liberal state, in which the very structure of the separation of power permanently manifests political antagonisms and the laws only seek to contain them, the state-sovereign must reign and exercise its defining legal power, which is the power to define the enemy of the state (Hofmann, 1986: 212ff.). Schmitt's decisionist theory builds on the assumption that the state has the power to make a sovereign decision about the limits of its own *universum* and thus define its own legitimacy in legal terms.

Politics has a polemic nature. According to Schmitt, it is structured and determined by inconsistency and conflict and the enemy is the source of polemic (Schmitt, 1963: 29, 31). Politics is pluriversum, not universum (Schmitt, 1963: 54). The state, on the other hand, is an integrating institution because it subjects political enemies by imposing its supreme will on them. Therefore, the legitimacy by legal normativity formulated by liberal theories of the rule of law system is not possible. Behind any legitimacy, there is a capacity to impose a state decision and apply it (Schmitt, 1980: 7f.). A decision, will (voluntas) and command are integral to legality, which therefore can never be explained purely by the concepts of normativity, rationality (ratio), and formal legislation.

Schmitt's theory of the state and its political enemy depicts the liberal democratic and parliamentary regimes of the rule of law as profoundly unstable systems and rejects the whole concept of the liberal democratic rule of law. It admits that democratic legitimacy is typical of modern mass societies. However, this legitimacy, though originally linked to the idea of parliamentarism, has also been connected with different regimes which emerged in the conditions of modern mass society, namely with dictatorships (Schmitt, 1985a: 30). Parliamentarism turns out to be weak because it cannot overcome the heterogeneity of interests and political goals within the context of mass society. According to Schmitt, the state must be identified with a power mechanism which will be able to control what shall be tolerated and legally defined as acceptable. A sovereign is defined by its power to impose a state of emergency (Schmitt, 1985b: 5). Consequently, any state and therefore any legal system are made up by *a decision and not by a norm* (Schmitt, 1985b: 10). No normativity can be treated as a foundation of any legal system, be it conceived in the sense of the norms of natural law and rights or as the basic norm of the democratic rule of law. The foundations of every legal system and all laws are within the sphere of a sovereign decision which is always able to overcome social heterogeneity (for a critique of Carl Schmitt's legal and state theory, see, for example, Dyzenhaus, 1997).

Whatever is objectionable in Schmitt's concept of politics and parliamentary liberal democracy, his understanding of politics as a permanent conflict or dispute, which reproduces itself in an irreducibly pluralistic environment, is of fundamental importance. The distinction between the state and politics, respectively between the universum and pluriversum, must consequently lead to the question whether it is possible to draw a strict dividing line between these two worlds. Do not they finally influence each other so that the world of universum always manifests characteristics of the world of pluriversum and vice versa? Can legality be established purely from the unity of a state decision, or is it also determined by the plurality which is characteristic of the world of politics?

A possible answer to these questions, setting out powerful objections to Schmitt's theory, is to be found in Weber. In Weber's sociological theory, the problem of legitimacy cannot be reduced to the very popular metaphor of 'the iron cage' of modernity (Mayer, 1956: 127-8) which is mentioned in almost every introduction to sociology. *The aspect of a belief in this cage and the power to persuade others about its rightness and necessity to obey it turn out to be of the same importance.* While Weber seeks to generate this belief from the sources of modern rationality and its normative power, which reveals itself in the field of law (and other social fields), Schmitt supports the idea of the closure of the pluralistic world of politics by a state decision. However, even Schmitt is well aware of the contingency and temporality of such a decision.

In *Politics as Vocation*, Weber concludes that the typical character of modern politics in a constitutional state is a demagogue (Gerth and Mills, 1958: 83). The rhetoric of a demagogue is behind all the ideal types of legitimate domination and authority. The exponents of the rhetoric of demagoguery are journalists who become a part of the legitimation political game in the modern democracy, in which the state and its law must be legitimated by those who are their subjects (Gerth and Mills, 1958: 81). These comments about the rhetoric and political role of journalists and their persuasive power make Max Weber's theory radically different from any theory, which derive the concept of legitimacy from rational discourse and its normative force. Unlike all theoretical attempts to contrast legitimacy and contingency,[1] Max Weber's theory defines legitimacy as a capacity of the political will to impose a certain opinion and worldview or ideology. Legitimacy is a matter of imposition (Connolly, 1984: 12, 16).

This close connection between the legitimacy and contingency immediately reminds one of Nietzsche's concept of the force of will and the will to power (Kronman, 1983: 42f). Legitimacy is an outcome of a sophist competition and struggle between wills. This outcome involves contingency and hardly can be reduced to any normative framework of rational discourse such as could be defined by the structures of discourse ethics (For Habermas' normativism and its connection with the Frankfurt critical school, see Sumner, 1983: 120f).

[1]A typical recent theory, which contrasts the legitimacy and contingency, is obviously the famous Habermasian theory of communicative rationality and discourse ethics (Habermas, 1997: 72).

The rule of law and the dilemma of normality: functionality and comprehensibility

It is pointless to question the fact that legality is the only technique for organising a modern state and its power. This is the meaning of the rule of law. To politicise any social conflict ends up in giving it a legal form. The concept and the political rhetoric of the rule of law have enjoyed an extraordinary renaissance in post-communist societies and represent a solid ideological scheme for the new, emerging, political systems of those countries. The revolutions against communism must find their legal form. They must go through a process of juridification in a similar way to other modern revolutions and direct their energy into devising formal constitutional reforms and a vocabulary of human and civil rights.

Legitimacy by legality is the fundamental condition of the liberal rule of law, which, as Roberto Mangabeira Unger suggests, cannot be treated just as some kind of ideology. When Unger was considering methodological aspects of his analysis of the rule of law and liberal society in his book *Law in Modern Society* (1976), he said:

> [I]n societies with a heavy commitment to the rule of law, people often act on the belief that the legal system does possess a relative generality and autonomy. To treat their understandings and values as mere shams is to assume that social relations can be described and explained without regard to the meaning the men who participate in those relations attribute to them. This ... would be to blind oneself to what is specifically social about the subject matter and to violate a cardinal principle of method in social theory (Unger, 1976: 56-7).

A brief analysis of Unger's understanding of the rule of law reveals that he takes a view very similar to Weber's. He argues that the rule of law in the broadest sense is defined by:

> [the] interrelated notions of neutrality, uniformity, and predictability. Governmental power must be exercised within the constraints of rules that apply to ample categories of persons and acts, and these rules, whatever they may be, must be uniformly applied.
>
> ... As long as the lawmaker must manifest his will through general rules, he is stopped from directly punishing or favouring particular individuals and therefore from bringing them under his immediate personal control (Unger, 1976: 176-7).

Unger is, of course, very critical of the modern concept of the rule of law and modern liberal politics. He refuses the inadequate formalism of modern law, which, through a mediation of seemingly general rules, can discriminate, exclude and persecute against whole social classes. Unger's notion of the historical development and limits of modern liberal society and its rule of law system is accompanied by his statement of the necessity of a post-liberal society which is to keep the principle of human rights and rule of law and found it on communitarian political values.

The transformation of individualistic liberal society into post-liberal communitarian society is a product of the Hegelian philosophical tradition and romantic political imagination which is present in Unger's works (for the romantic features of Unger's political and social philosophy see Rorty, 1991b: 184ff.). In spite of all his criticisms of the legalist formalism and the rule of law, Unger emphasises that without the notion of autonomous legal regulation freed from particular political pressures it would be impossible to set up welfare state institutions and move beyond modern liberal society and its politics. The communitarian is already present in the liberal.

Together with the autonomous legal regulation of politics and the legal legitimacy of modern political domination, Unger also appreciates the historical evolution of the modern bureaucratic administration and its importance for the development of the western liberal democracies. According to him, the universality of law, the limitation of the political power by law, and the principle of legality helped to overcome the traditional limits of individual freedom (Unger, 1976: 192ff.).

The principle of the rule of law and legality is undoubtedly a necessary and more or less effective filter of momentary political interests. Such qualities of law as regularity, foreseeability, integrity, or the minimal principle of justice of 'treating like cases alike', have significant political value. The idea of general legislation and formal equality of all humans before the law and political authority contains the modern ethos of emancipation, the ideal of the inclusive society, and a practical technique for the struggle against all possible forms of discrimination. To establish an order of rules and norms with general validity means a great breakthrough and shift in the realisation of the idea of justice.

The formal concept of justice is inseparable from the idea of humankind and its universal overarching standards (Heller, 1987: 35ff). The modern rule of law, constructed as the impersonal order of general rules, provides citizens with stability, security, the possibility to participate in democratic decision-making procedures, and personal freedoms established on a knowledge of the limits of political power. In this context, human action really seems to be legitimate only when it does not trespass the limits of legal rules.

The rule of law is a modern political institution which typically identifies legitimacy with legality. The legal nature of political domination constrains political subjects both by means of the force of the state and by means of the force of rational argumentative framework which 'must be accepted by all sensible citizens'. The belief in the legitimacy of legal domination must be supported. Political power and reason must therefore make a coalition and subject belief in that legitimacy by their united force. Modern politics is consequently exposed to its greatest perils when legality and its normative, impersonal and formal structures occupy the whole sphere of legitimacy and reduce it to the impersonal and automatic subjection of citizens.

This dilemma is typical of the relation between modern legality and its legitimacy and can be called *the dilemma of normality*. Max Weber kept it in its original double structure, in which the neo-Kantian concepts of impersonal and formal rationality coexist with the Nietzschean concept of will and human action. Habermas opposes formal legalism to the domains of the life-world, but even he finally reduces the concept of legitimacy to the procedures of communicative reason and their power to generate normative structures of discourse ethics (Habermas, 1999: 329f.). Another view of this problem is presented by Thomas S. Kuhn in *The Structure of Scientific Revolutions* (1970). In his analysis of scientific knowledge, Kuhn defined legitimate steps as those steps which corresponded to the rules worked out and imposed by a scientific paradigm (Kuhn, 1970: 10f.). A paradigm defines the meanings of 'normal science' (Kuhn, 1970: 10-1). and all moves accepted within a particular scientific discourse. Legitimacy then means normality in the sense of a set of conventions which must be adopted by everyone who wants to communicate and pursue his/her own goals within the framework of a paradigm and a community which has been established by epistemic commitment to this paradigm.

The paradigm of legal science is a reaction to the social need (Kuhn, 1970: 19) for order and the subordination of human behaviour to the governance of rules. Legal science must therefore create structures of rules and normality within its own paradigm and transform them into the existing structures of the system of positive law. Legal science is to help the system of positive law by creating new ways of communication about it and its social functions. Science supports the functioning of law and the system of positive law, on the other hand, adapts to what legal science says about it. Social normality is thus generated both by social structures of positive law and the paradigmatic structures of legal science.

Legalist fictions are exactly such an attempt to establish normality by means of legal positivist discourse. Legitimacy by legality is a restriction of legitimate steps to those defined by the language of law. *Normality must be identified with legality.* However, this attitude contains the threat that any behaviour proclaimed by the law as illegal will be immediately prosecuted and excluded as illegitimate and therefore pathological and deviant. The function of legalist fictions is to establish the conditions in which legality, by the means of scientific speculation on the fiction, will pretend to have set up a unified social space. All kinds of human behaviour falling outside its limits will then be declared illegitimate. The complicated nature of social reality is reduced by its 'transcription' into legal concepts. The legitimation fictions of legality can, as was argued in the second chapter, mitigate many differences and conflicts between legality and ethics, but only when legality has the final say. Under the rule of law, legality always contains that threat that the modern contradictory, complicated and complex world of beliefs in what is legitimate will be finally 'confiscated' by legality.

Legalist fictions are an attempt to translate the conflictual nature of politics and social reality into the codified world of legal normality. Their main function is to provide the legal system with a scientific definition and therefore set up *the limits of positive law and legitimate human behaviour*. It is eventually juristic and legal philosophical arguments that justify the democratic rule of law. In this system, the fiction of the just law is to resolve the paradox of the legitimacy of the modern democratic rule of law, which consists of the need to define universal ethical foundations for liberal democratic society and the need to enforce those foundations by the means of a particular legal system. The universal is definable and enforceable only by the particular.

The 'normalisation' function of legalist fictions helps to reduce the complexity social reality and set up the structures and social communication framework of the system of positive law. Nevertheless, if the legitimate shall be identical with the legal, the criterion of functionality and effectiveness of legality must be accompanied by *the criterion of comprehensibility of law* and individual legal rules. Law must be both accepted and understood. The problem of legitimacy and the belief in what is legitimate reveals the more general criterion of social comprehensibility.

This ability to understand and comprehend also makes political community possible. Joseph Raz means exactly this when he considers trust between government and its subjects to have a fundamental importance for any legitimate political order (Raz, 1994). The intrinsic value of political consensus is determined by this trust. Trust is the right basis for government. That the government is governed by reason makes it possible to trust that government and with that trust, it becomes legitimate. Political consensus, according to Raz, is not a contingent result of some utilitarian individual interests. It is right government by rational argument that makes modern political domination and its legal system legitimate.

Transformation of legitimacy into legitimation: legitimation by procedures and the disappearance of the centre of the legal system

Law as a social system and the expression of systemic rationality cannot provide society and individuals with good political reason for belief in its own legitimacy, which a citizen-layperson can understand and therefore accept. The systemic rationality of law cannot serve as the foundation of comprehensible political arguments. Comprehensibility goes beyond the internal operations of the system. In contemporary societies, law has become completely incomprehensible from the political perspective! This is the problem formulated in Niklas Luhmann's concept of legitimation by procedure [*Legitimation durch Verfahren*]. Unlike Habermas' theory of communicative reason and discourse ethics, which regards the loss of political and civic comprehensibility of law as the cause of the crisis of law's legitimacy, Luhmann's theory of autopoietic social systems admits and in fact enjoys the disappearance of modern human subjects in contemporary social conditions. According to the autopoietic theory, social systems (including political and legal systems) are determined exclusively by their inner rules and their main criterion has become the criterion of function (Willke, 1991: 109). Comprehensibility is subjected to functionality.

The theory of autopoietic social systems regards the mutual influence of modern political ideals, values, and legal procedures only as a historical movement which is not characteristic of contemporary social conditions. It defines the legal system as one of the autopoietic systems of a modern complex society, one which has differentiated itself from systems of politics, morals, and economy during the process of historical evolution.

Luhmann's theory of autopoietic law and legitimation by procedure hardly can be seen only as a political product of ideological conservatism. As Habermas himself admits, it can also have a strong critical impact because it assumes that law is independent of the concrete conditions of a political system, or of a given system of morals and economic interests (Habermas, 1997: 47ff). Autopoietic law develops at the historic moment when the principles of division and limitation of state powers and civil freedoms have become social facts. Legal systems must reflect and regulate those political and cultural facts in constitutional legal documents. Law is systematically ordered and founded on the principle of general legislation. The definition of what is legal and illegal is done exclusively within the complex system of positive legal rules. Legal systems of complex modern societies concentrate on future actions, so that they can reduce growing social complexity and work as one of many social decision-making mechanisms.

Luhmann admits that there is no simple and persuasive answer to the question of the legitimacy of modern law and political domination (Luhmann, 1981: 132). In modern societies, there are nevertheless no sources of legitimation of law that can be sought outside the framework of positive law. Legitimacy of law is a matter of positive law. It is not related to the concept of truth and the correspondence of positive legal systems to it. Modern societies do not require true law, but law enabling social action and decisions (Luhmann, 1969: 24ff). Theories of natural human rights are only a historical ideology which had meaning for the development and formation of positive law, because it limited the sovereign power of the king by invoking the laws of nature (Luhmann, 1981: 119-21). In contemporary social conditions, natural law and any other transcendent foundations of positive law have lost their formative function.

Due to the growing complexity of the modern social world and its law, individuals cannot make their own judgments about every single legal case or problem. They cannot invoke transcendental principles and values. All they can do is accept certain legal procedures which define and manage legal cases and problems (Luhmann, 1990: 227ff; see also Lenoble, 1996). These legal procedures embody modern political ideals and principles, but their acceptance depends purely on their *operative capacity, not transcendent value*.

Luhmann comes up with a radically different concept of legitimacy which emphasises the moment of *social communication and cognitive processes of learning* and criticises essentialist approaches to legitimacy.

The legitimacy of any social structure is not formed or determined by values and principles. This structure is legitimated by its power to communicate and inform its subjected elements about its own decision. Instead of legitimation based on transcendentally founded values, procedural legitimation begins to dominate and its main function is to teach subjects to accept systemic processes and procedures (Luhmann, 1969). *The problem of legitimacy becomes the problem of the permanent process of legitimation!* The whole project of legitimation by procedure shifts the social science perspective on the problem of legitimacy from essentialist to a proceduralist view. The problem of legitimacy changes and becomes the problem of legitimation. This transformation of legitimacy into legitimation and its strict separation from any transcendent values or socially and politically supreme cultural principles makes the autopoietic theory one of the currently most inspiring paradigms.

At the end of the 60s, Luhmann used some schools of German legal theoretical thinking and the common legalist notion of a proceduralist legitimation for the purposes of his own social theory. The central problem is the acceptance of decisions within the existing social system. Procedures must be flexible in order to translate and convince subjects about the necessity to accept a decision. The social function of procedures is to create a general framework of acceptability of decisions, the content of which has not been yet specified.

Luhmann's concept of legitimation by procedure reduces legitimacy to passive processes of learning and subjecting to the pre-existing procedures and structures of unequal and power determined communication. Acceptance is not conditioned by some qualified consent, such as we have seen is required in Raz's political and legal philosophy (Raz, 1994: 364ff.). This difference must be emphasised especially because Raz and Luhmann both closely connect the problem of legitimacy with cognitive processes of learning (Raz, 1994: 369). Legitimacy is not a matter of fundamental principles and the character of political community, and therefore it exceeds the common legal philosophical discourse (for this kind of discourse, see, for example, MacCormick, 1978: 55). Acceptance depends on system rationality and inner structures of communication.

Luhmann rejects the idea of consensus derived from the concept of communicative rationality, and also Weber's concept of belief as the condition of the legitimacy of legal domination. The concept of legitimation is reduced to the question of procedures inherent in the autopoietic system of law. Legality becomes the dominant element in the legality-legitimacy relation. This legality is however much more dynamic than the concept of legality formulated by the positivistic legal philosophy and theory, which, unlike autopoietic systems theory, prefers the structural-normative to procedural-dynamic perspective. Although Luhmann defines procedures from a much broader sociological perspective and the main criterion is the functionality of legal procedures, his concept of legitimation sometimes recalls Carl Schmitt's concept of legitimacy by legality.

Luhmann defines legitimacy as a '... general readiness to accept, within certain limits of tolerance, decisions which are still without content ...' (Luhmann, 1969: 28). Legitimacy depends on the processes of learning and an assumption of the acceptability of legal decisions by those who are affected by them. It depends on the social climate (*sozialen Klima*), which institutionalises the acceptance of binding decisions as something taken for granted, and understands it not as a consequence of personal decision but as a consequence of the validity of administrative bureaucratic decisions. Instead of the Habermasian *consensus*, legitimacy remains a matter of passive *consent* with pre-existing procedures. The symbolic level of consensus with all its democratic connotations is transformed into acceptance and learning to anonymous procedures. Instead of the passionate symbols of modern politics, this is a cold legitimation established by cognitive processes of learning which are a technique for securing the acceptance of the anonymous procedures of legality.

Luhmann refuses psychological explanations about the legitimacy of law. The decisive fact, according to Luhmann, is whether the system enables the procedures of learning, that is, whether it enables citizens as subjects of the system to grasp cognitively the normative expectations involved in the autopoietic legal system. Describing the theory of autopoietic systems, one could speak about the process of auto-legitimation of law, or self-legitimation of law (Lempert, 1988).

Luhmann's concept of legitimation by procedure has provoked many criticisms and misunderstandings. It obviously makes a radical break with the common understanding of the problem of legitimacy within the field of social and politititical philosophy working with the concepts of ideology, democracy, democratic political morality or natural human rights.

It is also criticised for its decisionist view, according to which the problem of legitimation is always about arguments and explanations of the decision-making of the powerful. While other theories legitimate decisions from the outside and require democratic procedures and liberal civil rights, the autopoietic theory defines a decision as legitimate when it effectively transmits information to the addressee and makes it possible for the addressee to adapt to commands. This kind of decisionism in fact dismantles the centralist model of political domination, in which the decision-making centre dictates its moves to the subjects. Decision-making processes are not one-sided communication processes and legitimacy in fact grows in the process of communication between a decision-maker and addressee (Luhmann, 1975: 11).

Unlike the common legal positivist critique of natural law, autopoietic systems theory castigates the whole tradition of legal humanism and rejects the notion of a person who, together with other individuals-persons and within generally binding pragmatics, put rules and limits on their own actions, rules articulated around the modern transcendent ideals of freedom, equality and democracy (for the critique of this approach see Cornell, 1992). According to Luhmann, '[S]tructural changes ... do not require any special 'legitimating' principle, *ius eminens*, or super-norm. They are in any event only possible in law' (Luhmann, 1988: 18). Besides the essentialist concept of legitimacy and broader political and ethical legitimation framework, Luhmann's theory also dismantles the positivist notion of law being a product of sovereign political power. Behind the law, there is only law. This statement can remind Kelsen's concept of the basic norm because it excludes all extra-legal elements from the legal system (Teubner, 1988: 4). Nevertheless, the autopoietic concept of legitimation by procedure goes further because it does not require *any centre* to found the law as a functioning and self-referential system. The autopoietic legal system can be conceptualised without the basic norm or the fiction of the political sovereign deciding finally about the distinction between the legal and illegal. Luhmann's concept of law can hardly be seen as primarily coercive because it accommodates surprisingly many features of the 'living law' socio-legal paradigm, abstracting law from patterns of human behaviour (Tamanaha, 1997: 112; for the difference between Luhmann's systems theory and common legal positivism see Rosenfeld, 1998: 92). The sovereign political power is only an element of the environment of the autopoietic legal system and therefore cannot directly influence its procedures and structure (Luhmann, 1982: 122-37).

It would be a fundamental mistake to simplify the interpretation of the autopoietic systems theory and take it as just one of many theoretical fields in current legalist science. One of the facts that make this theory different is the way it employs the concept of *contingency.* While the legal positivists usually understand law in its direct opposition to the contingency existing in modern society and define it as a system of hierarchical social and political integration, the autopoietic systems theory has chosen the opposite perspective. Law is defined as a structure of expectations of a contingent nature (Luhmann, 1983: 208ff.). Modern society as a whole is complex and contingent. There is no hierarchical order in it, but only contingent mutual relations between different social systems. Such a society cannot be held together by some ideological framework, or ruled and determined in its development from just one centre of the political power. The concept of legitimation by procedure confirms the autonomy of law in relation to politics. Politics is law's environment and therefore cannot be its legitimation foundation.

Autopoiesis dismantles the popular notion of society as a system ruled from one centre. The command centre has disappeared because every procedure becomes such small command centre which seeks to establish communication and the functioning of different elements of a social system. In a society consisting of different autopoietic social systems, there is no sovereign norm or procedure. Instead of this organising master centre, a social system is united and strengthened by its differentiation. Flexibility and differentiation have become the most decisive characteristics of the system.

The master discourse is impossible in any social system including law, in spite of the fact that lawyers and legal scholars conceive of modern legal science as a supreme science about law and the sovereign standing behind the creation and application of law (see, for example, Schutz, 1994: 149-64). Society and its law go through a process of their *horizontalisation* (Murphy, 1997: 163, 183). Borders between social systems are not borders between superior and inferior subsystems of modern society. They are horizontal borders which make it possible to distinguish one social system from another (Murphy, 1997: 164). These systems cannot be explained one by another. Law cannot be explained by politics or economics. Law can be explained only from law. The normative closure of autopoietic systems makes them independent of their environment.

The process of the horizontalisation of law helps to isolate and separate the 'sovereign' vocabularies of political and moral discourse from the problem of the legitimacy of law. All essentialist and foundationalist attempts to legitimate law by reference to the universal validity of the external discursive framework only make it harder to understand law in the plurality and variability of its social functions, in its flexibility and ability to respond to the growing contingency of our social world (Teubner, 1992).

The relation between legality and legitimacy cannot be a relation of superiority and inferiority. Autopoietic theory correctly analysed the fact that the universal acceptance of anything is impossible and indeed unthinkable in contemporary social conditions. Although we might have universal demands for legitimate law, their universality is immediately dissolved on contact with social reality.

The derivation of the legitimacy of law from a 'higher order of norms and principles' which ignores the inner mechanisms of legality is abandoned by the autopoietic systems theory (Luhmann, 1995a: 317). The reasons for this are the facts about the actual functioning of contemporary law, which can seemingly operate without ethical or fundamental political legitimation. Values and virtues of democracy or human rights and freedoms do not have a primary impact on the functioning and therefore the legitimacy of law. Law is enforced in society independent on those values, which belong to the political system. The process of the legal system's differentiation and the expansion of its regulations into different social spheres make it also legitimate. Consequently, the matter of legitimacy must become a matter of social facticity (Murphy, 1997: 184).

....

In his later works, Luhmann paid little attention the topic of legitimacy. In the 90s, he completely separated legitimacy from legality and understood the former as a problem of the political, not the legal, system. The problems of the sovereignty of the people, democratic decision-making, and human rights belong to politics. They do not determine the legal system's operations. They are law's environment. Such, as it were, legal-political problems must be understood as a structural coupling between two different social systems. The political system must incorporate into its own operations the demand for the legitimate expression of a political will by democratic procedures within the limits of civil freedoms. The legal system must incorporate into its own operations the legal expression of this will in the form of the constitution and laws. The legality-legitimacy relation copies the system-environment relation.

The autopoietic theory of law contains the problem of the legitimation of law within the sphere of the positive legal system where it is a matter of the procedures supporting the system's self-reproduction. The main shortcoming of such legitimation by procedure is not its decisionist character or its narrow identification of legitimacy with social control. Its main shortcomings are its reduction of legitimation to passive processes of learning procedures and its deliberate exclusion of the social contingency of belief in legitimacy. Luhmann and others ignore the problem of legitimacy, which is one of the instability and changeability of the acceptance of a legitimate order, such acceptance being a matter of understanding and volitive acts of individuals and groups as social actors. Legitimacy and legitimation cannot be explained only as a matter of compliance with procedures. On the contrary, they can involve the need to break with or destroy legal procedures. The concept of legitimation by procedure focuses on what happens inside the system. It ignores what is different from the system and happens outside its borders. Even within the paradigm of autopoietic systems theory, the problem of legitimacy thus remains a matter of *normality*. Everything that is outside the system is its noise, illegitimate environment and parasite (Luhmann, 1998: 661).

This noise, however, has an extraordinary importance for the problem of legitimacy. If it is impossible to found legitimacy in some kind of universal master discourse or superior social system, this does not mean that legitimacy would have to be defined exclusively in terms of what is normal and functional within the framework of existing social systems. Legitimation, although its goal always is the stabilisation and normalisation of thought, communication or action, also contains many elements of instability. If legitimacy is normality, the social space of this instability and constant confrontation is the space in which legitimation takes place. System's noise is not only contingent, but also often subversive in respect to what has already been recognised as legitimate and normal.

A parasite is inherent in the problem of legitimacy. Legitimacy is not only a matter of a system's operation expressing social normality. At the same time, it also points to the system's environment, which is not yet described by the language of the system and controlled by its procedures. The problem of legitimacy consequently breaks into two different spaces which must be analysed separately. The first space is already normalised legitimacy. The second space is a plural space of various legitimation strategies, many of which have an openly anti-normative, parasitic or subversive character.

Legitimation between the noise of politics and the order of law

This reduction of legitimacy to normal procedure is surprising because autopoietic social systems theory centrally builds on the assumption that difference is the most important part of the whole system-environment relationship. Difference embraces that which is always waiting to be described and grasped by the system and thus contains the open, contingent possibility of social evolution. Legitimation by procedure cannot resolve a tension central to legitimacy, which is the tension between *ratio* and *voluntas* which finds one of its forms in the system-environment loop.

The technical rationality of legal procedures is to isolate legitimacy from the instability of the political world, with the polemic, contradiction and partiality which are the consequences of unorganised expressions of the political will. The legal system has to take political communication, which in all modern societies consists of disputes between the constradictory wishes of individual wills, as its environment. It cannot exist without it. Legitimation is impossible without legal procedures (the principle of the rule of law), but it also must be clear that the whole legitimation strategy is directed beyond the limits of legal system and into its political environment.

Umberto Eco's semiotic theory of the artwork might help us to understand this situation. According to Eco, every work of art must translate disorder into a system of language or conventions in order to be able to convey information (Eco, 1988). Legitimation of law may then be seen as the translation of political forms of information into the organised and systemic language and rules of law. Legitimacy and the legitimate must have the form of law. Legitimacy is an outcome of the process of legitimation, which belongs already to the context of law and legal system. Legalist fictions are to establish the domain of the law (Teubner, 1993: 3) and prohibit us from leaving the framework of legal procedures or eschewing the language of legality, whenever we are in the legitimation process. The function of every fiction is to transform noise into order and normality as they are defined by the system of positive law. Fictions have a very important legitimating function, because they establish order from noise (von Foerster, 1960). *The legitimating fictions of legality are to translate the noise of politics into the order of law.* Fictions support the movement from pluralistic reality to a legitimate order which is considered normal.

That different social systems are linked only horizontally lacking hierarchical relations, determines the relationship between legal legitimacy and the processes of legitimation. In philosophical, sociological, political and legal texts, this process of the horizontalisation of social systems is described in various ways, as the postmodern condition, anti-foundationalism, or the end of man and philosophy as a perspective with the power to take the 'God's eye view' (Putnam, 1981). Because only God can possess the ultimate, all-encompassing and objective concept of the truth and because man is not God, a transcendental concept of truth is useless in human life and thinking. This opinion, quite common in current philosophy and social science, assumes furthermore that man should accept this situation of contingency and insecurity as a basic social fact. Contingency is unlimited and pervades all structures including law. Is it, however, possible to imagine law as a contingent structure, if normality, order, security and regularity are crucial qualities of law and legal legitimacy?

One of the most consistent advocates of the anti-foundationalist concept of law and the rejection of transcendental principles of law is Stanley Fish. According to Fish's legal theory, law is not a dominant or integrating system in modern society and does not incorporate transcendental political values. It may not be regarded as an *a priori* normative structure. Law is contingent in the same way as all other spheres of social reality, language and thinking. In the legal system, the pragmatic use of norms and anonymous force manifested in different legal interpretations and concepts are more important than normativity itself.

The contingent character of law cannot be defined theoretically because every theory (and consequently all fictions produced by various theories for their own purposes) is a manifestation of the false hope that we may construct a general discourse about law which would encompass the legal system in its complexity and fully describe all its aspects and functions (Fish, 1994). Law cannot be explained through philosophy, literary criticism, psychoanalysis, or economics. Law may not be even deconstructed in the sense that scholars would be able to provide an interpretation of law, which would be different from and superior to legal interpretation itself.

According to Stanley Fish, law is a closed context with its own 'informing rationale'. In spite of the fact that political conflicts are disguised by legal terminology in contemporary societies, there is no reason to be worried that these societies would be 'colonized' by law. Law as a context is surrounded by many other contexts independent of legal procedures and terminology. Interpretive practice is what puts law in motion. All law is created by interpretation and therefore subject to forces existing within the framework of the interpretive community. The law is therefore the product of the forces, strategies, and particular interpretive rules established by an interpretive community. Law is self-referential because its legal interpretive practices produce their own limits. These limits are not, nevertheless, set up by some principles, as suggested by Ronald Dworkin, but again by a contingent constellation of the forces and strategy which produce law.

Law is a momentary and contingent outcome of the interpretive practices of a community. The reproduction of law is a matter of the enforcement of what at that moment was the most persuasive interpretation, which prevailed over other interpretations and therefore defines the future limits and rules of legal interpretation and decision-making. In this sense, law is always political, like any other system. Interpretation of law is always conflictual. Such interpretation is an internal mechanism of functioning and self-reproduction of law. No interpretation however may be founded in the 'right' theory and lead to a better, more just or theoretical concept of law.

This anti-foundationalist approach to law involves a forceful rejection of that theoretical legitimation of law which is based on a claim to provide knowledge of better and more just interpretive techniques in the processes of legislation and enforcement of law. Legitimacy is no 'ready-made' (Fish, 1994: 170). The legitimate is determined by contingent forces standing behind interpretive practices and rules set up by them. Contingency is an important characteristic of every social communication. All participants in social communication experience it. According to Luhmann, contingency structures social systems and exceeds the very concept of social action (Luhmann, 1995b: 108). Contingency has a fundamental importance for establishing meaning in the social world. Social communication cannot be derived from some generally shared symbolic order or system, as is suggested by Parsons, or from moral value consensus as claimed by Durkheim, or from a Weberian belief in the legitimacy of a political order (Luhmann, 1995b: 123-5). Meaning is not given by *a priori* consent. It develops in the process of permanent communication about this consent. Meaning changes because communication between social actors or systems is a contingent structure of expectation of expectation. Meaning is always a correction or specification of social expectations, which cannot be fully predicted because the other party to the communication is in the same position.

The growing contingency of modern world makes the question of what is legitimate a much more difficult problem. Because of our experience and acceptance of a particular version of reality, we know that social development could run differently. We know that there are always more possibilities of action than the action taken. Legitimacy is always a product of contingency. It is not derived from the subjection of law to political principles, because the only principle in contingent societies is that there is no principle or starting point. Law is politics, but politics is not the foundation of law, and law is not the foundation of politics. Between law and politics in their traditional sense, there is an irreconcilable difference.

Legitimacy must be understood as a legally formulated strategy which has momentarily won in the context of law. Its status nevertheless is always open to question, because, at the same time, there are present many other legitimation strategies inside the legal system which look for their own ways of coming to dominate. This mechanism of legal self-reproduction and self-reference is exactly what makes every law political but it does not mean any simple subjection of law to the political framework.

We may therefore sum up by saying that legitimacy is a contingent outcome of the legal definition of a particular social strategy. Legitimation is a permanent struggle to obtain this outcome, which does not initially have a legal form and represents what has not been defined, conceptualised and enforced by law, yet.

The law's cult of impersonality and its limits

Legitimation is a permanent struggle for and against legality. It is inseparable from the tension between the legal system and its environment. The environment cannot be understood only as a political space, which penetrates legality from outside and thereby determines the behaviour of the system of positive law.

The complicated nature of the relationship between a system and its environment is nicely reflected in Teubner's distinction between the actual and constructed environment of the system, which must be addressed by the autopoietic theory of law: '[F]or the theory assumes that, although the environment actually exists, it is inaccessible to the operations of the system. The system can deal only with its own internal construct of the environment' (Teubner, 1993: 74). This double character of the legal system's environment raises important problems, the most basic of which is whether the legal system has the capacity to conceptualise the difference between the actual and the constructed environment? Teubner's concept of reflexive law as a system able to interfere and interpenetrate with its environment (if it is at the same ontological level) (Teubner, 1993: 89) does not seem to offer a satisfactory answer, because the decision about the environment's ontological status ultimately belongs to the episteme of a particular social system and therefore is an internal construct of the system. It appears that even autopoietic systems theory is confronted by the duality of a system's environment: the first environment being established by the system, while the second one is escaping the language of the system.

As a consequence of its effort to satisfy the idea of justice as formal equality before the law, legality must represent *the cult of impersonality.* In order to become legitimate, law must be without human qualities and, in this sense, inhuman, in order to preserve its functionality. The autonomy of law must be secured by the generality of its internal procedures, which excludes all elements of subjectivity. The only permissible element is the passive capacity of learning and adapting to those procedures, which nevertheless has only an operative meaning. Coeval with modernity, state power expresses itself in the language of impersonal legality. General legislation codified liberal principles and ideals. Law could legitimate modern politics and state power because it used the most general language and could satisfy the universal aspirations of modern rationality. Its impersonality and power to operate seemingly without qualities made it a very effective strategy of modern state power.

Besides the objectivity of science and the autonomy of art, the universality of law and morality was the main feature of modernity (Habermas, 1987a). The universality of law required the development of the internal logic of law able both to assert law's autonomy and represent modern rationality connecting law with science. Modern legality must define its centre and finds it unsurprisingly in Leviathan, this 'mortal god' that is the first and most persuasive picture of the modern legalist fiction of the political sovereign (Hobbes, 1952: 100). God as a power transcending human political society was transformed into a sovereign possessing (almost) divine force in ruling that society (Fitzpatrick, 1992: 73). Modernity is obsessed with looking for the centre. Legality is also deeply affected by this obsession. All modern political utopias seek to create a 'divine community' which would be governed in a geometrical spirit of regularity. For instance, F.L. Aubry proposed to create an entirely new city corresponding to the spirit of revolutionary France in which logic would prevail over irregularities and impersonal reason secure social transparency. Time has its new beginning, new cities with new centres are founded and modern legality also has to find its own centre. *Legalist fictions are to help to define the centre.* The existence of law is even conditioned by its capacity to identify its own centre, be it the basic norm, the political sovereign, or the principle of the just law. As Peter Fitzpatrick points out:

> [Law] takes on the impression of the *imago mundi*, affirming the ordered, normal course, often by correcting deviations from that course. The creation and enforcement of any law is a ritual reassertion of the foundational strength and ordering of the centre (cf. Eliade 1965: 20). What is being affirmed is not just a particular order in opposition to disorder but the very being and force of order itself (Fitzpatrick, 1992: 86).

The force of the modern law derives from the centre's power to set up its limits by distinguishing between the legal and illegal (Fitzpatrick, 1992: 62). Legalist fictions then connect jurisprudence and the modern legal system in order to produce the power of the law's centre. Jurisprudence must establish 'law's truth', that is the truth about what is its part. This truth is obviously different from, for instance, the truth of science, yet it cannot exist without claiming to have a scientific nature (Nelken, 1998). Positive law cannot exist separately from jurisprudence, which both claims a scientific status and performs important functions within the framework of positive law.

The cult of the impersonality of law may be understood as a consequence of modern efforts to establish universally binding law and morality. The concept of the rule of law is the concept of law being the centre of political life subjected to impersonal rational rules and not human arbitrary will. In this sense, Hart's concept of law as the unity of primary and secondary rules is an attempt to bring the rule of law concept to its perfection because it conceives law as a self-regulating system of rules in which the role of political sovereign as an external element of positive law is limited to the minimum (Cotterrell, 1989: 98ff).

Law should not be an instrument of power. Quite the opposite, every power must enforce the principle of the rule of law. Political power and administration however have an eroding effect on the rule of law principle because it turns out that law and power are rather in a complex relation of horizontal interdependence (Fitzpatrick, 1992: 150, 153) and not in a simple hierarchical relation of law's domination. On one side, political power and many other spheres of social life are subject to the law and have to accept its language. This development is sometimes referred to as juridification of social reality (Teubner, 1987). Legal procedures organise more and more of social life and adjust to its growing complexity. On the other hand, a consequence of this juridification is the loss of the declared autonomy of the regulative system of law and its transformation into the administration of society which reacts to the demands of social regulation. *The unity and cult of impersonality of law are dismantled.* In order to perform the role of the political centre of modern society, law must incorporate all its elements in the same way as Hobbes's Leviathan did in 17th century. Such incorporation however dismantles law's internal unity because law as a means of regulating social conflict must adapt to the structure of these social conflicts.

A higher social reflexivity of law causes law to become as complicated, incomprehensible and inaccessible as modern society itself. Legitimacy of law is not so much a matter of the symbolic function it had (when it represents the constitutive principles and ideals of state power), but rather of its capacity to reflect and respond to the growing complexity and variability of social reality. Variability also means contradiction. What is a legitimate solution for some individuals may be entirely illegitimate for others. Legality tries to re-describe the complexity of the world and to offer it its own solutions, but the legal need for generality and universal validity then becomes a problem without any solution.

Modern legality and its internal logic seek to eradicate what cannot be subjected, conceived and calculated in the language of general rules and norms. An Austrian novelist Robert Musil understood that logic as a desire to rule the life itself and compared the logic of law to *ice flowers*, the blossoming of which is in care of lawyers (Musil, 1997: 586, 646-7). Unlike critical legal scholars, Musil would never say that those, whose minds have thawed have overcome falsity and achieved an insight into the right state of things. Thaw brings just the knowledge of contingency and instability of any such flower as the ice logic of law.

The empty form of a rule is the only fabric of our depersonalised world. In this context, Musil's own definition of the 'banality of evil' is not so surprising. In the language of bureaucratic organisations, any order creates a feeling that the moral is impersonal. Bureaucratic consciousness is a consent to and performance of an order, whatever its content may be (Musil, 1997: 696).

Rationality and the logic of our world cannot, however, be demonised in the way it sometimes is in legal and political philosophy. The law's impersonal world may not be opposed to some fundamental order of principles and universal norms. It is impossible to live either without the logic of the law, or in the blind automatism of exclusive subjection to this logic.

The impersonal logic of rules and rationality ends up in the world of fantasy. Reason leads to excesses (Musil, 1997: 234-5). The logic of rules spreads from the centre, shapes a clear fabric of human thinking and acting, but breaks and denies itself at the periphery. The 'luxury of pure rationality' (Muşil, 1990) expressed in mathematics is not only a matter of economy and effectiveness. Behind effectiveness, there is passion and pure intellectual fantasy, which may not be programmed in advance as is a machine. Even the purest rationality involves the irrational elements which call for it to exist and function. The periphery of reason and impersonality turns against its centre and foundations. The common logic breaks along a centre/periphery distinction and denies itself.

This movement may be detected in law. Legality and its impersonal world of rules, foreseeability, repeatability and security are the absolutely necessary legitimation framework of modern political societies and of law itself. Legal legitimacy creates the centre of legitimation strategies and it is hard to imagine that the state organisation could be legitimated without any reference to legality.

At the same time, the centre of legality, mainly human rights arguments, corrupts the sovereignty of legal discourse and legal legitimacy. Freedom of expression and other human rights involve an ideological plurality which it is impossible to contain within legal language. Legitimation strategies may often be disconnected from legal rules. The legal logic therefore creates a periphery which can be eventually anti-legal.

In contemporary societies, law is decentralised and the common concept of legality as the only source and criterion of legitimacy has vanished. The decentralisation of legality coincides with the dissolution of the sovereign as the central mechanism of modern political society. In post-modern pluralistic societies, law does not have the capacity fully to legitimate political power and its decisions. Legal procedures have only a limited and not a sovereign legitimation force. Legality can never colonise the problem of legitimacy.

6 The Centre and Periphery of Legality: The Strategy of Dissent

The gap in the legitimation of law

The condition of law's legitimacy is often specified only as its correspondence to democratic decision-making procedures and the moral demands of a liberal community. According to this view, legal normativity must correspond to a broader framework of political and moral normativity (see, for instance, Dyzenhaus, 1997: 10ff). Legitimacy is perceived as a problem of stabilising the standards which are to operate as *the foundations* of rightness and therefore can justify the exclusion of other, 'incorrect' practices and normative demands. This perception is common to the legal theoretical concept of legitimacy as law's correspondence to political morality and the Habermasian concept of discourse legitimacy of law. Legitimacy is conceived as correspondence with a pre-existent normative framework defining the limits of acceptable social action. The legal system must be built up according to this normative framework.

This decisive role of a moral vocabulary in the definition of legitimacy is not, however, typical only of those streams of legal and political philosophy which base legality and legitimacy on some 'foundations' or complex 'theory'. Acceptance of moral conditions of legitimate actions and institutions may also be detected in those current paradigms of social sciences and philosophy which are critical of 'foundationalism'.[1] In the post-modern version of pragmatism set out by Richard Rorty, there is a very strong call for the abandonment of all transcendent foundations or humanist principles in the Kantian sense. But Rorty also holds that

[1]In respect to law and politics, Stanley Fish and Richard Rorty seem to be two most representative authors criticising 'foundationalist' views (see especially Fish, 1989; Rorty, 1980).

concepts such as 'rationality', 'morality' and 'the common interest of humanity', though it is impossible to treat them as universally binding, have a vital role in our own culture (Rorty, 1991a: 198). The contingency and particular character of the democratic culture of contemporary western liberal democracies does not mean that one would have no moral conviction in them. Morality is not founded by transcendental principles and universally binding norms of human action, yet it persists as a cultural and historical tool which is used by human beings both in their self-creation and in their political existence.[2]

Rorty's 'offer' is a moral version of the world which is to make possible democratic consensus in a deeply pluralistic political and social situation. This consensus is radically different from Habermas' discourse concept of consensual democracy because Rorty refuses to make a distinction between 'true consensus' and 'false consensus' (Rorty, 1991b: 165). Democratic consensus is a historical and contingent product (Rorty, 1998: 33), the purpose of which is to secure unity, coherence and the decision-making powers of a democratic political community.

Rorty looks for *the common* in a situation 'without principles', when no grand legitimation narrative such as Habermas' discourse theory or Dworkin's liberal legalism. He expresses the post-modern ironical morality which is to harmonise heterogeneity with inclusion and plurality with consensus. Democratic and sentimental education is to replace transcendent principles and knowledge the source of the legitimation of our culture, and this will eradicate the *a priori* from our political vocabulary:

> [T]he best, and probably the only, argument for putting foundationalism behind us is the one I have already suggested: it would be more efficient to do so, because it would let us concentrate our energies on manipulating sentiments, on sentimental education. That sort of education gets people of different kinds sufficiently well acquainted with one another that they are less tempted to think of those different from themselves as only quasi-human. The goal of this sort of

---

[2]It is typical for Richard Rorty's philosophy that it strictly divides the private and public world. The public world involves solidarity, while the private world in modern societies may be characterised by irony or protest. Rorty adjusts his reading of contemporary political philosophers to this distinction and, consequently, Derrida becomes a private ironist, while Unger or Habermas are considered important representatives of modern thought and democratic vision of the public space. According to Rorty, intertwining the private and public worlds is an example of metaphysical thinking (see Rorty, 1998: 308; for the relation between the private and public, see further Rorty, 1989: ch. 4; Rorty, 1991b: 164-98).

> manipulation of sentiment is to expand the reference of the terms 'our kind of people' and 'people like us' (Rorty, 1998: 176).

The problem of normativity in such a contingent situation becomes the problem of life of a democratic political community rather than the problem of setting up the transcendent principles which can guide all the practical political and moral steps of members of this community. According to Rorty, the common is shaped by the human community and this is also the reason why it has a contingent and historical nature. Community is legitimate when it can consensually contribute to the utopian ideal of inclusive democratic and liberal society. The validity of these consensual procedures cannot, however, be secured transcendentally from some super-legitimating procedures of knowledge and correct thinking. It can be secured only as a reflection of the life of democratic political community.

....

A brief analysis of the legal system of any liberal democratic society shows that this system enables us to secure plurality of legitimation, but that it also remains a solid framework of the legitimate rule of law. Legality and the legal system is only one of many legitimation narratives, but it also has the role of the common and it is the common that creates the very possibility of the public world of politics (Arendt, 1958: 58-9). Legality seeks to define this common even when growing social pluralisation radically fragments the public world of politics and turns morality cannot provide the conditions of universal validity and legitimacy. In early modernity, legality was supposed to provide a basis for cohesion in the light of the fading morality. Legality was to prevent all moral fundamentalists from dominating the public space and Kelsen's liberal legalism was one of the most complex statements of the values of legality in opposition to the conservative moralism and traditionalism of natural law ideology. Legality was to be an empty, impersonal form which would be accepted by all as legitimate just because it is empty and impersonal. According to the concept of legal legitimacy, the common was to be shaped by the logic of the ice flowers of impersonality. However, this common turned out to be too rational, 'cold' and inaccessible.

Legality seeks to stabilise and close the legitimation space by framing it in procedure, rules, and logics of impersonality. This is a necessary condition of the legitimacy of modern law and political domination. Without the impersonality of law, no modern political society would have the power to communicate, reproduce itself and therefore exist at all. The liberal democratic rule of law relies on the legitimation power of legality, and legality, up to a certain point, can successfully perform this legitimation function.

The impersonality of law is a consequence of the modern ethical and political demand for the equality of all citizens and people. Legal justice and generally binding laws must express the ethical and political principle of equal treatment. In any modern legality, there consequently is an element of external legitimacy formulated in legal vocabulary and eventually conceived as an internal part of modern legality. However, at the moment of legitimacy's reduction to legality and the exclusion of all other discourses from the space of legitimation, the rule of law system may place itself in a similar situation to that in which totalitarian regimes justified their crimes. Because the Holocaust was carried out in obedience to the law, it was legitimate. Because the enemies of Soviet power were punished with 'due' process of law in Stalin's political trials, their punishment was legitimate. Even liberal democracies may find themselves indulging in the 'banality of evil' if they justify themselves exclusively by reference to legality and exclude all other vocabularies from the legitimation field.

The fiction of the just law, which is to fill the empty formal structures of legality with the substantive principles of democratic and liberal morality, was formulated as a reaction to this threat hidden in the formal character of the modern rational system of law. The fiction of the just law wants to define politics in moral terms, but maintains the modernist structure of legal legitimacy and continues to give an ultimate supremacy to legal discourse in the context of politics. Legality is to be revitalised by morality in order that it may continue to function as the sovereign legitimation framework.

A morality of this sort must be universal to the same extent as legal rules and it therefore must manifest a similar level of impersonality. But the principles of liberal democratic morality cannot exist outside of juridified reality and therefore must manifest similar features of impersonality to legality. The logics of impersonality and the ice flowers of rationality are not in peril. But this means the continuation of the crisis of legitimacy disclosed by the failure to satisfy the demand for comprehensibility of the law. This moral legitimation of law does not solve the problems of legitimacy by legality. It only shifts them into the extra-legal context.

Rational and impersonal legality is just one of the many manifestations of modern knowledge which:

> [d]oes bureaucratise nature, and must necessarily do so; but, serious cognition need not pervade all aspects of daily life. On the contrary, the insulation of various spheres of life, the division of labour and specificity of function, makes it easier to permit any degree of fantasy in those aspects of life which are distinct from the serious business of knowledge. The disenchantment of cognitive life, together with the severe separation of thought from play, can actually liberate the latter from constraint (Gellner, 1974: 193).

Because law and politics combine thought and play, no contemporary legal framework, even if it is strictly founded on the principles of political morality, can claim to have the character of *a sovereign discourse* implicit in the strategy of legitimation by legality. The moral foundation of legality formulated by the fiction of the just law is, in a certain sense, just an attempt to re-establish the sovereignty of moral discourse in modern societies with the help and in the form of legality. The erosion of the sovereignty of rational and impersonal legal discourse is a consequence of the strategy of legitimation by legality, for the attempt to confine all politics to their expression in law encounters resistance by many forms of political life. This juridification of politics leads to the creation of parallel and resistant political structures.

The legitimation process is the *extra-territoriality* of politics and law. It works as an 'agent-provocateur' (Gellner, 1974: 16) permanently exposing the legitimated politics to external judgments and critique. In legitimation, the search for correctness and rightness implies both the acceptance of legitimated structures and resistance to them. This tension is ignored by legalist fictions although '[t]he real starting point was a justified sense of chaos, of cognitive breakdown.' (Gellner, 1974: 205). Although the problem of establishing an order is central to legitimation, legitimation also creates a need to challenge the existing order.

The limited legitimacy of fictions is evidence of the 'gap' character of law and legal legitimacy, emphasised in the various strains of legal realism, which signifies the impossibility of establishing a completely sovereign legal discourse. *The gap legitimation of law* is not a pathological aspect of legality.[3] It is its necessary character in the conditions of liberal democratic society. This gap legitimation of law was first manifested in the fiction of the social contract. The social contract assumes the establishment of the generally binding framework of law and sovereign political power with the monopoly of legitimate violence. This general framework, however, depends on the individual decision of people to make the social contract. The contract creates the symbolic order of the sovereign power, but in this order, there is plurality and the possibility of different interpretations of the norms and symbols of legality. Political plurality and heterogeneity create the permanent threat that the legitimacy of legality will be denied. The internal construction of the contract fiction puts in doubt the possibility of the total legitimation of political reality by the language of law and opens up legality to interpretative plurality.

Leviathan can never fully control a general belief in its legitimacy in Weber's terms. In the social contract, individuals and social groups may create the legitimation strategies which may call for radical departure from the existing state. The fiction of the social contract is contradictory because, whilst its purpose is the establishment of one political body, the means by which this is sought depends upon individual wills, which can never be determined by any collective body. The gap legitimation of legality, which necessarily is left by the social contract, is inevitably present in every liberal democratic society. In this society, dispute concerning the content of legality and therefore its legitimacy must be permanently reproduced. The gaps are in fact a source of the legitimacy of law because they help to reproduce a range of legitimation strategies. The sovereignty of legal discourse as an exclusive source of legitimation contradicts the ideas of democracy, freedom and political plurality.

Democratic procedures expressed by legal rules are perceived as an internal part of the legitimacy of the rule of law. However, these procedures cannot be fully stated in legal language because the referential field of democracy is not identical with the referential field of legality, despite their many common 'territories'. The legal protection of human rights and freedoms, the liberal aspect of the rule of law system, plays a

---

[3]The concept of 'the legitimation gap' in the negative sense is used by Jürgen Habermas (Habermas, 1989: 148).

similarly important role in legitimating that system as democratic procedures. It is another part of the legitimacy of the rule of law, which has a legal form yet cannot be limited to the legality. Even legal positivists acknowledge the supra-legal character of human rights and freedoms. The legal system of contemporary liberal democracies is permanently engaged in disputes about the interpretation of these rights and freedoms, their mutual relations, priorities and hierarchies.

Decision-making and the attribution of meaning to specific legal texts is variable and often even contingent in spite of all efforts of modern legality to enhance predictability and diminish contingency. The universal nature and unity of legal discourse is dismantled by the rhetoric of human rights. *Human rights and freedoms constantly open new legitimation fields and use legality as an instrument or key to enter this field.*

Centre vs. periphery; forgetting vs. memory

Legal legitimacy involves both an effort to achieve sovereignty and an effort of social reflexivity. Law, originally the sovereign discourse of modern politics, has been found to be diluted or thwarted in many spheres of social life. The vocabulary of legality clearly dominates the public world of modern societies. This domination is, however, possible only when law adapts to the dynamics of social development in contemporary societies. The growing social reflexivity of law, or law's tendency towards socialisation (see, for instance, Rehbinder, 1977: 128ff), leads to its dilution in society, and such dilute law cannot play the integrative role attributed to it by lawyers and politicians. Effective legal sovereignty requires the acceptance of legal legitimacy as a closed framework. Social reflexivity, however, respects the culture of plurality, and this is to legality's sovereignty.

The function of legality is to limit and control pluralistic political culture. Law is to set up a sovereign normative framework of legitimation, but this can never be entirely successful in liberal and democratic society. The horizontalisation of law means the loss of political sovereignty by legality. No system or discourse can fulfil the demands of universality. And this is exactly why the question of legitimacy remains a crucial question not just of modernity, but also in the situation described as postmodernity (Lyotard, 1984), late modernity (Giddens, 1990), or new, reflexive modernity (Beck, 1992).

The topic of legitimacy remains urgent because the absence of a unifying normative framework of society which is the core of postmodernity has followed the collapse of the grand attempt of modernity to overcome this feeling by means of technical rationality. *The agora* of modern political societies was one of the normative force of rational knowledge and transcendent principles of ethics and politics (Bauman, 1983: 238). The internal rationality of the political system forms only the normative framework of politics, not the whole society.

The modern *agora* established on the basis of the sovereign legitimacy of law and rational knowledge has disappeared. Instead of legitimacy by legality, Jean-Francois Lyotard has put forward his concept of legitimation by *paralogy* (Lyotard, 1984), which criticises sovereign legal normativity and, generally speaking, any concept of legitimation by some meta-narrative or meta-language game. The heterogeneity of language games, according to Lyotard, dismantles the possibility of a master, grand narrative and a fundamental normative criterion. There is no superior argumentation of 'litige' which can specify the winner of a dispute. There is 'differend' among individual language games and no common criterion may be identified among them (Lyotard, 1988a: n. 12, 13). Lyotard attributes only a particular meaning to every language game, including legality and morality. Legal legitimacy, derived from the sovereign power of state, always threatens the terror of a system and the total control.

In his book *The Postmodern Condition: A Report on Knowledge* (1984), Lyotard described the pluralisation of, and consequent loss of a common normative framework of culture in, contemporary liberal democratic societies. Lyotard's marginalisation of legality contradicts the claim that our social reality is being juridified, which means the imposition of legal regulation in more and more spheres of social life. Discussion of both President Clinton's scandalous actions with Monika Lewinski and the case of Dolly, the genetically cloned sheep were notably juridified. But neither legally defining the sexual intercourse nor legally prohibiting the cloning of the humans has, however, provided a higher level of stability or security in contemporary society.

A typical example of such useless efforts to enhance social and moral security by the means of a legislative act is *The Human Fertilisation and Embryology Act* adopted by the British Parliament in 1990. Long and careful discussions and consultations with many experts, from medical doctors and genetic scientists to moral philosophers and theologians, preceded the enactment of that law, yet its provisions could not surmount the contradictions between technological possibilities, the legal principle of expressed consent, and the feelings of moral or existential satisfaction and human solidarity in the famous case of Diane Blood (for legal details, see, for instance, Morgan and Lee, 1997).

Legality and attempts to establish legal legitimacy turn out to be politically and socially less marginal in the post-modern condition than is claimed in Lyotard's concept of legitimation by paralogy. Under the conditions of liberal democracy, legality actually initiates the pluralistic play of legitimations. Not all language games enjoy the same status in the heterogeneous post-modern condition. Some are more dominant and agressive. Instead of a simple paralogy, an irregular placement of different language games is to be observed.

Although not being a master discourse or grand narrative, legality manifests a strong capacity to dominate even in contemporary liberal democratic societies. *The picture of centre and periphery* appears, then, to be of primary importance. The legal system is a centre which seeks to produce legitimacy of the liberal democratic rule of law system. However, the legal system also has a periphery that cannot be fully controlled from the centre. This being so, the overally system, constituted in/by the centre, loses its clarity at the periphery, its borders become diffuse, and its rules less effective.[4] This periphery is a world of legitimations and all possible de-legitimations, which may not be specified in advance by the legal system. *The centre produces the periphery in order to persist as a centre, but it is unable to control it.* This is the important part of the definition of the gap legitimation of the rule of law in liberal democracies.

The relationship between legal legitimacy and the plurality of legitimations is, then, one of the functional interdependence in which the legal legitimacy is characterised by normative regulations but this characterisation is contradicted by an irregularity produced in the very process of the creation of a legitimation strategy. Legal legitimacy assumes

---

[4]The difference between centre and periphery was extensively discussed within the sociological paradigm by Edward Shils. Shils's concept of centre is, however, somewhat different from my difference because it takes symbols, values and beliefs governing the society as criteria of a centre, and not functionality, reproduction and procedures, which are crucially important for my own analysis (Shils, 1975).

a space which is not normatively defined in advance. In this space, everything is in the state of 'waiting for normativity'.

....

Legal legitimacy requires the *forgetting* of the complexity of our reality and all possible alternatives and worlds. This mechanism of forgetting establishes the possibility of social action, communication and the reproduction of law and politics. Forgetting is therefore one of the main features of consumer society (Bauman, 1998: 82). It affects legal legitimacy both as a political technique and the symbolic expression of political morality. All pragmatic steps taken within the framework of the legal system must adjust other social meanings to their legal interpretation and translate the social environment into the language of legality. Subsequently, they have to forget this adjustment and translation. Other vocabularies and interpretive practices and their rules must be forgotten and re-told, 're-codified', within the legal system.

Legality must ignore its environment. Ignorance and forgetting constitute pragmatic actions, theory, rhetoric and knowledge itself (Fish, 1994: 236). Forgetting is a mechanism for the discrimination and isolation of all social facts that are irrelevant to legal practice. The forgetting of non-legal elements makes possible the behaviour required by the legal system. Forgetting is intrinsic to the operations of any social system that reduce the variability of social actions and define systemically relevant behaviour (Luhmann, 1995b: 56, 565f).

It is an important condition of the functioning of any social system, not just the legal system. Nevertheless, forgetting is also central to modern legitimacy built on the principle of the sovereignty of the people. The people is a political sovereign, but its one body of People-Leviathan must be translated into the language of legality and 'cut' into specific legal procedures and the constitutional rules of the separated political power. The people may be one sovereign only if it is separated into different power centres. The people must forget its symbolic unity in order to be subject to impersonal legal procedures. The emotional political vision present in the revolutionary moments of modern societies must become an empty legal automatism. Forgetting transforms the conditions of the legitimacy of modern political domination into legal procedures.

Like the sovereignty of the people, legitimation by human rights is turned into an automatic procedure of the legal system. Their primarily moral meaning must be transformed into a legal meaning. Moral and political virtues and human rights must accept legal procedures as the way they may be enforced (for the proceduralist concept of the legal system, see Ladeur, 1986).

Consensus and other fundamental political values do not have a place within the legal system as its constitutive elements. If they appear in it, the criterion of their presence is the functioning of the legal system and not its constitution. In order to function and reproduce its operations, legality must forget its moral and political context and deny its subjection to any other social system. The operation of forgetting involves the restriction and discrimination of all political and social elements defined by the legal system as its environment. In his critical reaction to this operation of forgetting, Peter Goodrich speaks of it as a dangerous threat and seeks to establish the art of rhetoric and reconstruct the forgotten in defiance of the politics of forgetting practised within the legal discourse (Goodrich, 1995: 210).

Legality contains a field where two strategies meet: *the strategy of forgetting and the strategy of memory*. While forgetting constitutes the unity of legal system and enables it to function, memory represents a political challenge going beyond the framework of any system (Goodrich, 1996: 112f). Goodrich's call for cultivating a jurisprudence and law which would respect the art of memory and allow the heterogeneous structures of contemporary societies to speak through the language of legality may seem to be too ambitious and to ignore the key structures of legality. The political dimension of forgetting, nevertheless, must not be marginalised. Milan Kundera has said that forgetting is a big ally of political power and tyranny. Struggle against this tyranny is always a struggle of memory against forgetting (Kundera, 1990: 1). George Orwell also warns against the totalitarian control of the present, which means the control of the past and therefore the control of the future (Orwell, 1990). Such statements call for resistance to the dangerous forces of politics and public world, which threaten to allow us to be controlled and prefabricated through the repressive process of forgetting.

The politically dangerous character of forgetting is closely tied to the tyranny of silence, which is the worst violence (Derrida, 1978: 117). The art of writing must be supported against silence. It is necessary to speak and write about the limits of our thinking, politics and law and therefore also formulate what is beyond those limits. It is necessary to remind ourselves of what differs (for this political aspect of the art of memory, see, for instance, Lyotard, 1990) from us and may be driven to oblivion by the expansion of our own limits or borders. Memory strengthens the awareness of the heterogeneity of world, while forgetting creates the illusion of homogeneity and systemic unity.

Legality and legal legitimacy cannot exist without forgetting. Forgetting eliminates all elements complicating the functioning of the law as a systemic whole. The everyday reproduction of law must suppress communication about constitutive principles, ideals, maxims and values of law. The stabilisation of law proceeds by means of a separation of law from external elements, from politics, morals and economy. When these external elements are not questioned and challenged, they are stabilised as factual modes of social action and consequently enhance the acceptance of normative legal structures. In this moment, legal legitimacy grows.

Legality is one of the most important contexts separating normality and abnormality in modern societies. However, the problem is that legality is not the only context of contemporary politics and cannot claim itself to be a sovereign legitimate framework. The normal and the abnormal must be separated by the language of legality in order to establish the political context at all. Under the liberal democratic rule of law, however, 'normal' legality requires the support of, and *supplements* from, its 'abnormal' context.

The normal cannot be divided from the abnormal. Legitimacy rather oscillates between normality and abnormality and cannot successfully lead only to the sovereign normative framework of legality. *The problem of legitimacy is a problem of setting up limits, which can never be resolved from a position inside the system.* Legal legitimacy is constituted in the process of the transformation of legal principles into everyday legal practice. While those principles have primarily a non-legal character and enter the language of legality from its political, economic and moral environment, legal practice seeks to operate as an automatic reproduction of legal texts, decisions and actions. *Forgetting the primarily non-legal character of legal principles enables us to establish the normality of law and legitimacy by legality.*

Forgetting the non-legal sources of legality supports *the self-legitimation of law* in stabilised modern societies. In times of complex social changes and reconstructions, however, people retreat to the entirely opposite strategy in the field of legality. The self-legitimation and reproduction of law are interrupted and, instead of forgetting, memory has the primary importance. Any complex political change initiates the perspective which takes law as a highly political normative system that must be re-defined and re-constituted. *In times of complex social and political change, social memory reveals the non-legal sources and conditions of legitimacy of law.*

The politics of memory eventually assumes the same key importance as the politics of forgetting in modern societies. Every political ideal has its roots in a reflection upon the past. Natural rights and the ideals of liberty, equality and fraternity are the idealisation of the fictitious natural state existing in fictitious historical time and reconstructable by political action such as revolution. The question of legitimacy oscillates between memory and forgetting. A dialogue with the past leads to an acknowledgement of the relativity of present political demands and denies any legal system its universal validity. The politics of memory can name the wrongs of the past, and it also challenges the authority of the present demands. Memory is the mechanism of naming the injustices and the protection against the potential authoritarianism of the present which would like to claim universal validity for the existing state of things.

The whole process of de-Nazification is based on the politics of memory, which nevertheless has its internal limits prohibiting the possible paralysis of the constitution of the new political and legal system in Germany after 1945. Memory must be used economically. It must not become a never-ending mourning about the past. In order to constitute a legitimate political order and law, memory must observe political limits. One example of a proper recognition of this necessity may be *The Truth and Reconciliation Commission* in South Africa, which was such an institutionalisation of political memory of wrongs, injustices and violence (Dyzenhaus, 1998). Setting up such limits in the institutionalisation of memory can, however, mean that the past can never be fully grasped and reconciled. Memory cannot be fully politicised because it always escapes every form, rule or institution.

Legitimation as the environment of legality

I argue that the problem of legitimacy is one of setting up the limits of legality and this cannot be resolved entirely within the legal system. One may conclude from this that *the problem of legitimation is a problem of re-defining the context and variability of the limits of legality.* Legitimacy requires a form. Legality can, to some extent, provide this form. In order to have the power to deal with social conflicts, law must reduce the complexity of social reality to legal forms. In modern society, no form may be declared to be completely sovereign. Legality consequently must always suffer from a deficit of legitimacy. In his essay 'The Conflict of Modern Culture', Georg Simmel says that there is an irreducible tension between life and form and the exceptional quality of modern culture is that it gives constant challenge to the very category of form and replaces it by the category of life (Simmel, 1987).

According to Simmel, modern society does not involve the struggle between old and new forms of social life. Modern culture is unique in its attempt to break down every form as such, attacking the rigidity of forms. Life itself is sovereign, with all the implications of this for authenticity, freedom and self-containment (Simmel, 1987: 172). The difference between life and form in modern culture shows that culture to be one which refuses to accept that there can be any ideal form of thinking or social system (Simmel, 1987: 167ff), the best expression of this being the pragmatic turn in modern philosophy with its rejection of truth as an ideal form. The conflict between form and life also reveals the temporary, variable character of any life form. Life must formalise its spontaneous movements, but the result of such formalisation is the enforcement of this movement. The denial of form therefore is a never-ending process because form can never be fully removed. It is subject to the spontaneity of culture and social dynamics.

This perspective on modern society and its culture obviously is inspired by Nietzsche's philosophy which embraces both the continuous breaking of formal limits of ways of life and the necessity of providing those ways with a temporary form at every stage of their development. A similar conclusion, unencumbered by the metaphysical ambitions contained in the concept of life, is reached in Rorty's critique of epistemology. Rorty gives a decisive importance to the distinction between epistemology and hermeneutics. While epistemology sets up norms and codifies knowledge, hermeneutics embraces revolution and change. Hermeneutics builds on the knowledge of differences and of shifts in thinking (Rorty, 1980: 315f.; this difference is also analysed by the Italian philosopher Gianni Vattimo, who treats it as an important sign of the end of modernity in Vattimo, 1988: 145f).

The dynamic, imaginative and innovative aspect of human thinking and cultural heterogeneity reflected in hermeneutics is contrasted with the codifications of the rules of thinking pursued in epistemology. This 'political reading' of the difference between epistemology and hermeneutics is expressed in the following:

> [I]n the interpretation I shall be offering, 'hermeneutics' is not the name for a discipline, nor for a method of achieving the sort of results which epistemology failed to achieve, nor for a program of research. On the contrary, hermeneutics is an expression of hope that the cultural space left by the demise of epistemology will not be filled – that our culture should become one in which the demand for constraint and confrontation is no longer felt... [H]ermeneutics sees the relations between various discourses as those of strands in a possible conversation, a conversation which presupposes no disciplinary matrix which unites the speakers, but where the hope of agreement is never lost so long as the conversation lasts. This hope is not a hope for the discovery of antecedently existing common ground, but *simply* hope for agreement, or, at least, exciting and fruitful disagreement (Rorty, 1980: 315, 318).

Substituting hermeneutics for epistemology means giving up the philosophical ambition of defining the correct and right foundations of our culture and having a 'scientific' or philosophical control over them. Hermeneutics dismantles the hierarchical concept of modern knowledge and favours equality of different discourses operating inside our heterogeneous culture. Cultural differences are overcome by mutual compromise and not by their subjection to one sovereign discourse (Rorty, 1980: 316-7).

Rorty more recently has stated the distinction at issue between horizontal and vertical thinking. While the first kind of thinking is associated with ironical distance and the reflection of contingency in the world of liberal democracy, the second kind evokes the metaphysical passion for principles and foundations of our thinking and political society (Rorty, 1982: 92). Drawing on this tension between form and life, rule and spontaneity, or norm and revolution, as they have been formulated by

Simmel, Rorty, Kuhn, and others, allows us to penetrate more deeply the relationship between legality, legitimacy and legitimations. Legitimacy requires a form and, in modern political societies, finds it in legality. The general, highly formalised language of rational legality, however, does not lead to higher clarity and trust. The growth of generality paradoxically leads to the decline of clarity of language and communication. The Italian novelist Italo Calvino describes this phenomenon as a plague in contemporary society because the generality of language establishes an *automatism* in communication and thinking which threatens to erode meaning (Calvino, 1996). The form of legal legitimacy contains this danger of automatism and therefore must be confronted with different legitimation strategies coming from the outside of legality. *Legitimation becomes the outside of legality without the fundamental destruction of the concept of legal legitimacy as such.*

Our liberal democratic experience is too dynamic and open to be reduced to the structures and rules of legal legitimacy. This legitimacy indeed is strengthened when legal rules are more open to their outside. The level of legitimacy of the legal system of liberal democracies directly depends on the level of plurality existing in its legitimation environment. *Legal legitimacy* is paradoxically strengthened when it dismantles itself as *a sovereign political discourse and opens the space for other legitimation strategies in the public world.*

The problem of legitimacy obviously may not be resolved by the amoral legalist fiction of law as a 'cold' and therefore legitimate technique of the organisation of modern society. The problem of legitimacy also may not be resolved by any other fiction translating a purportedly fundamental moral discourse into legality. The problem of legitimacy may be resolved only by a proper determination of the *functional* relation between legal legitimacy and the plurality of legitimations. The legitimacy of legality is not determined by legality's subjection to moral and political values and principles. It is determined by law's variability and openness to the range of opinion and belief that may be formulated and enforced by law (Ladeur, 1986: 265-74). Instead of consensus as the purpose of communication, the liberal democratic legal system shapes an environment in which the plurality of opinions and meanings finds its legal procedural expression. Legal procedures reflect and serve the changeability, openness, plurality and contingency of opinions.

Legitimation as a strategy goes even beyond the distinction of centre and periphery existing in the legal system of liberal democracies. Legality as the formal centre of legitimacy must remain diffuse and open to other legitimation strategies. At the periphery of the legitimate, however, it is impossible to determine in advance whether a different legitimation strategy enhances the stability of the legal system and existing legal legitimacy, or leads to its weakening. This is the reason why the legitimacy cannot be an internal product of the legal system. The legitimacy of law is never constituted by legality itself. It comes from the outside. Individual actors in a system of positive law introduce external elements into this system (van de Kerchove and Ost, 1994: 110). It is therefore necessary to perceive *legitimacy not as a matter of form, but rather as a process of legitimation, which is never fulfilled or finished, yet extremely important for the functioning of societies in the contemporary postmodern condition.*

What is legitimate can never be decided only within the system's framework. It is decided at the system's periphery and is affected by many elements from *the system's outside*. Legitimation involves external elements which can both stabilise and disrupt the system. Legal legitimacy is obviously determined by the internal conditions of the law's validity, coherence, and the logical unity of the system. Legitimacy is, however, also determined by the law's outside, which may not be reduced to the normative system of morality and its arguments.

Socialist legality as an example of automatism in legal legitimacy

The general character of modern legality is a necessary condition for the establishment of legitimate political order in modern society because its rational structure establishes political equality before the authority of the law. However, the general character of legality also diminishes legitimacy because it easily turns public political discourse into a kind of nonsense comprehensible only to a bureaucrat or a legal expert. In one of his plays, Václav Havel used the word *ptydepe* to describe such nonsensical political discourse (Havel, 1965; 1991: 48ff).[5] A legal expert and bureaucrat are equipped to use and benefit from this discursive consequence of modernity.

[5]The term *ptydepe* designates an incomprehensible language, the real social purpose of which is power manipulation and the reproduction of one's own position and benefits from impersonal bureaucratic structures.

The danger of the transformation of legal legitimacy into an empty automatism of general language is endemic in all modern legal systems (see, for instance, Fitzpatrick, 1991: 18ff). This automatism is, however, extraordinarily strong in the communist totalitarian legal systems, where it is usually described as the principle of 'socialist legality'. This principle uses some constitutive formal features of modern rational legality whilst actually dismantling the whole system of the rule of law and the proceduralist concept of legal legitimacy. Moreover, socialist legality is open to a very effective legitimation, or rather delegitimation, strategy targeted against the automatism of general legal language. This is the strategy of *dissent*. This strategy is not only a potent form of protest against the law and political systems of totalitarian or undemocratic societies. Dissent also has an exceptional political value within the liberal democratic rule of law system.

In the last part of this chapter, an analysis of anti-communist dissent will be used to formulate the relation between legal legitimacy and legitimation strategies emerging from the environment of the legal system. Anti-communist and in fact any dissent exemplifies the fact that the relationship between legality and legitimacy may never be limited to the legal system but extends into its environment. The example of anti-communist dissent also shows that in contemporary social and political conditions legitimations cannot be founded on 'God's eye view', that is, on some transcendent order of norms, principles and virtues, which law would have to adapt in order to become legitimate. This may seem to fail to capture the moral aspect of the dissident criticism of the communist system. Dissent, however, does not have direct legitimation force by saying what law has to do. It rather indirectly and from the law's outside points to possible alternatives to existing legal normativity. Dissent is an ironical struggle against systemic formalism. It is the uncontrollable outside of law and a permanent challenge to law.

....

At first sight, socialist legality seems to be incompatible with the rule of law, a view which is strengthened by consideration of Hannah Arendt's brilliant analysis of totalitarian regimes. Arendt suggests that these regimes represent the rule of instability and uncertainty which enables the population to be effectively controlled by terror and violence. Both the

Nazi and the Bolshevik political systems are characterised by the lack of predictability in their legal, constitutional and political orders. Distinctions between Party and State are blurred, legal institutions are overshadowed and dominated by Party decisions. Law becomes a facade for political voluntarism (Arendt, 1956, ch. 12). This description captures Lenin's concept of a dictatorship as a rule which does not require law, because law just blurs the violent nature of every government (Lenin, 1936).

When they ran up against the political reality and problems of the soviet system, Lenin's revolutionary concepts had to be re-shaped or, indeed, abandoned by the official ideology. The developing communist totalitarian state had to take a legal and constitutional form, so as to cover repressive party policy with an image of stability and legality. New legal doctrines emerged which attempted to explain the nature of the new political system in legal terms. Vyshinsky's legal theory retreated from, and indeed denounced, Stucka and Pashukanis and backed Stalin's unpredictably repressive policy with the concept of socialist legality (Vyshinsky, 1949: ch. 3). The communist totalitarian system developed under Stalin during the 30s which survived in the Soviet Union and other countries until his death in 1953, declared itself to have its own historically 'higher degree' of legality and to act constitutionally. In 1936, Stalin even adopted a Soviet constitution which would have brought rights and decent social and political conditions, if that constitution was ever obeyed. In fact, it was just a rhetorical veil for terror and arbitrariness. Isaac Deutscher described Stalin's constitutional and legal efforts as a political tactic enabling him to execute opponents and innocent citizens under the mask of constitutionalism, the rule of law, and liberalism (Deutscher, 1949: 381f). In reality, no constitutional provisions, and certainly not those which incorporated the humanist ideals of enlightened, free, democratic society, were obeyed by the ruling political élite, especially not the secret police. Under this constitutional and legal surface, political crimes and atrocities stretching the limits of human imagination were a part of everyday social life. Socialist legality became synonymous with the sheer political terror practised by the totalitarian political power (Skilling, 1966: 172), and the role of communist constitutions was always more ideological than legal (Skilling, 1966: 50f).

Besides this rule of arbitrary terror speaking the language of general legislation (Podgorecki, 1996: 11f), the communist societies also had a vast legal apparatus functioning in a similar way to law in liberal democratic societies. Parliaments controlled by the communist party enacted laws which were applied by courts and provided citizens living in those countries with legal security and stability. This security was obviously very fragile because it could at any time be broken at the will of the communist party. This 'system' is described as *telephone justice*, in which courts could decide independently until their deliberations were interrupted by a member of the Party élite who exercised the power to influence the case, destroying the autonomy of the system of justice.

The parallel enforcement of law according to legal rules and arbitrary political interests is a typical characteristic of the communist totalitarian regimes. These regimes, however, underwent significant changes in the course of their historical development. The open political terror common to the early 50s disappeared after Stalin's death and the XXth Party Congress, and every country of the Soviet bloc had always represented a specific variant of communist totalitarianism.

In the Czechoslovak case, it is important to realise that the repression following the invasion of the Warsaw Pact armies in 1968 never had the character and intensity of the repression of the early 50s. Communist repression affected hundreds of thousands of people and created new 'second class citizens', but the regime did not resort to mass imprisonment and execution (Oxley et al., 1973). It preferred to introduce a policy of 'normalisation' which discriminated and persecuted mainly through an elaborated mechanism of social and economic sanctions and remuneration (for an analysis of political 'normalisation' in Czechoslovakia during the 70s, see Kusin, 1978; Pelikan, 1976).

Reflecting political, cultural and social changes in Czechoslovakia in the 70s, Václav Havel and other dissidents started to speak about a 'post-totalitarian' political system (Havel, 1985: 27). Havel did not mean by this that the totalitarian nature of the communist system would disappear, but that it was, in a way, fundamentally different to totalitarianism as usually understood. It was not founded on open political terror or violence, but on the ritualisation of public life and a kind of 'blind automatism which drives the system' (Havel, 1985: 30). The overwhelming majority of the population was not involved in open confrontation with the regime and only had regularly to express loyalty to the existing political system.

Another Czechoslovak dissident, Milan Šimečka, brilliantly described this state of petrified stability of the communist regime as a special kind of social contract between the ruling Party élite and the population subjected to its government (Šimečka, 1990: 168f.; quoted also in Skilling, 1981: 53). The population was provided with some guarantee of its material existence but in return was required not to interfere in political affairs. Furthermore, they were guaranteed a certain autonomy in the private sphere which was limited to material wealth. P.G. Lewis, for example, calls this unique political and social condition a 'consumer-based conservatism' (Lewis, 1994: 178f). The distinction between the political and the private represented a profound distinction between official enthusiasm and private cynicism. Ritualised accommodation to the regime was to some extent compensated by an improvement in economic standards of living which, nevertheless, subsequently appeared to be only temporary.[6]

If the original modern fiction of the social contract created the conditions of modern dynamic politics, the communist social contract is a quite opposite attempt to maintain a political status quo. Communist political power had a total control over population, yet, in this unequal condition, it offered its subjects a minimum of social welfare and consumerism in exchange for ritualised loyalty. Even though the purpose, namely the creation of political stability, is the same, two contracts are quite distinct because the communist social contract exists between unequal subjects, and its primary goal is the creation of a depersonalised, ritualised political environment with which citizens can never identify.

The legal system was an important a part of the political sphere where such official enthusiasm had to be manifested. Under the surface, the Communist Party continued to control the whole social body. Nevertheless, it must be said that many legal norms never had a primarily political or repressive character and even the communist totalitarian system generated legal security, predictability and some other virtues emphasised by ethics of legalism and considered moral foundations of the rule of law.

Political terror did not vanish, but was limited and exercised only against a tiny minority of dissident groups and human rights activists. This

[6] 'Consumer-based conservatism', based on a specific kind of social contract between the communist élite and citizens, is a phenomenon well known in Czechoslovakia and other countries of the Soviet bloc. While in Czechoslovakia people spoke about 'dumpling socialism', in Hungary the term 'gulash socialism' was preferred. The economic reforms of the Polish communists in the 70s were also driven by an attempt to neutralise growing tensions in the socialist economic welfare system. Private life was reduced to a reproduction of consumer goods and was politically controlled only in order to avoid any free political will formation.

'limited use of terror', limited in its intensity and social targets, nevertheless had a significant political function because it reminded the population to approve the system ritually and as all the instruments of political violence and open repression were still alert.

Human rights and the double language of dissidents in the communist countries

It turns out that even in their late stage the East European communist systems did not lack legal stability and the arbitrary use of political violence was not their dominant mode of government. The systems contained the strong tendency to autarchy. Socialist legality was to contribute to the stability of socialist societies in a way similar to legality under the liberal democratic rule of law. Law and order had a totalitarian character, but the whole system was looking desperately for legal legitimacy, both in internal politics and at the international level.[7]

The basic strategy of the Czechoslovak dissidents was to exploit the distance between the concept of socialist legality and political reality. Charta 77 and other dissident organisations constantly tried to point out that the whole nature of the regime, which claimed to be socialist, legal and constitutional, was in fact bluntly discriminatory, repressive, and broke all international standards of human rights and civil freedoms, and therefore was illegitimate. The dissident struggle in the 70s and 80s was a struggle to expose the illegitimacy of the Czechoslovak communist system.[8] From its very beginning, Charta 77 strategy was to operate within the discourse of legality. It used the need to respect the law to point out the 'double-speak' nature of the principles of socialist legality and the communist regime (see, for example, Skilling, 1981: 125). The drafters of the Charta 77 document

---

[7]A typical example of these efforts to achieve legal legitimacy was the Helsinki peace process in the 70s, which eventually led to the strengthening of the position of dissident movements in all the countries of the Soviet bloc. 'The third basket' of the Helsinki Final Act concerning human rights protection inspired Charta 77 in Czechoslovakia and other dissident activists throughout communist Europe.

[8]A Czech historian and journalist Jan Urban says of the difference between 1968 and 1989 that: '... while twenty years ago it was predominately a matter of a crisis of legitimacy within the governing Communist élite in one country of the Communist bloc, in 1989 it concerned a phenomenon of a greater degree. It was the Czechoslovak variant of the crisis of legitimacy of the whole Communist system' (Urban, 1990: 108).

appealed to the International Covenant on Civil and Political Rights, the International Covenant on Economic, Social and Cultural Rights and to the Helsinki Final Act (Skilling, 1981: 209-12). It was argued that, as the Czechoslovak Socialist Republic signed these legal documents, they were now incorporated into its legal and constitutional order. This legalist strategy appeared to very effective and clearly showed that the language of law meant absolutely nothing within the communist system of justice, where the decisions of the judiciary ultimately were made outside of judicial institutions.

Totalitarian domination by the Communist party is constituted on three main pillars – the secret police; the army and paramilitary organisations; the courts and prosecutors. It is typical of the post-totalitarian communist regime that it diminishes and blurs the role of the paramilitary organisations and the army and shifts much of their power into the system of judicial power. This merely serves as an example of the illusory nature of general obedience to law. Instead of the party militia, it is courts and prosecutors who become the real 'iron fist' of the Party and working class. To show the discriminatory and repressive character of this phase of the system therefore requires the unmasking of the machinery of justice and socialist legality by showing its real political function.

The Charta 77 declaration was not a political programme but a list of human rights and civil liberties violations by the communist regime. It emphasised the well-known fact that the political and legal actions of the regime were inconsistent with international human rights conventions. Although very mild and careful in its criticisms and demands, the Charta 77 declaration met with a hysterical reaction from the regime and its media, and the anti-Charta campaign was reminiscent of previous ideological emergencies, and their demands for extraordinary rituals manifesting the popular support for the communist regime.

From a legal and political philosophical viewpoint, the Charta 77 and other dissident movements raised a fundamental question about the legitimacy of the political system and its law. The issue of the nature of legality had to be addressed because the communist system had a paradoxical double structure. It was based on a widespread and arbitrary abuse of power, but also declared its acceptance of the principle of legality (Havel, 1985: 69ff). The dissident movements used this doublespeak in which communists declared a respect for the principle of legality because it was the most vulnerable part of the system. Because communist law was never only a set of regulations for human behaviour but also played a symbolic ideological function, in order to disclose the nature of the system it was necessary to operate within legal discourse. Havel even called this dissident strategy 'legalist' and found it to have the greatest value in the possibility of demonstrating the ideological nature of socialist legality, its inconsistency with the liberal rule of law, and also the absurdity of the excuse that communist officials have observed the law and therefore could not commit any crime (Havel, 1985: 74). The dilemma of the Nazi and Stalinist political crimes still existed in the post-totalitarian political system. According to Havel, legality was so important for the system because it established the system's legitimacy as a whole before its own citizens, before the international public, and before history (Havel, 1985: 75). It established the illusion of legal justice. To show the paradox of use of the rhetoric of legality and its constant abuse by the communist power was to show the illegitimacy of the communist system and its law.

On the surface of this 'legitimation battlefield' between the communist regime and its dissidents, it may seem that the dissident strategy is really legal or even 'legalist'. Looking more carefully at the whole issue, it is, however, possible to unveil a more fundamental strategy. The dissidents never demanded that the communist system of justice and administration should obey its own law. The legitimation question was, in fact: 'What content should the rule of law and legality have?' They argued that not everything that was commanded by the sovereign political power automatically had the character of law. From a more general point of view, this argument calls into question Bentham's or Austin's definitions of law or the early Kelsenian definition of the *Rechtsstaat* (Kelsen, 1922). According to the dissidents, neither the legal procedures, nor the legal rules of communism could be squared with the principle of legality and the rule of law. So far as the principle of legality and the rule of law is concerned, legal rules and procedures must represent certain values, political principles and procedures supporting the separation of political power.

The legitimation strategy chosen by Czechoslovak dissidents in the late 70s and 80s was deeply influenced by the concept of universal validity and inviolability of human rights rooted in existential ethical discourse. It is highly symbolic that one of the first Charta 77 spokesmen was a Czech philosopher, Jan Patočka, who always emphasised the ethical dimension of dissident opposition to communist power and who had an enormous impact on Havel and other dissidents. Patočka, who collapsed and died after two days of police interrogation in March 1977, criticised the western concept of technique and was convinced that the communist state was an implication of the technical hopes in politics (Skilling, 1981: 217ff). According to him, the concept of human rights is:

> [n]othing but the conviction that states and society as a whole also consider themselves to be subject to the sovereignty of moral sentiment, that they recognise something unqualified above them, something that is bindingly sacred and inviolable even for them, and that they intend to contribute to this end with the power by which they create and ensure legal norms (Skilling, 1981: 218).

Czechoslovakia was then a country with a political dictatorship founded on ideological mystification and it was, therefore, a crucial task to show its inconsistency with human nature.

It is obvious that the dissident strategy of legal legitimation goes beyond legalist discourse and is entrenched in a moral and existential vocabulary which does not perceive morality as some sphere of rules, prescriptions and governance, but as that sphere which opens up the possibility to experience human authenticity and independence. This call for authenticity and independence is contained, for example, in the dissident project of a 'parallel polis' worked out by Václav Benda, advocating the creation of parallel structures of intellectual, cultural and spiritual life which would ignore the official structures of social life colonised by the communist party, its coercive power and aggressive ideology (Skilling, 1981: 183).

This expression of legitimation discourse in a moral and existential vocabulary is typical of Havel as well. In spite of his comments on the importance of using a legalist approach against the communist regime, Havel talked of a 'higher responsibility' and a decent 'human order' that must stand behind any critique and civil action aimed against the repressive power. Kafka's concept of 'living in truth', central to the 1989 Velvet revolution, is also very close to Patočka's own philosophical and ethical perspective. The dissident movement thus was hardly only a legal struggle against a political power. It also was an attempt better to understand humanity itself in the extreme situation of communist totalitarianism and its repressions.

Although the concept of natural rights was not commonly used in the dissident literature and political texts of the late 70s and 80s, the ethical universalistic vocabulary standing behind the legal critique of the communist power had the same implications as the natural rights and natural law criticism of positive law and legality. It is possible to speak of a 'weak version' of natural rights and natural law discourse within the Czechoslovak dissident movement. Under the surface of the legal battlefield and legalist language, it is possible to unveil the real reasons for the dissident struggle against communism to be an ethical commitment to 'the will to truth' (Keane, 1985: 97). Pragmatically speaking, it would be hard to imagine someone who would risk so much of his/her life and comfort only to prove that the communist law did not fit within the positive principles of formal legality.

The systemic role of dissent

The dissident struggle to delegitimate communist law and political domination certainly has moral features. That it involved the revival of human rights, humanity and human nature should, nevertheless, not be understood as an attempt to deal with the problem of legitimacy in a transcendent natural law framework. The existentialist standpoint of dissent makes it impossible to found legality in political and moral principles. Dissent involves a different formulation of the problem of legitimation of a political and legal system. This formulation is determined by communication between the system and its environment.

The experience of anti-communist dissent may be generalised to apply to all modern societies (for communist totalitarianism is a product of modernity as is liberal democracy) as a challenge of any systemic language claiming sovereignty. This is why the ideological background of the different dissident groups does not have to be analysed here. People became dissidents for many different moral and ideological reasons. While Catholicism and national patriotism was enormously important in Poland, these ideological influences were significantly weaker in Hungary and only marginal in Czech society. Each national society had different ideological streams of dissidents and the Charta 77 movement is a good example of this.

The illegitimacy of the communist regime could be exposed from the position of reformist communism, Catholicism, economic liberalism or non-conformist anarchism. None of those ideologies could, however, establish one common moral framework of legitimacy and create a common legitimation discourse. This was not even a goal of the dissidents.

The moral reasons for dissent were different, but *the concept of dissent as a delegitimation strategy against the communist system and socialist legality* was common to all of them.

The strategy of dissent is applicable to the liberal democratic conditions of the rule of law because legality seeks to declare itself the sovereign legitimation framework there as well although this is done with the help of the moral vocabulary of human rights and democracy. Dissent is not only a political position and action. It is first of all an expression of the social requirement of understanding and comprehending every social structure and normative system in order to make them legitimate. Dissent represents a pragmatic moment in the reproduction of any social system.

As a general strategy, dissent is more than a critique of the system. Critique is often limited to the structures of a given system. It uses the vocabulary to suggest an improvement to and stabilisation of the system. Such critique implies the removal of the dysfunctions of system and represents, in fact, systemic functionality. In contrast to critique, the purpose of dissent is not just some improvement of law and politics. Dissident activities often start knowing that many apparent dysfunctions are a part of the system's behaviour and not its failure. Many injustices are not removable by legal means and the system of law may be a source of injustices even in liberal democratic societies. Dissent shows that the principle of 'justice according to the law', so important for the formation of modern liberal democratic societies, is not sufficient and it is sometimes necessary to leave the system of law in order to challenge 'legal injustices' from the outside.

The strategy of dissent has a uniquely powerful effect on the system of law because it has the power to disclose and point to the danger of every legal *ptydepe*. It is interesting that dissidents accepted the vocabulary of legality as their starting point of their discussions about legitimacy, but the real purpose of this seeming subjection to the legal discourse was to reveal its absurdity when faced with the deeply unjust and discriminatory political system. Dissidents demonstrated both the incapacity of socialist legality to provide the political system with legitimacy and the limits of legal legitimation in general.

No law is legitimate because some political authority declares it to be the law. Legitimacy of law cannot be fully determined by the character of this authority, or by the content of the law. Legitimacy is neither a matter of the political system creating the laws, nor a matter of their moral content. It is a matter of the permanent communication between the legal system and its environment. Without this communication, legality degenerates into *ptydepe* and codes itself into incomprehensible rules.

As it is external, dissent functions as one of the possibilities how to translate the law and make it comprehensible. This translation however cannot be reduced to systemic language because dissent is irreducible to the element of the legal system. Dissent translates legal rules into a concrete situation which represents only a fragment of our complex social reality. It is a strategy of exposure of legal legitimacy to the demands emerging in different fragments of contemporary societies.

It would be an inappropriate simplification to say that the purpose of dissent is only the delegitimation of the principle of legality. Justice according to the law and the rule of law were the most important original political demands of dissident movements in the communist countries. In this sense, the 1989 velvet revolutions have been a great success. Their modernisation efforts were centred around the idea of social order established on rationality, negotiation and a clearly defined argumentative framework. Legality represents this order.

But beside this re-modernisation of the post-communist societies, it is important to remember that the demand for the rule of law was not the only demand and the strategy of dissent was merely the starting mechanism of the whole revolutionary process. Together with the modernist demand for the subjection of politics to the strict rules of legality, the revolutionary process included the element of dissent, *a supplement of modernisation*, distant from legal techniques and rules, which can define the limits of legality itself. Dissent as a supplement to and distance from legality cannot be identified as an external objective perspective on social systems. Dissent is entrenched in the relationship between system and environment and its externality provides another contextualisation and relativisation of every social system, including the system of law.

Dissent goes beyond the systemic framework of modernity without the fundamental destruction of modern social systems. Justice according to the law is not destroyed. It rather becomes relative in the sense that the problem of justice may not be reduced to the problem of law. The strategy of dissent reveals the limited validity of every social system without attributing universal validity and binding force to itself. Dissent as a legitimation strategy means the end of all attempts at a universal legitimation.

Legality remains an important legitimation technique, yet it cannot own the definition of humanity. Humanity reduced to human rights and freedoms, that is, humanity as a category of the system of positive law, is a parody of the human condition. The 1989 revolutions expressed this dissident experience, in spite of the strong use of the rhetoric of the rule of law and human rights. The modernisation process of post-communist societies therefore lacks homogeneity. Instead of homogeneity, the very centre of the revolutionary process is dominated by a heterogeneous space divided into legal legitimacy on one side and dissensual legitimation strategies on the other. The first cannot exist without the second and no vocabulary can consequently function as universal and sovereign. The 1989 revolutions identify themselves with the universality of human rights, yet they do so reflecting the profound particularity of social and political motives, interests and beliefs. A growing space of heterogeneity, pluralisation and particularisation is an immediate consequence of this revolutionary movement.

7 Legitimation Fictions and Power of the Contractual Model

Legitimacy - an old-fashioned or an unfinished project?

The problem of legitimacy can be approached in three different ways in the current intellectual and social conditions. The first is the modernist search for universally binding, general and neutral criteria of the system of law and political domination. Political institutions and order may be called legitimate if decision-making procedures can claim universal validity established by rational argumentation. Knowledge and humanity are universal categories with the power to legitimate political violence and law's enforcement. If law and political power are outcomes of rational argumentation, violence is transformed into a legitimate political structure. Political structures cannot be a mere social convention emerging contingently from the process of social communication. This communication must have its elaborate order corresponding to rational argumentation. Knowledge is the transcendent source of the validity of political norms and conventions.

We have seen that legitimacy is conceived in this way in, for instance, the work of Jürgen Habermas. According to Habermas, communicative rationality may be called a language game, yet its procedures and rules are not mere conventions (Habermas, 1996a: 18f). This particular game is exceptional because in it empirical conventions are transformed into universally valid principles of political decision-making. Knowledge and truth keep their transcendent foundations and cannot be considered as only the results of unspecified social communication and agreement (Habermas, 1968). Their legitimacy is derived from transcendentally valid principles of free rational argumentation and the normative structures of *correct thinking*, which is the exclusive source of human knowledge.

Ernest Gellner approaches the problem of legitimacy in a similar way. According to him as well, it is necessary to defend the Enlightenment project typified by Isaac Newton's scientific thinking or Immanuel Kant's philosophy and universal ethics. The Enlightenment is unique because it replaces the authority of tradition with the impersonal authority of reason, in which the criterion of correctness and legitimacy is not some arbitrary political power but rather the transcendent force of knowledge. Legitimation of political belief always proceeds as a rationalisation of the irrational and a translation of the complicated and ruptured world of social conventions and prejudices into the clinically clean and ordered world of rational argument. The process of rationalisation is a legitimation strategy, the goal of which is the codification of legitimate political structures.

In Gellner's political philosophy, which is a complex mixture of the Cartesian critical method, Kantian rationalism, and Weberian ideal type analysis of modern society (Gellner, 1974: 206), these political structures remain the foundations of the open character of modern society and therefore of free thinking. Legitimating beliefs and knowledge or political and social structures is a matter of finding the *external* criterion (Gellner, 1974: 20) which can judge the correctness or incorrectness of this knowledge or structures.

This first, modernist approach to the problem of legitimacy also dominates in the legalist fiction of the basic norm. The Kantian notion of the correspondence of empirical normative systems of law (and morality) to the transcendent and universally binding norms of thinking as a condition of their legitimacy prevails in this fiction. Hans Kelsen's legalism is a form of transcendent and not positive thinking.

Similarly like Kelsen's fiction of the basic norm, Stammler's fiction of the just law also has a transcendent nature. The just law becomes just when it corresponds to universally valid principles of rational thinking and decision-making. What is morally right derives from what is cognitively right. The fiction of the just law, currently described usually as the ethics of legalism, has nevertheless many different forms, and it has found its support both among adherents of transcendentalism and of conventionalism. The legitimacy of law is provided either by transcendent rational procedures, or by existing social and political conventions. The legitimate is always something that is primarily extra-legal and takes its own normative perspective on the legitimate system of positive law.

The second approach is to *ignore* the problem of legitimacy. This is typical for Niklas Luhmann's later works of the 90s in which he suggests:

> Nowadays, people look for moral rules or values to found the legal system in nonlegal norms - the famous Jellinek-Weber-Habermas line of 'legitimation',

> or the American discussion of moral aspiration versus original intent as a guideline for an interpretation of the constitution. My advice would be to unask such questions - or to 'deconstruct' them - and to replace them with the question of how the system organizes its own closure, its own social autonomy, and its own immunity in fulfilling its function (Luhmann, 1992: 1426).

Luhmann's effort to describe the specific character of law by analysing its internal operations and structures, by understanding *law from law*, partly resembles Kelsen's efforts to establish a pure legal theory. For Luhmann, this theory obviously is a part of the autopoietic system of law. Unlike Kelsen, Luhmann nevertheless does not believe in a basic norm which might organise law into a centralised and hierarchical order and system. Together with Kelsen and others, Luhmann is convinced that all efforts to legitimate law by extra-legal structures, be they transcendent or conventional, are useless. According to Luhmann, law legitimates itself by its own internal resources, if one has to mention the probem of legitimacy at all. This reminds one of the basic norm, the main epistemological function of which also is to prove that law's validity is entirely a matter of the positive system of law, although the final source of validity (of the basic norm) must be formulated in a transcendent logical context.

Autopoietic social systems theory gets a juridical character when it defines what still belongs to the sphere of theoretical analysis of law and what has to be excluded from it. Binary coding, which operates within the system of positive law as the legal/illegal distinction, gives a legal form to the distinction between scientific and unscientific and defines the problem of legitimacy as falling outside the sphere of socio-legal theory and social science discourse about law. Autopoietic theory refuses to address the problem of legitimacy and legitimation just for the reason that it exceeds the framework of social systems behaviour. Excluding the problem of legitimacy from the complex of socio-legal questions nevertheless makes it only more urgent.

The third approach to the problem of legitimacy is to identify the difference between legitimacy and legitimation and perceive the legitimation processes as shifting between the legal system and its environment. The legitimation of law is a matter of the difference between law and its social environment.

This difference is irreducible to the matter of a different social system which could have sovereign legitimation force over the legal system. The legitimation process cannot be centralised and anchored in some transcendent normative order. The legitimation of law occurs in a horizontal communication between the legal system and its environment, as is made manifest in the strategy of political dissent.

It is impossible to decide in advance which vocabulary from the legal system's environment will be used. Legality may accommodate it only after it penetrates the internal grammar of legal language. A legitimation strategy is then transformed into legal procedure and becomes a part of legality. Legitimacy can nevertheless never be founded by legality because the legitimation movement always starts from the law's outside.

Legitimation by authenticity?

This quality of the legitimation process is important to the already analysed strategy of dissent and its influence on the revolutionary events of 1989. The political, legal and social transformation of the Czech and other post-communist societies in Central Europe revealed that the legitimation by the system of positive law has its limits and the principle of legality, although being an absolutely essential filter of momentary political interests, cannot satisfy many post-revolutionary demands of citizens for historical and social justice. Many legal norms primarily enacted to achieve the moral rehabilitation of former wrongdoers were highly controversial in terms of justice. *The Act on the Lawlessnes of the Communist Regime and Resistance Against It* analysed in the fourth chapter of this book, may serve as a typical example. No law directly pursuing justice obviously can establish justice in its complexity. Any such law, paradoxically, produces new conflicts in the field of historical and social justice. The post-revolutionary legislation clearly manifests the limits of every system of positive law in relation to the demands of justice. Law cannot directly 'speak' the language of justice!

The duality of natural law and legal positivist discourse typical of both dissent and post-revolutionary legal reconstruction cannot lead to any 'new' synthesis between positive and natural law. It can create only new paradoxes and conflicts, against the background of which it is nevertheless possible to re-think the concepts of liberal legislation, civil society and the rule of law.

Dissent was a complex strategy, the divergent strains in which were marked by a use of the moralist vocabulary of natural rights and an emphasis on legalist arguments to point to the serious human rights violations by the communist regime. This double character makes it impossible to understand the dissensual legitimation strategy as a transcendent critique of legality. Dissent was not only a matter of either natural rights or the ethics of legalism. Dissent is a constant *oscillation* between various vocabularies, demands and criticisms of law and political domination.

We must assess whether the existential nature of dissent, which so strikingly determined the character and development of the 1989 anti-communist revolutions, is not finally a hidden attempt to entrench a foundation of politics and law in *the authenticity of human being.* We must ask whether dissent is not a specific foundationalist narrative of authenticity.

The incorporation of the existentialist demand for human freedom and the authenticity of the human being into the politics of dissent was typical of every protest movement against the totalitarian and authoritarian regimes. Writers, artists and intellectuals, for which authenticity of being is inseparable from their social role and freedom of expression, therefore usually played a very important role in these movements. People like Etienne Leroux, André Brink, Mario Vargas-Llosa, Suu-Tyi, Gyorg Konrad and many others have one thing in common. It is their belief in politics as a guarantee of personal freedom and of the possibility of authentic human expression in an open society. Their dissident position is not a primary position. It is a reaction to the political regime which stabilises itself by the denial of exactly those freedoms which writers, artists and intellectuals find the most important for the inherent meaning of human existence and identity.

In such a political situation, the system stands against individuals and suppresses them by its violence. Therefore, it is not surprising that the dissident struggle takes the form of an ethical call against the violence of the system. Dissidents confront the system from the outside (Brink, 1983: 35). The position of the dissident writer and intellectual usually oscillates between a more narrow understanding of writing as a political instrument and a broader concept of the politics of writing. A writer can be 'the rebel who fights in the name of the essential human values - against everything which threatens the human, against everything which is essentially *inhuman*' (Brink, 1983: 51). In this sense, a writer's expressions in art are conceived as a directly political act seeking social and political change.

Together with this political rebellion by writers fighting deliberately against a repressive political system and formulating every word in respect of its political consequences, writing of any sort may become an act of dissent. Every act of uncensored writing in a society without political freedoms becomes subject to political repression and therefore has a primarily political meaning, even when it is intimate poetry or a diary.

Due to the political situation, what began as an authentic personal artefact achieves the status of a political text which irritates the repressive political regime. Political protest against totalitarianism begins as an attempt to secure authenticity against an empty and 'immoral' system. The struggle for authenticity is an ethical call. Its political value is not, however, given by its ethical meaning. Ethics is not above politics. The ethical nature of dissent does not depend on the content of what dissidents do. Dissent is ethical because it invokes structures, expressions and texts parallel and independent to the politically sovereign and ideologically codified repressive system (for the concept of 'parallel polis', which was introduced by the Czech dissident Václav Benda, see Skilling, 1981: 183f).

What begins as a struggle for authentic being and later transforms itself into the language of law as a movement for political and basic human rights, finally has the highest value in its strategic position within the repressive political regime. Dissident moralist language is not in itself interesting and important. The most important thing is the fact that dissidents question the normative systems of politics and morality and do not construct such systems themselves. Dissent is not a positive political programme. It is a negative call speaking the language of warnings and is close to Socrates's *daimonion* (Patočka, 1996: 135). Dissent begins in persecution and deep insecurity which is a consequence of a free decision to step outside of the borders of the existing system. Therefore, dissent can never speak the normative language of rules. On the other hand, it cannot be silent because to be silent would be to tacitly approve the system's violence. It is necessary to take the position of a dissident who must speak and consequently enter a 'battlefield' defined by the totalitarian system. This is how dissidents become 'the enemy of the people'.

For instance, in Havel's essays one can find strong elements of anti-normativism and morality. For Havel, dissent is first of all a matter of human performativity. The dissident struggle against forgetting is also a matter of performativity. The purpose of such a struggle is always prospective, although the whole strategy focuses on the injustices and bad experiences of the past. This performative tension between the past and the future is a typical feature of all dissent.

Modern wo/man looks for authenticity, but cannot achieve it. Individual expressions of authenticity are always corrupted by some structure to which they are subject as in Milan Kundera's novel *The Joke* (1991), in which Ludvík's personal, ironic comment on a postcard takes on a different meaning, with catastrophic consequences, within the system of communist power and ideology. Ludvík's irony cannot stand by itself and the postcard becomes an irritation to the system, which decides that it is threatening to its stability.

The main characters of Kundera's other novels also find themselves victims of false games, lies, and intrigues, yet they are never entirely their prisoners. To be a prisoner means to resign one's own identity. Winston Smith knows this fact very well and his first task is therefore to write his own diary; a task actually carried out by many dissidents living under real totalitarian systems. This is also why he writes that freedom is the ability to say that two plus two equals four. However, which is more important, the reality which Winston tries to describe in his diary and to which he attributes the quality of truth, or the very fact that he writes his diary, which is a threat to the Party and its system? The Party fears the diaries not for their content, but for their existence.

Every totalitarian system fears that the political space might be invaded by unauthorised opinions and expressions which would be *uncontrollable.* However, authenticity assumes exactly such an absence of political control. Totalitarianism tries to suppress intimate diary records because they represent a form of social and political reflection which is impossible to subject to official totalitarian ideology (for the diary as a literary form with an extraordinary value for the description of all totalitarian regimes, see Garros and Korenevskaya, 1997). Intimacy is the political obverse of totalitarian terror. This is the reason why writing a diary must be declared a crime against the Party, State and Mankind.

Dissent is ethical because it refuses to establish politics on normative principles and functions as an outside confrontation of the system of politics and law. This involves an extraordinary amount of danger as it certainly will lead to political persecution. Dissent has a parallel existence to, and an independence from, the political system; its original attempt to save the possible worlds of authentic being finally brings dissidents to the situation where they have to refuse to 'live like others' (Marcenko, 1989) in the same uniformity and political suppression. The dissident position assumes a certain amount of elitism because dissidents refuse to accept the 'normal' living condition defined by the authoritarian or totalitarian system, and that system can therefore criticise them as a very small group of people.

If ethics emerges where living for others precedes living with others (Bauman, 1993: 165, 185), the dissident position can hardly be understood without a use of the language of ethics. At the same time, it is however impossible to derive a normative framework of social morality, 'good' politics or 'right' law from dissident ethics and calls for human authenticity.

Authentic life is life, which, according to Jean-Jacques Rousseau, is achieved by 'le sentiment de l'existence' (Rousseau, 1959: 1047) and consists of the harmonic relation between man's thinking and acting and his own nature. The question of morality becomes a question of listening to the voice of nature, which speaks through individual human existence. Politics and laws, if they are to embody the virtue of justice, also must be an expression of the voice of Nature. This concept of authenticity is deeply entrenched in modern thinking and contains the contradiction, which cannot be satisfactorily resolved, between individual will and thinking on one side and natural laws and rules on the other. This contradiction may be found in 'the ethics of authenticity' formulated by Charles Taylor, which seeks to harmonise the authentic life of individuals and social groups with the 'impersonal machinery' of the modern political system and representative democracy ruled by instrumental reason (Taylor, 1991). Taylor criticises the narrow concept of instrumental reason, which takes it to be only a tool of man's domination over the world. He seeks to disclose a deeper ethical background to modern rationality which would guide us in our attempt to reformulate democratic politics so that they become more than the working of a decision-making machine ruled by the political majority, and instead respect all social differences so that individuals and groups can freely express themselves and come to the authentic life and self-fulfilment.

Despite his noble goal, Taylor finally subscribes to the ideal type of political community based on the concepts of domination and manipulation and thus finds himself again in the heavily criticised 'iron cage' of modern instrumental rationality when he states, for example:

> [I] have described some of the sources for the strength of our culture of an ideal of self-determining freedom. We are free when we can remake the conditions of our own existence, when we can dominate the things that dominate us (Taylor, 1991: 101).

Rationality can be a legitimate basis for domination of the world only when it is tied to ideals of freedom, autonomy, critical, and self-generating thought. The relation between the technology of power and the ideal of a free community in which all have the possibility of authentic self-generation is an unending struggle of contradictions (Taylor, 1991: 107). Differences and uniqueness are recognised and respected in this community, but political decision-making and changes are impossible outside the framework of state machine and the political majority principle. The problem, however, is how this machine, which is an expression of instrumental rationality, may be adjusted to the plurality and differences existing in modern societies.

Despite this deep reflection of plurality and political inconsistencies, Taylor's argument ultimately is no more than a version of the common scheme in which political recognition means adaptation to the general norms defining the space of modern politics. A fragmented society must unite and different groups must act as one force in order to secure political recognition, equal treatment, independence and political freedom. It is then not surprising that 'the politics of resistance is the politics of democratic will-formation' (Taylor, 1991: 118). The formation of a common political space is done through democratic decision-making procedures and all humans subject themselves to these knowing that they will have to abandon part of their authenticity in order to form a common democratic political will. The force of the political system determines the conditions which turn the call for authenticity into a political problem. Even Taylor must accept the language of technology of power when he looks for political protection of the ethics of authenticity in democratic political society. Rousseau's problem of the subjection of political society to the laws of Nature remains unresolved. It only finds another form in the ethics of authenticity.

....

The ethics of dissent finds itself in just the same trap of modernity. Dissent originally was expressed in existentialist language, but it also must be transformed into the political and legal language so that the political system may be criticised. Dissidents stood against the political regime because it deprived them and other citizens of the possibility of self-generation and self-creation. Individuals subject to this deprivation find it impossible to speak in the language they perceive to be their natural one. The remedy for this existential deprivation, however, posits the necessity of leaving the framework of authenticity and stepping into the impersonal language of politics and law. It is hard to imagine a more inauthentic language than the language of law. Dissidents go a long way when they translate their call for authenticity into the meta-language of legality and criticise the political regime with the help of the concepts of the rule of law and the protection of human rights. In dissent, the search for natural language goes hand in hand with an entirely opposed adoption of the highly artificial language of legal and political concepts. In order to protect the space of authenticity, it is necessary to use an inauthentic vocabulary, the concepts of which are deliberately impersonal.

Every law must dismantle and silence calls for individuality and uniqueness. This is the law's condition. As condition of its existence, personal freedoms must be transformed into impersonal procedures. The legal language of human rights, although it starts as a moral political call for modern wo/man in her/his uniqueness to stand sovereign over any political power, must finally get rid of humanity and establish a structure of general rules. Furthermore, law must impose this artificial structure on a civil society as a natural structure of its existence.

Law turns out to operate as a second-order semiological system stealing the natural language, similar to myths as Roland Barthes describes them in his analysis (Barthes, 1993: 129, 131). Dissidents must accept this theft and fight for natural language by the use of formalised meta-concepts. In this dissident dilemma, the force of law is nevertheless not real. Although dissidents are forced to accept the use of this formalised language when formulating their own demands, they are never colonised by it. Because dissent starts as an existential call, the acceptance of the language of legality may be only pragmatic. Legality is only a powerful instrument, not a sovereign structure.

Dissidents are forced to leave the existential frameworks and accept legal language. However, this acceptance is not internalised but rather is accompanied by a constant distance and sense of irony. Dissent simply forbids legality to become the only and ultimate legitimation vocabulary and keeps it in a permanent tension with its environment. The dissident acceptance of the legalist language means the political relativisation of that language and manifests the dependence of legal legitimacy on the non-legal structures of society. Instead of taking a fragmented society to be, from the political perspective, something pathological, the pluralistic nature and ethos of dissent supports the acceptance of the fragmented environment as a form of political existence.

The common assumption that fragmented groups must politically unite if they want their differences to be recognised looks very weak. Dissent builds on the politics of pluralisation and evidences the possibility of constructing democratic politics and law even in fragmented social and political conditions (see, for instance, Bauman, 1995). The ethics of the original dissident call for authenticity is an ethics of pluralisation, not unification. This ethics, derived from existentialist experience and not from general moral categories or the governance of rules, is primarily negative. Its political purpose is to avoid the situation in which general democratic decision-making procedures would become only a tyrannical arbitrary power, supported by impersonal legal rules.

To answer the question in the title of this section, it must be said that legitimation by authenticity is impossible because authenticity never enters the field of law and politics uncorrupted. Authenticity does not have an ultimate legitimation power, yet it is present in modern legitimation strategies including the strategy of dissent and plays an important role in the legitimation processes of modern law and political domination.

Authenticity, fictions and the social contract

This dilemma of authenticity faced by dissidents is not only a political problem. It is a general problem of the relationship between language, thinking and authenticity.[1] Soren Kierkegaard was aware of the fact that authenticity cannot be reached directly and it is therefore necessary to take the disguise of a seducer and use aesthetic, indirect, descriptions to express what is authentic in human life. It is necessary to retreat to narratives and fictions. It is only this indirect way, using inauthentic tools, that we can point to the ethically more valuable, higher and true world, which hides the authentic life in itself. A seducer's disguise is a necessary condition of authenticity, yet Kierkegaard does not understand the relationship between facts and fictions only dialectically, but also as a hierarchical relation in which the function of a fiction is only secondary and subject to the order of authentic existence in the real world (Norris, 1983: 88f).

Unlike the philosophy of the Christian existentialist Kierkegaard, Nietzche's philosophy dismantles this hierarchical relation between facts and fictions and turns it into a play of various meanings, confrontations and

---

[1]This problem is sometimes understood as purely modern although its roots may be traced to Plato and Socrates. For Plato, the main philosophical and political goal was to separate right thinking from false and he gave real and authentic thinking a supremacy over false fictions (for details, see, for instance, Nehamas, 1998).

riddles, which finally makes the difference between fiction and reality unimportant. The authentic order of ethics, truth and reality is pulled down. According to Nietzsche, all moral and philosophical concepts including the concept of will are only a grammatical fiction (Holt, 1997: 60) and human existence is thinkable only within the structures of language.

Transforming philosophical speculation into grammatical structures, Nietzsche anticipated what is nowadays referred to as the linguistic turn in philosophy, and radically changed our approach to all social structures including law and politics. Authenticity itself is already a metaphysical concept and the uniqueness of human existence present in the natural language or expression is always entrenched in the grammatical structures of language and the system of signs and names. The unique and authentic are thinkable when they are a part of the classification system of language (Derrida, 1976: 109-13).

No structure may be regarded as constituting a simple contradiction of the authentic life of the subject. A call for the natural language is vain. Fictions are not a corruption of reality and authentic life. They are its necessary expression at the moment when language must express and represent what is primarily unrepresentable. Freud's 'theoretical fiction', the function of which is to refer to the unconsciousness, is an example of this (Bennington, 1991: 22-3). Fiction is a secondary representation of what otherwise escapes our knowledge and descriptions within the structures of our language. At the same time, no fiction is able to reconstruct and renew authenticity and human nature. It may be an indirect expression of something signified as authentic, yet it cannot reconstruct authenticity. Nietzsche renounces the western metaphysics and instead establishes the will to power, which means *the will to fictions*, that is, a commitment to the active process of signifying and writing (see, for instance, Milovanovic, 1992: 21).

Authenticity may certainly be conceived as a specific and independent part of the social world and, in a certain sense, as a pre-social/pre-systemic reality in the life of human beings (Heller and Féher, 1989: 31-2). However, even if one refuses to take the problem of human existence only as a problem of different contexts and grammars and attributes a status of authenticity to everyday reality, the difficulty begins when this reality is to be specified and its social framework and consequences defined. Authenticity is always affected by some symbolic order which shapes subjective opinions and beliefs by the force of constructed social reality. Legitimation takes place through the impact of symbolic universe on individual beliefs, not as the establishment of social symbols from authentic human life (Berger and Luckmann, 1967: 115ff). Everyday life requires 'institutionalised programmes' (Berger and Luckmann, 1967: 155) establishing, shaping and differentiating human identity.

Rousseau's fiction of *a noble savage* more ethical than a civilised man, contains many serious threats. Here, the authentic behaviour of man in the natural state stands in opposition to the artificial order and symbols of political culture. Ethics stands in opposition to law and state and, because it is founded on authentic human nature, has precedence over any legislative power. If civilisation is to recapture the dimension of ethical community, it must subject itself to this original nature and its imperatives.

Human nature and authenticity stand in contradiction to the 'inhuman' structures of politics, economy, legality and science. This anarchistic and libertarian protest against law and state (Derrida, 1976: 138) eventually leads to the metaphysical principle of authenticity, which founds a new ethics and consequently posits new just and legitimate political order and laws to those ethics. The renewal of human civilisation will be the product of the power of an authentic natural law which acts directly and reveals a true face of humanity.

The belief that the development of social forms and structures leads to the progress of civilisation but also to the decline of morals and humanity, is transformed into the call for a *brotherly* community in which no forms of social organisation would lead to the exploitation (such as in the modern capitalist economy) or denigration (such as witnessed in modern states and their legislation) of humanity. This belief is present, for instance, in the work of Claude Lévi-Strauss, when he describes in his famous book *Tristes Tropiques* the implications of the lecture of writing in a village of Nambikwars. Lévi-Strauss shows a nostalgia for an authentic human nature which has not been corrupted, and describes how civilisation, with its 'writing', laws, power, economic exploitation and ideological indoctrination, comes to dominate the system of education (Lévi-Strauss, 1985). Civilisation is inauthentic and corrupt, while the small community of a 'primitive' Indian tribe, in which everybody knows everybody, is closer to the ideal of humanity and authenticity. Jacques Derrida calls this approving attitude of the anthropologist to the subject of his study a myth, when he writes:

> [w]e, like Lévi-Strauss, conclude that violence is writing. But, coming at it another way, this proposition has a radically different meaning. It ceases to be supported by the myth of myth, by the myth of a speech originally good, and of

> a violence which would come to pounce upon it as a fatal accident. A fatal accident which is nothing but history itself. Not that, by this more or less overt reference to the idea of a fall into evil from the innocence of the word, Lévi-Strauss makes this classical and implicit theology his own. It is just that his anthropological discourse is produced through concepts, schemata, and values that are, systematically and genealogically, accomplices of this theology and this metaphysics (Derrida, 1976: 135).

The legitimation force of the 'myth' or 'theology' of authenticity is extraordinarily strong just in the fiction of the social contract and the difference between the natural and political state. The natural is authentic, while the political is always already an artificial construct, the legitimacy of which is founded on the act of contract. Contract is possible only as a departure from the natural state, which means that it is the result of an authentic acceptance of the conditions of political society.

The authentic natural world determines the conditions of the legitimacy of political order and its law because natural laws and rights create the foundations of legitimate positive law. In this interplay of authenticity and the impersonal order of laws and politics, there lies the threat that politics and law may be legitimate only when they introduce by violence a 'pure' life-world, in which human existence achieves original and therefore ethical forms.

The fiction of the social contract and the natural state of mankind involves *a danger that political institutions and laws function only as a form of the imposition of the fundamental ethics of authenticity and human nature.* Politics then becomes a mediation of the authentic happiness of wo/man. This intellectual construction lies behind all modern political catastrophes, and defines totalitarian politics and laws. If a legislator is also a guardian of human happiness and a sovereign body that defines this happiness, then the conditions of totalitarian domination are established. Paradoxically, this totalitarian domination of happiness also typically claims to represent human authenticity, which it transforms into structures of the state control of citizens.

Happiness and authenticity are organised exclusively along lines approved by the Party and the state and the sovereign power of the Party is manifest in many ritual displays of this happiness. To Orwell's doublethink and newspeak slogans 'Ignorance is force', 'Freedom is slavery', 'Peace is war' and 'Love is hate' may be added 'Authenticity is Impersonality'.

The communist concept of the historical law of the working class and the Nazi concept of the supremacy of race and nation also have pre-political foundations which were to be respected by every political authority. Historical reason and order define the foundations of positive law and expressions of will enacting such order finally achieve the status of law. The Leader or the Party express historical reason and use political violence for the imposition of the natural order of history and political reality. True nature and the authentic existence of a nation or class is to speak through these structures guided by the will of a totalitarian political leadership. These structures finally impose authenticity upon an individual. Rousseau's notion of authentic freedom returns in the form of a map of the Gulag Archipelago and Auschwitz. In these structures of political violence, the original call for human authenticity and the modern revolutionary ideal of brotherhood was changed into an impersonal technique of human extermination. Authenticity was eventually eliminated by those very political institutions, which, according to the original plan, were to produce it. The social contract fiction can never completely get rid of the dangers posed by the concept of authentic ethics and the understanding of law and politics as instruments for the pursuit of human happiness because those dangers are inherent in the contractual construction of the difference between the natural and political.

This difference between the natural and political shows that it is impossible to found the legitimacy of modern political domination and law 'purely' from their inner structures. They cannot be self-sufficient sources of their own legitimacy. The social contract fiction gives rise to the danger that legality will be eliminated by the external legitimation strategy founded on human authenticity and nature. On the other hand, this fiction makes it impossible to identify the legal and legitimate within the system of positive law and political domination. *In the social contract, the relation between legality and legitimacy is always established in between the system of positive law and its environment.*

Legitimacy by legality or democratic vote cannot, for instance, explain the principles of minority rights or civil disobedience. They can only translate them into their vocabulary. Legitimation is therefore both inside and outside the system of positive law, and this is made manifest by the dissident 'legalist' strategy. That strategy always must be in law because every modern political power rules by law, but it also addresses external aspects of law and its environment.

Legality, in order to be legitimate, must be comprehensible. It must be translated and accepted in its social environment. When legality becomes an instrument of political repression and seeks to codify the sovereign ideology in the language of law, *dissident legitimation strategy is one of many possible formulations of the demand for comprehensible law*. Dissent is a strategy which avoids treating the relationship of legitimacy and legality as matter of political ideocracy (Gellner, 1995).

Dissent thus points to another vital structural element of the social contract, which is *a necessary plurality of legitimation strategies, if the fiction of the social contract is to represent the legitimation of human autonomy and freedom*. Dissent protects what the social contract defines as individual autonomy and represents a necessary condition of a legitimate political order.

The unique character of the social contract as a legitimation fiction for modern law and political domination is furthermore manifested in the fact that, under it, it is *individual wills which shape the common political will and its laws*. This uniqueness finds its very strong form in dissent, which always emphasises political and social plurality and defends them against the political violence of the state and law. Individual autonomy is the first condition of legitimate law and political domination. However, this autonomy also means that no legitimacy may be entirely codified, and legitimacy becomes therefore a matter of dynamic legitimation strategies.

Instead of stable legitimate structures, modern society embraces an enormous dynamism of legitimation strategies opened up by the fiction of social contract. In fact, this fiction sets up conditions for its own negation because individual autonomy leads a growing plurality of vocabularies and fictions to enter political discourse and thence the language of law. The social contract therefore lies behind what we have called 'the gap legality'.

Performativity of dissent and legitimation fictions

After this analysis of the social contract fiction, we are challenged by the question: 'To what extent can legitimation fictions be identified with the expression of authenticity?' Authenticity is not achievable in the field of legitimation, despite the fact that the social contract, many other legitimation fictions, and the dissident struggle against 'unjust' political regimes embrace authenticity. The legitimation force of authenticity is extraordinary, yet legitimation itself is a process of the transformation of authenticity into a highly structured political reality.

The dissident position is a fascinating example of its being necessary, in defence of authenticity, to leave the referential framework of authentic expression and accept or challenge arguments formulated by the impersonal general language of legality. The defence of authenticity requires the use of *indirect* arguments which respect the order of political power and normative system of law. *The demand of authenticity may be formulated only in its dependence on 'impure' structures of our social life and thinking.* In the dissident struggle, authenticity is most commonly translated into the demand for protection of human rights. Although these rights have a strong resonance in both ethical and legal discourse, the force of the dissident legitimation strategy is significantly weakened without legal arguments. The force of a legitimation depends on its referential power within the system of positive law. Plurality, groundlessness and the existential aspect of dissent are manifested in the fact that this force can never be *universal.* Within the framework of dissent, there are many different legitimation fictions, ideological views and political goals.

Dissent is a specific example of structural changes in the nature of the social contract. The original purpose of this fiction was to disclose a mechanism which would have the power to establish a united community and legitimate political order. In the social contract, political unity was originally founded on the ideas of consensus and the moral integrity of a political community. These features have been discussed widely in the second chapter of this book. On the other hand, every dissensual strategy shows how disunited every modern political society is and even how every seemingly legitimate order, defined by the language of legality, is finally exposed to many argumentative challenges from the outside. In the past, the social contract was a fiction of unity. Nowadays, it is turned into a fiction securing the pluralistic character of political communities.

Dissent also shows that legitimation strategies may not be *a priori* normatively defined. Legitimation is formed according to narrative rules of fiction. In the legitimation strategy of dissent, a key role is played by the concept of living in truth, which precedes the world of normativity, has a mainly negative meaning, and represents only a potential to be secured by legality. This *anti-normative aspect of the legitimation of law* radically changes the whole problem of legitimacy. The social contract originally had distinctive *constative* features. The act of contract establishes a solid structure of political laws held to be legitimate because of general consensus expressed by all parties-individuals to the contract. By their expressed will, those parties become citizens who must subject themselves to the general force of legitimate laws. The final purpose of the contract was to produce law and order. The social contract transforms the violence of the state of nature into a legitimate and stable power structure. On the other hand, dissent emphasises *performativity* in every political community, treating individuals as autonomous beings with the power to manifest and enforce their political will. Dissent is derived from the unique character of every human being and his/her power to influence political life.

Every dissent includes a negatively formulated *will to power*, which is established on the resistance against political power and attempt to confront it with a different power protecting the political system from any totalitarian or authoritarian rule. Dissent cannot be formulated without any relation to existing power structures. A performative dissident action must be formulated against a constative 'state of affairs' (for the constative/performative duality, see Derrida, 1992c: 21). There is a permanent communication and mutual irritation between the constative and performative, which establishes modern political societies and their legitimation fictions (for political meaning of relations between the constative and performative, see Derrida, 1986). Dissent is imaginable only in the political condition, not as an anarchistic and spontaneous action, which would be a pure expression of human nature.

....

The plurality of contemporary societies and the consequent impossibility of formulating a legitimation fiction by one generally accepted vocabulary is fully revealed in dissent. Modern legality was to have the status of such vocabulary in the modern past and jurisprudence therefore produced its own fictions which were to reflect this unifying and integrative role of law in modern society. Dissent makes it clear that no fiction and vocabulary can achieve general validity and the political space does not have such a solid normative framework as it might seem from a superficial reading of the constitutional principles of the democratic rule of law.

All fictions are possible; the pluralistic play of different legitimation vocabularies is open. The constative structures of legality are inseparable from this play, yet they have only secondary importance; the most important is the performative character of every legitimation strategy and its fiction. Although some particular legitimation fictions employed in dissent may claim search for a perfect language which would provide laws and political power with universal legitimacy, the very fact of plurality within dissent makes this universality impossible.

The plurality which leads to the construction of the social contract finally prevents the contract from serving its function as a universal legitimation fiction in which the authenticity of human uniqueness and the impersonality of legal rules are reconciled. Authenticity functions as a starting point of legitimation when dissent struggles against the political system and its laws, but its use is circumscribed by the knowledge that it can never be fully realised. Every legitimation fiction formulated, even those devised by dissent, finds itself forced to ask 'What should be the content of laws under the democratic rule of law?' Legality, political violence, and the structure of state organisation are the goal of legitimation fictions. Legality is deprived of the universal legitimacy, yet it keeps the position of a *referential centre* which must be addressed by all legitimation fictions.

Legality still is the vocabulary used for the justification of the state (Schmitt, 1980: 8, 14f). Political power must be enforced only by legal means. Formal legality is the unquestionable technique for enforcement and discipline. Nevertheless, the legal definition of a state does not mean that the power structures of modern political societies are legitimate (Hunt and Wickham, 1994: 1994: 39ff). Legitimacy and legality are not identical. Arguments about legitimacy are not coextensive with legal arguments. But every legitimation strategy must refer to the rule of law. The politics and strategy of dissent is a vitally important case study of how the problem of the legitimacy of law and political domination is transformed into the performative framework and how the plurality and dynamics of legitimation fictions must go beyond the framework of legality.

....

What, then, is a legitimation fiction and how does it emerge in the social field defined by legality and its environment? The strategy of dissent reveals that *legitimation fictions can never be the product of an authentic individual act.* The indispensable individualism of the social contract fiction cannot survive in current political and social conditions. Subjectivity in a legitimation fiction is impossible in the same way as subjectivity in language games (Wittgenstein, 1972). In the dissent and revolt, wo/man discloses the universal nature of suffering and comes to realise human solidarity (Camus, 1971). What looks to be individual and anarchistic is, nevertheless, finally entrenched in social structure and the normative system of politics, ethics, language and law.

The search for authenticity in structures of modern depersonalised society has been the main concern of the whole existentialist philosophy (see, for instance, Santoni, 1995). That authenticity is an alternative to the nihilism of rational technique in modern western society is one of Heidegger's fundamental claims. Heidegger's popularity with the Czech dissident movement needs to be understood against the background of the special political position of dissidents and their attempt to develop parallel forms of social life independent of the dehumanised techniques of the repressive political power (Day, 1999: 11ff). People like Václav Havel or Jan Patočka formulated the problem of authenticity with the help of Heidegger's vocabulary of being and existence because it corresponded well to the tension between individual life and the highly organised structure of political automatism which sought to control and pervade even the most intimate spheres of human life.

When Bruce Ackerman criticised Havel's use of Heideggerian language, he was concerned about the power of this language to back liberal democratic changes (Ackerman, 1992). Ackerman showed, however, his misunderstanding of what the dissident movements actually meant and used a typical cliché of Anglo-American political philosophy that Heidegger's philosophy must be conservative, anti-modern and anti-liberal because its author had some links with the Nazis. The dissent against the communist system clearly manifests the political ambivalence of Heidegger's philosophy. Dissident pamphlets, essays and manifestos accommodated both poetic language calling for the authenticity of human being and the classical arguments of political liberalism and democratic politics. In the dissident 'liberal reading' of Heidegger, it is very clear that authenticity cannot be understood as a political project. In the book *The Way of the Masks*, Lévi-Strauss says that we never wander alone on the paths of creation (Lévi-Strauss, 1999). The social character of every sign or symbol also determines the character of all legitimation fictions. These fictions are not individual understandings of law and political power because their referential framework is entirely social and wo/man can formulate them only as a social being inhabiting a certain space of social signs and symbols. Because the target of every legitimation fiction is a social structure, every legitimation vocabulary must always return to society and every *legitimation fiction dismantles the possibility of a fully authentic action.*

Between law and justice: the social space of legitimation fictions

Legitimation strategies belong to the world of *social facticity*, and this exceeds the sphere of social norms, principles and values. Legitimations can embrace, for instance, not only moral, but also aesthetic, historical and economic aspects. Arguments and attractions, calculations and compassions, and descriptions meet in legitimations. Every legitimation is nevertheless oriented to the political space, which is defined by legality in the rule of law system. Because of this orientation, legitimations must be limited and adopt some structures of argument. A *legitimation strategy must be self-limiting and this function is performed by a fiction.* Fictions enable law to reflect any legitimation in the normative argumentative framework. In the process of legitimation and its transformation into legal legitimacy, two major steps may be detected: a) the nominalisation of a certain strategy into a legitimation fiction; b) the establishment of the rules and normative framework produced by a legitimation fiction. This is how specific anonymous strategies can be transformed into the form of legal legitimacy.

The process by which a strategy and its network of particular social forces becomes a fiction shows that the claim of legality to general legitimacy is impossible and there is something incalculable that cannot be translated into the procedures of the rule of law (Lyotard, 1993: 166-7). In order to become legitimate, a legitimation strategy must create a fiction which has effective power to identify it as generally valid because it expresses universal values. *The process of transformation of legitimation into legitimacy is a process of turning the particular into the universal, the specific into the general, the anormal into the normal.*

This process of the universalisation of the particular is the internal process of politics. Its principal modern form is the transformation of the people from an amorphous political mass into a sovereign of political power informed universal political principles and moral values. The French and American Revolutions, in spite of many differences, have in common just this process of the transformation of a particular political force into a guardian of universal human ideals and moral political values. Modern democratic discourse is new and exceptional because it changes the political power into a purely symbolic construction which can never be adequately represented by any real political force. The purity of the general will of the people must not be questioned but nobody can really claim that s/he can express this will on behalf of the people (Žižek, 1991: 268; see also the second chapter of this book).

The fiction of the people is posited by legality in order to give political will a legitimate form. This form must be as general as possible so that the democratic power of the people is not identified with certain actors that have constitutional power. This is why democratic power must be separated into different branches. The constitutional principle of checks and balances prohibits (with the exception of the referendum) the sovereign power of the people from being given direct effect, for then there would be no difference between freedom and tyranny.

Legality must protect the empty character of democratic power. The revolutionary slogan 'We are the people!' and the closely related call for basic human rights are concrete historical expressions, but they obtain political effect when they become universal demands. This transformation is done in the language of legality which transforms political power into general procedures. At this moment, the rule of law state becomes a political value and the legitimation fiction of the just law, based on the assumption of the correct procedures of legislation and the correct application of law, pervades political structures. Reflection on the fact that our political universality emerges from many different particularisms should help us to avoid the view that the legal structures are the sovereign source of legitimacy. Legitimations always start from particular forces in a political society. Legitimation fictions are nominalisations of these forces and it is just *through the establishment of a fiction* that the apparent *universal validity* emerges.

What is the character of the space in which legitimation fictions emerge to give dominance to certain legitimation strategies? The answer is somewhat traditional: it is the space of *the difference between law and justice.* Legitimation fictions may be understood in two ways: either as narratives hiding a true nature of things, or as narratives the function of which is to translate the incomprehensible body of positive law into a politically acceptable form. For instance, Michel de Montaigne draws on analogy between legitimation fictions and the ivory teeth of women who are missing real ones. This artificial supplement is necessary for the legitimation of positive law which is unable to legitimate itself by reference to its own political nature (Derrida, 1992b: 12). Derrida, basing himself upon Montaigne's analogy, takes legitimation fictions[2] to be a supplement to legality, which is to separate law from political violence and link it to the principle of justice. In Derrida's reading of Montaigne's analogy, legitimation fictions are defined as that which is to hide the violent nature of law so that law might be socially and politically accepted. In order to make legality legitimate, law must disguise the close links between law and violence. This is the task of fictions which make a redefinition of law's nature possible and thereby secure its social acceptance. The falsity of fictions is socially inevitable. The fictions are extraordinarily important in every society because their manoeuvre of disguise makes the existence of social order possible. Due to the existence of legitimation fictions, people may be subjected to sovereign political violence in the form of law.

The concept of legitimacy has a marginal role in Derrida's concept of law. Legitimacy belongs to the sphere of the calculable and therefore is closer to law than to justice. Essential importance is given to the difference between law and justice and the concept of legitimacy is only a derivation from this. The difference between law and justice, Derrida states, comes from the fact that law is the calculable, while justice is the incalculable. Derrida writes:

> [J]ustice remains, is yet, to come, venir, it has an, it –venir, the very dimension of events irreducibly to come. It will always have it, this –venir, and always has. Perhaps it is for this reason that justice, insofar as it is not only a juridical or political concept, opens up for l'avenir the transformation, the recasting or refounding of law and politics. 'Perhaps', one must always say perhaps for justice. There is an avenir for justice and there is no justice except to the degree that some event is possible which, as event, exceeds calculation, rules, programs, anticipations and so forth. Justice as the experience of absolute alterity is unpresentable (Derrida, 1992b: 27).

Contrary to the Kantian concept of justice, which assumes the calculability of a just action and the horizon of justice, Derrida connects his concept of incalculable justice with a possibility of deconstructing and crossing any horizon and breaking with any form of 'juridical' structure of the world, for instance communicative rationality, the metaphysical concept of happiness, etc (Derrida, 1995: 97-8, 107). Legitimacy and legality are already a transformation of incalculable justice – originally understood as a

[2]Michel de Montaigne speaks about a legitimate fiction, but it is clear from the context that he understood it in the dynamic and performative sense and attributed it the function of legitimation.

heterogeneity, endlessness, absence of symmetry, or rebellion against any rule (Derrida, 1992b: 22) – into a system of regulated and codified prescriptions.

The main problem coming with this understanding of legitimacy is that it reduces legitimacy to being of the same genre as legality. However, legitimacy is neither legality nor incalculable justice. The legitimacy of law and political order stands outside the legal rules, although it is only the existence of law that enables us to develop legitimation fictions and the topic of legitimacy in general. If the problem of the legitimacy of law belongs to the sphere of difference between justice and law, what is the status of legitimation fictions?

It is possible to draw a more general conclusion from Derrida's approach to fictions as a disguise for the violent nature of law which goes beyond the moral, political and epistemological implications of the analogy between a fiction and ivory teeth. It is not only the political violence present in law, its manifestations and social and political consequences, which calls for the production of legitimation fictions. The creation of the legitimation fictions is necessitated by the complex nature of social reality. *The main function of these fictions is to translate the complicated world of legality and reduce its complexity to such an extent that it can become an acceptable framework for social and state organisation.* This reduction does not mean that every fiction would automatically support the existing system of law. Reduction may also be critical and can in fact delegitimate the laws in force. The purpose of a concrete legitimation fiction may be the delegitimation of the law in force and a demand for its change. A legitimation fiction is *the reduction* of legality, but the reduction does not occur according to the internal procedures of the legal system. It happens as *an external reflection* on law and its social functions. *Every legitimation fiction*, because it is not limited by legality, *is also potentially a delegitimation fiction of law. The extent of the legitimacy of law is given by the extent of the free creation of legitimation and delegitimation fictions.*

Legitimation as the in-fiction of legality and human rights

The facts that the relationship of legality and legitimacy is one of a centre to a periphery and that legitimation is a dynamic process uncontrollable by legality means that every legitimation fiction is an *in-fiction of legality*.[3] The legitimacy of law and political domination is not a matter of consensus or the acceptance of law and power by its subjects. It depends upon a paradigmatic interdependence between the legal system and its environment. The legitimation fictions are a functional condition of legitimate law, and they exceed the legal system.

The legitimation of law does not give security to political participation. I borrow William S. Borroughs's idea that language is a virus from outer space in order to say that the legitimation of law is an infection of the seemingly value-neutral system of law from its social outside. Legitimation fictions are these infections of law – we can therefore speak about 'in-fictions' of law. Any system of positive law must constantly struggle with these 'infictions' and reflect them. The anonymous impersonal structures of legal rules are constantly confronted by different narrative rules and exposed to infection by them.

This account of the in-fictional character of legitimation allows us to say something more about the legitimation fictions of legality analysed in the third chapter of this book. The fictions constructed by legal positivist philosophy, which were to legitimate the existing system of the rule of law as an integrative social mechanism, possess this 'external' character. Legal theory seeks to translate legality into a form in which it can claim scientific legitimacy. Legal theory seeks to reduce legality's complexity, give it a scientific background, and provide it with a theoretical canon making it legitimate.

Legal theory does not belong to the system of positive law and is not a part of legality. Yet jurisprudence seeks to impose a common legitimation scheme, founded in scientific discourse, on this system from its outside. Legitimation by legal positivist science also finally proceeds as communication between legal system and its environment. Any legitimation fiction of legal science must intrude into legality from its outside and become its scientific in-fiction.

Every legitimation fiction is an in-fiction of legality. It is not individual and does not depend on subjective beliefs and opinions. It is the formulation of a legitimation strategy which responds to the grammar of modern law and confronts the formal framework of legality, political values and terminology of the democratic rule of law. In-fictions go beyond

[3]The concept of in-fiction draws on biological metaphors which are popular in social and legal theory. It is also a reaction to the theory of autopoietic systems inspired by the evolutionist perspective.

a legal rule in the sense that they encompass the question of law's justification. They are a challenge to law posed by justice. *Legitimation is a movement, which, in the form of a fiction, narratively unites justice beyond the rule limits and the system of rules of positive law.* Law and legality therefore cannot use the binary opposition of legitimate and illegitimate and turn it into an opposition of the legal and illegal. Legitimacy is framed by narrative rules of a legitimation fiction on one side and impersonal legal rules incorporating the concept of regulative justice (as even-handed decision-making and equality before the law) on the other side.

The process by which the concept of human rights is translated from its ethical into a legal context was analysed in the previous chapter. The double character of human rights and the constant oscillation of this concept between its legal and ethical context makes any sovereign legal definition of legitimate political domination impossible. Human rights set up the conditions of the legitimacy of the democratic rule of law, but it is impossible to give clear definitions of the content and extent of those rights. Perennial issues of political and legal philosophy, for instance whether social rights are a part of human rights or whether the right to life involves the banning of capital punishment, arise because of the semantic 'impurity' of human rights. Emmanuel Lévinas pointed to the broader context of human rights, exceeding the ethical or legal technical social framework, in his essay 'The Rights of Man and the Rights of the Other' (Lévinas, 1993: 116-25). In this essay, Lévinas understands the development of modern society as an ever-growing elaboration of the concept of human rights and says:

> [T]hus the dynamic and ever-growing fullness of the rights of man appears inseparable from the very recognition of what are called the fundamental rights of man, from their requirement of transcendence, in a sense, of the inhuman that may be contained in pure nature, and of blind necessity in the social body. The uniqueness and irreducibility of human persons are respected and concretely affirmed by the diminishing of the violence to which they are exposed in the order, or disorder, of the determinism of the real (Lévinas, 1993: 121).

This transcendence does not give any moral foundation to human rights. Transcendence refers to exactly what disappears in the world of fictions and is entirely neutralised in the context of legality, namely to the concrete existence of man, his unique nature and irreducibility to any category or general concept. The rights of man must respect this uniqueness and reality. According to Lévinas:

> [t]he defence of the rights of man corresponds to a vocation *outside* the state, disposing, in a political society, of a kind of extra-territoriality, like that of prophecy in the face of the political powers of the Old Testament, a vigilance totally different from political intelligence, a lucidity not limited to yielding before the formalism of universality, but upholding justice itself in its limitations. The capacity to guarantee that extra-territoriality and that independence defines the liberal state and describes the modality according to which the conjunction of politics and ethics is intrinsically possible (Lévinas, 1993: 123).

Concepts and the logic of rules do not govern ethics and our uniqueness is revealed in our responsibility for the other as a unique being. This difference and *proximity* between I and the Other, which is established in the initial event of meeting (Lévinas, 1993: 124) and not by some logic, the ethical nature of human rights as responsibility and obligation to the other is disclosed. This provides the rights of man with a stability, which is not secured by legal rules and state power or violence. This stability is secured exactly by the event of meeting.

Pre-normative ethics and obligation to the other is irreducible to the obligations of man as a rational subject, the will of which is commensurable with the will of other citizens and creates the foundations of their political community. *The liberal democratic rule of law system is legitimate if it protects human rights by its power and technique. Yet, the legitimate structure of legality is defined by the crucial fact that the content and meaning of human rights escapes state institutions and the logic of social morality.* The strategy of dissent, so central to this book about legitimacy, legitimation and legality, is unique exactly because it is inseparable from the ethics as life for the others. The most dangerous threat of totalitarianism is that it fights to eliminate any event (Havel, 1989) and possibility of meeting the other face to face in his/her uniqueness. By eroding this uniqueness, totalitarianism creates a shapeless crowd of subjects of political power and systematically destroys human responsibility.

The difference between I and the Other and the ethics present in this difference, precede the concept of an autonomous subject. The ethics present in the event of meeting with the Other expect that a wo/man in her/his uniqueness and responsibility will give him or herself entirely into the hands of the other. This situation, which is the authentic experience of otherness and humanity, nevertheless also threatens to turn into the worst violence (Derrida, 1978: 152). This authentic world, in which face to face social relations dominate, is not automatically a free world in which an individual has a bigger freedom of choice and individual self-creation (Luhmann, 1986: 16). This world is more comprehensible, closer and intimate in comparison to the world of 'big' social systems of law, politics and economy. On the other hand, the impersonal rules of big systems such as law make possible a higher flexibility of human action. The control and surveillance of the intimate and authentic experiences of a modern man may be extraordinarily strong, and the threat of 'authentic' violence may be transformed into social relations of intimate surveillance of individual action. *The desire for a comprehensible world, which is a primary impulse of the social process of legitimation, may also lead to the creation of rigid social frameworks defining very restrictively the behaviour possibilities of an individual living in such an 'authentic' social world.*

The ethics of otherness has very ambivalent implications for freedom. Logos and laws therefore must supplement this ethics by the foreseeability and power of rules. The uniqueness and authenticity dominating the face to face relations with the other is inseparable from the impersonal social techniques of law and political power which divide social reality into private and public spheres and thus secure individual autonomy. Unlike authenticity, autonomy is always a function of structures of law and politics. Autonomous subjects cannot, however, exist without the possibility of authentic being. Legality is not self-sufficient and also needs its alterity for legitimation.

Man as an autonomous being is a result of the juridification of reality and necessity to establish the government of rules. 'Citizens' and 'the rule of law' are mutually dependent concepts. The social sphere providing the possibility of authenticity, which is the crucial condition of the legitimacy of the rule of law, must be protected by the impersonal order of legality. The nihilism of modern civilisation does not stand in opposition to authentic being. The nihilism present in 'the iron cage of modernity' and human authenticity may be conceived only in their mutual interdependence.

In the distinction between the private and the public sphere, legality only redescribes the condition of its legitimacy, but this cannot be fully translated into legal language. If authenticity were to be the foundation of legality, it would lead to the terror of human 'nature' against 'inauthentic' social conventions. The distinction between the private and the public redescribes in legal language the space outside legality from which legitimation fictions enter legality.

Legitimation fictions may lead to an open revolt against any rule of laws if legality is conceived only as a limit which must be dismantled. The plurality of legitimation strategies therefore must not lead to another attempt to define lost human nature, in the name of which legality is denied. The new legitimation vocabularies and the descriptions of legality contained in legitimation fictions always must respect legality as a 'hard fact' without which they themselves would not be imaginable. This state certainly is not a state of naive or endless pluralism (for this critique, see Dews, 1995: 110). Legitimation fictions cannot exist without legal frameworks in the same way as legitimate legality cannot exist without a space beyond its control.

Legitimation and delegitimation

Any attempt to understand and accept or criticise and change existing political and legal structures, formulated as a fiction, is the product of the difference between the legal system and its environment and therefore cannot be reduced to the rules of that system. This difference also makes it possible to set up independent narrative rules of fiction. Legality in liberal democratic societies must not interfere with these rules and attempt to control all legitimation fictions by its inner pragmatics. It has to be their guardian without placing limits on what it guards. In such conditions, it is impossible to guarantee that all fictions about law will automatically legitimate the liberal democratic system of law. Legality must protect the difference between the legal system and its environment, but this will lend support to both legitimation and delegitimation fictions. Legitimation in-fictions therefore can operate as *strategies of irritation* (Boyne, 1990: 60) and not as strategies of acceptance.

A famous example of an exponent of the strategy of delegitimation by irritation is the eponymous hero of Josef Hašek's novel *The Good Soldier Švejk* (1974). Josef Švejk effectively destroys the Austro-Hungarian administrative machinery of war, and the impersonal language of legality which defended this war and prosecuted everybody opposed to its logic. The logic of war and law were identical in the Habsburg Empire in 1914. Švejk had chosen a very original way how to break into this logic and delegitimate the existing structures of state administration and its legality.

He deliberately abandons his individuality and exposes his thoughts, motives and idiotic behaviour to the public. This is the way of avoiding any punishment. Švejk completely adopts the logic of impersonality and legality, is fully obedient and never questions the content and consequences of a given order. This absolute acceptance of the logic and legality of war obviously reveals the law's absurdity. Švejk's non-identity irritates in the same way as his obedience. When somebody subjects him or herself entirely to the system of rules and accepts legitimation by impersonality and anonymity, s/he becomes an irritating element threatening the existence of that system. A seemingly total acceptance of the self-legitimating scheme of legality is in fact delegitimating and leads to its complete collapse.

In adopting this delegitimation strategy, Švejk differs significantly from another Central European hero, Josef K. Unlike Švejk, Josef K. struggles to have a dialogue with the Law. He seeks to understand it and become a part of its dominion. The consequence of such attitude is an absurdity which finally leads to the collapse and death of Josef K., not to the collapse of the world of legality as in the case of the good soldier Švejk. Josef K. wants to revolt against the Law (delegitimate it), but also to penetrate its structures (accept legal structures as legitimate). This contradiction is a perfect reflection of the absurdity of Law. It is only the death of Josef K. as an existential gesture which finally turns out to be a delegitimating act against the impersonal structure of Law (for one of numerous interpretations of Kafka's *Trial* and the absurd relation of Josef K. to the Power and the Court, see Žižek, 1995: 1511-32).

Both Josef Švejk and Josef K. challenge legality and the inseparability of their delegitimation strategies from the existential position is typical of them. Even their delegitimation strategies show the close links between legitimation, existential situation and possibility of authenticity as legitimation's referential point. This point has the *generative* meaning for legitimations. While Švejk chooses to abandon his identity and authenticity means nothing to him, Josef K. seeks to reconcile the world of authenticity and law, which is obviously absurd. The desire to live both in truth and before the Law means death. However, as a consequence of Josef K.'s death and Švejk's 'idiotic' behaviour, legality can no longer treat its legitimacy as a matter of impersonal rule.

Legality can respond to irritation only by developing its reflexivity and comprehensibility. Legality has to struggle to be translated into the languages of its environment. Every legitimation fiction of legality may eventually delegitimate the legal system. Modern legality 'suffers' from a permanent insufficiency of legitimacy. This insufficiency establishes the dynamics of contemporary liberal democratic societies.

Every fiction may *subvert* legality. Dissent showed that (de)legitimation strategies always involve moments both of denial and responsibility. Subversion and revolt are never pure anarchy and move at least within a basic structure of responsibility for what is being denied. Even delegitimation, then, takes form of a struggle for law because it cannot escape from the space defined by the difference between justice and law.

A delegitimation fiction is a threat to the system of positive law, yet, if one wants to use medical metaphors and the 'organic view', legality may also be immunised by such an in-fiction. This depends on the extent of legality's reflexivity towards the social environment, but also, paradoxically, on the level of its autonomy and power to define the limits of legal acceptability of individual delegitimation fictions. Legality must operate as a mechanism of political violence determining the extent of regulation of the legitimation space.

Subjects using the delegitimation strategy of formulating fictions which seek to dismantle the existing system of positive law find themselves in a similar situation to the dissident or, in a more theoretical context, de Certeau's tactician who overcomes the system (de Certeau, 1988: 34f). The law regulates social reality and formulates its normative structures, yet any norm creates the space for its avoidance and rejection.

Delegitimation must come from outside legality and weaken its legitimacy so that the legal system must communicate with its environment. Delegitimation is finally always a matter of the force of some fiction to intrude upon the system of legality.

'The right to Law' and force

The two decisions of the Constitutional Court of the Czech Republic, we have examined in the fourth chapter, manifested the basic problem of the relationship between legality and legitimacy today. This is the impossibility of deciding who has the right to write and constitute the basic law which, then, would give the existence to all other laws and rights subsequently protected by political power.

The question of legitimacy can be clearly answered only in societies with a well defined political sovereign. The concept of a political sovereign is a logical trap (Bataille, 1967: ch. 6, section 10, n. 10) because in liberal democracies there is nobody possessing absolute political sovereignty, not even 'the people', despite the fact that constitutions claim that this is the case. The people is not one body and cannot be the only author of the supreme law from which the normative discourse and regime of legal rules might be derived (Lyotard, 1988a: 144). The people must be represented in the process of drafting the constitution, and this 'basic law' must respect some pre-existent rights independently on the people's will. The contemporary social and political situation is one of *the absence of a sovereign.* The sovereign turns to be a rather useless concept which does not correspond to the current social dynamics and forces behind various mechanisms of social control and discipline (Foucault, 1990a: 150).

The human rights discourse established in modern society is exceptional precisely because of its inability to become a meta-narrative which would legitimate the position of a sovereign by legality. The different meanings of human rights give rise to the possibility of the (de)legitimation strategy of dissent, but they also open up a large range of arguments which are contradictory even within the framework of legality. Human rights introduce ethical, socio-economic, political, cultural and other meanings into legal arguments.

Legitimation escapes the contradictions of legal/illegal, theoretical/practical, constative/performative or general/particular. Legitimation may be descried only as a mutual penetration of those contradictions. Legality seeks to translate the plurality and spontaneity entrenched in legitimation fictions into the world of rules, balance, calculability and unifying order. Political violence and force are to exclude all fictions de-stabilising this order. Stability is the goal of legality, be it the legality of the liberal democratic rule of law, socialist legality, or the rule of apartheid law. The force and fiction behind such legality are nevertheless always deconstructable into their particularity, limited social validity and ideological framework. The stability of legality is established by the instability of force and its legitimation fiction. Yet, fictions also function as a framework and limit on irritations or subversive strategies (Derrida, 1992a: 216).

To the question 'Which fiction or narrative is more legitimate than other ones?', there is only one answer: a legitimation fiction dominates over other fictions if it has a better capacity to describe the pluralistic condition of which it is a product, and if it more precisely reflects the transformation of legality into a social context the legitimacy of which paradoxically is conditioned by the plurality and controversy of different legitimation strategies.

Such legitimation fictions have extraordinary *persuasive force*. However, their force also challenges the general validity and legitimacy of the existing structures of legality they are to legitimate. They must both intrude into the world of legality and reveal the contradictions existing in the very concept of legal legitimacy. The anti-communist dissent succeeded in just this effort when dissidents disclosed the particular forces, control, enforcement techniques and ideology standing behind the system of socialist legality.

Dissent confronts the political violence accompanying law and the mask of general legality slips. Even inside liberal democratic political culture, the neutralising force of legality exists together with the *'natural war'* of different vocabularies and fictions. Political conventions have a legal form, but this form is itself in a state of 'war' with its environment, and legitimation fictions which seek to translate the existing system of positive law into their own vocabularies consequently can approve, change, dismantle, or destroy this system by their inner pragmatics.

It would be a serious mistake to think that the social environment of legality is full of tolerance and the growth of plurality is its first principle. Zygmunt Bauman describes the relation between the *agora* of the liberal democratic rule of law and its rhetors on one side and a social environment characterised by tribalism and rupture on the other side as 'tolerance of the rhetors feeds on intolerance of the tribes' and 'intolerance of the tribes draws confidence from the tolerance of the rhetors' (Bauman, 1993: 238).

Political leaders, rhetors, are cautious and aware of the modern crimes against humanity committed in the name of reason, better political order, or the greater happiness for humankind. They hesitate to legitimate existing political order by reference to the rule of reason. The growing tolerance of leaders leads to bigger social insecurity and provokes tribalism, mutual clashes and intolerance. The modern democratic state and its laws continue to speak in the name of universality, but at the same time the social space is privatised and isolated social fragments are filled with an intolerance produced by social uncertainty (Bauman, 1993: 239).

The liberal democratic rule of law is a political form in which the political and natural coexist and permanently interfere with each other. One quality is common to legality and all legitimation fictions and represents the internal part of any legitimacy. It is persuasive force. Law and legality are always a part of a pluralistic political situation, although their purpose is to overcome it by establishing a formal, politically neutral context and transforming it into the impersonal language of general laws. But inside legality, there are always different interpretations and strategies. Legality is contradictory, conflictual, and comprises different ideologies, worldviews and political interests and beliefs (Fish, 1994: 154). All legal interpretations and legality itself are just the momentary outcomes of the struggle between different social forces and strategies using the law as their framework of reference.

This conflictual character of legality, nevertheless, does not mean that legality is unstable. Legality can only exist because these forces and conflicts operate within its structures (Fish, 1989: 139). Force lies behind every act of law's application and creation, and represents an irrational element inherent of law. This force is, however, not a principle founding the legal system. It is a movement full of concrete social networks and practices. As Stanley Fish suggests:

> [f]orce is the sole determinant of outcomes ... is understood not as 'pure' or 'mere' force (phenomena never encountered) but as the urging (perhaps in the softest terms) of some point of view, of some vision of the world complete with purposes, goals, standards, reasons - in short, with everything to which force is usually opposed in the name of principle (Fish, 1989: 12).

Legality is, then, not defined by a pre-existent framework of decision-making according general rules and universal political principles. It is politics in the sense of never-ending disputes between different particular beliefs, goals and interests which determines law and legality. According to Fish, the legal system is governed by the pragmatic (anti)principle of considering each situation in its particularity, or simply as it emerges (Fish, 1994: 111). However, there is no need to be worried about the Hobbesian war of all against all, because persuasive force itself constitutes the main regulatory mechanism of law's pragmatic operations and defines its limits. This force is a repository of norms, standards or rules, not, as suggested for instance by analytical jurisprudence, a mortal threat to them.

Law's neutrality is just one of the manifestations of this force, and legal positivist calls for the neutrality and generality of law are nothing other than an attempt to subject all other social and intellectual forces to the force of the neutral language of legality. The neutrality of legal language is, in fact, a regime of subordination of all particular convictions, beliefs, and ideologies (Fish, 1989: 517, 519-22). Neutral law is law which can better control and discipline the actions of members of our political society. The neutrality of legal language and rules is a manifestation of restrictive force. Law is a particular and contingent context manifested in the strategy of neutralisation, generalisation and universalisation.

All legitimation fictions must primarily reflect the force of law and legality. The fact that political violence and the disciplinary techniques of state power may be applied only through the principle of legality makes the relationship of legality and legitimacy *assymetrical.* Every *legitimation fiction must therefore reflect this movement from the particular to the general, from concrete political violence to its generally acceptable explanation and justification in the form of law.* The force of law initiates the necessity to create the legitimation fictions of legality. Fictions are a transformation of this force and violence (Derrida, 1978: 147f) to the level of communication between legality and its social environment, where the problem of the social acceptance of legality may be resolved.

Conversation, common sense and necessity of the contractual model

Justice and correctness are the starting point and external limit of all legitimation efforts and fictions. The force of legality makes all legitimation strategies reflect of the rule of law. The legitimation capacity of legality as a part of the Enlightenment project is not gone yet (Lyotard, 1984: 36-41). Rational legality as formulated in the modern political project of the liberal democratic rule of law still remains a necessary, though not an ultimate condition, of legitimacy.

The force of such legality protects the space of (de)legitimation fictions by violent means. General legal rules have their political limits, but still do protect the liberal democratic principles of individual freedom, political equality and fairness which are principles taken for granted in any realistic and pragmatic post-modern political discourse (Heller and Féher, 1989: 119f) which is concerned with the fragmented nature of the contemporary social and political worlds. In spite of all abuses and violations, modern political principles and ideals remain attractive and determine our liberal democratic politics. But now political domination and legality cannot be given theoretical or scientific legitimation (see, for example, Rorty, 1991a: 175f). Democracy, law and liberty must survive without ideological leaders of the institutionalised reason.

Some fictions will nevertheless establish the image that they are the only and ultimate expressions of the universal truth (Foucault, 1990b: 107) and therefore are entitled to claim a sovereign validity which would limit and possibly exclude all other fictions from the public space of politics and law. Legality must then guard the pluralistic legitimation space, which consequently means the relativisation of its own legitimacy, and act by force against those authoritarian delegitimation fictions which aim to destroy the public space in which they emerged themselves.

Legality is in a paradoxical position because it must enter the legitimation process and avoid the situation when some fiction would try to help it to achieve sovereign and exlusive legitimacy. The legitimation gap of legality cannot be 'filled' in the contemporary social and political condition. It is legality's main characteristic. This gap is therefore also a limit on all its (de)legitimation fictions.

....

The second limit of legitimation is justice. While legality means the power and force of impersonal rules, justice is a richer and less concrete concept than law. Justice is often understood to be in direct contradiction to empirical law for its character is similar to aesthetic judgments, judgments without *a priori* and universally binding criteria (see, for example, Douzinas and Warrington, 1994; Goodrich, 1995; Lyotard, 1988b: 40-1). Justice both involves and exceeds the concept of rule, though this concept is a pre-condition of the principle of equality before the law and equal treatment of all members of a political community.

By exceeding the concept of rule, justice radically changes a political community. Politics involving indeterminate judgments cannot have foundations or simply define political goals because they recognise the absence of knowledge of what the law exactly should be (Lyotard, 1985: 91). Such politics cannot rely on any final judgment and word which would have the Big Brother's authority and political monopoly of knowledge. Rationalist terrorism (Lyotard, 1985: 73) ceases to exist at the moment when politics becomes a matter of justice, for justice is not an attempt to establish the regime of truth, but to cope with the differences in society, culture and thinking. In such politics, there is not and must not be any *final solution*.

Justice in this unprocedural and anti-normative meaning is not a matter of truth in the sense of a mimetic correspondence to an origin or telos. Every law is constantly yet to be determined, every justice yet to come, 'a-venir'. Justice changes from telos into something that can be formulated only as *a just act* (Lyotard, 1985: 69, 72). A guarantee of such justice is that it is impossible to prescribe the framework of the law's interpretation.

Philosophers like Derrida or Lyotard refuse to subject justice to an epistemological regime of *a priori* existing criteria and rules. The concept of justice as alterity or a regulative idea similar to aesthetic judgment cannot, however, resolve the legislative and normative problems of our contemporary social and political situation. The power of rules, normativity and legality still represent a crucial part of our social life.

By exceeding the force of law and rules, justice changes every system of legality and structure of political domination. Law is not supported by any political foundation such as democratic consensus because it is always confronted with justice as its *alterity*. This tension and difference between law and justice gives rise to what have been described as legitimation strategies and fictions.

The strategy of dissent revealed that legitimation always encompasses *irony and distance* from law and politics. This irony and distance are not a part of the private world (for the identification of irony with the private world, see Rorty, 1989), because the whole dynamic of legitimation fictions shapes the public world of politics and enters the legal system. The dissident attitude is a nice example of the necessity of the private (in this case the commitment to freedom and the possibility of authentic self-expression) to enter the public (to be formulated as the dissident strategy) in order to keep a distance between politics and violence and the language of legality, especially when it is socialist or apartheid legality. Dissent may not be reduced to political resistance because its primary goal was to force the regime to respect social plurality and differences and abandon the politics of extermination of singularity and uniqueness.

Dissent is an example of a legitimation strategy with extraordinary persuasive force which exists without any normative foundations. Legitimacy is separated from the notion of sovereignty. The model of political sovereignty is insufficient because dissent resigns for the identity of truth and politics and, instead of this, demands to secure the absurd possibility of living in truth which may be formulated as the possibility to make steps with *a priori* unknown meaning (this concept is close to Lyotard's concept of legitimation by paralogy). The pragmatic connection between truth and politics (Putnam, 1981) was proved to be unimportant by dissent. The status of the rule of law system as a hierarchical and centralised structure of legitimate violence was successfully challenged, because politics and subsequently legal legitimacy turned out to be a matter of particularisation and pluralisation than a matter of unification and uniformity.

The legitimacy of law grows as an effort to cross the infinite gap between the ethical demands of justice, formulated often beyond the limits of rules from the existential position of the singularity and uniqueness of man, and the impersonal system of general legal rules and procedures drawn from the principle of equal treatment of all members of a political community. In contemporary liberal democracies, there is no single mechanism with the power to unite the political community as an autonomous body and thus secure its complete legitimacy. Political consensus is a contingent structure determining human behaviour only in certain parts of the political system of the liberal democratic rule of law. The sovereign people as a founding element of law and politics does not exist. It is therefore impossible to centre the rule of law on democratic decision-making procedures, as was proposed by the Constitutional Court of the Czech Republic in its judgments or in the discourse ethics. The principle of autonomy is being dismantled and replaced with heteronomy as the first condition of the reproduction of liberal political communities (Lyotard, 1993: 161).

The role of compromise as a mechanism for the maintenance of political unity grows in any politically heterogeneous community. Consensus is being replaced by a broader phenomenon - *conversation*. The purpose of conversation is not only the achievement of various political goals. It also functions as an instrument to express differences and contradictions. Unlike discourse ethics relying on the ideal starting point of political discussion under equal discursive conditions for all participants, conversation respects the plurality of the political community and does not seek to identify the winners and losers of political discussions. It is to strengthen and recognise the plurality of speaking voices (Putnam, 1990: 213).

The political life of contemporary liberal democracies is not founded in political consensus. It derives from the amount of freedom of conversation. Instead of the culture of consensus with its sovereign auditorium, the importance of ever-growing and permanent dialogue grows. This permanent character of dialogue and conversation between individuals, groups and even whole cultures and populations, stands behind the cultural movement (Lévi-Strauss, 1992) and supports the reflexivity of structures of the political power and law.

Unlike the culture of consensus, the political culture of conversation also involves a pre-political, existential dialogue as a search for identity and authenticity (Vattimo, 1988: 150f). Conversation corresponds more closely to the absurdity of this search because it, unlike Habermas' ideal speech situation, does not rule out the possibility that participants will not understand each other at all. Conversation does not presuppose a minimum agreement or consensus, yet it still can be a very important political structure.

This structure has a strong critical force and represents a necessary part of civic culture, which must not be the culture of assimilation founded on a politically enforceable *a priori* normative framework. It must be the culture of permanent communication, which is always 'yet to set up and define' this framework. In conversation, citizens can mutually acknowledge their existence and political position without the necessity of accepting a pre-existing framework specifying permitted and prohibited communication. Wo/man becomes a free citizen only through her/his language and conversation.

The space in which legitimations are put forward exactly corresponds to this culture of conversation and shares its structure, dynamics and plurality as a constitutive condition. Legitimation by democratic procedures represents a very important, yet only one of many, legitimation strategies. The modern political vocabulary of the people's sovereignty and the struggle for more democracy becomes only one of many expressions of the conversation existing in contemporary heterogeneous and heteronomous liberal democracies.

However, conversation is never completely spontaneous. It is regulated by a *common sense* which therefore becomes another limiting structure of legitimations and legitimation fictions. No legitimation fiction emerges without assuming that it will be understood and shared. Every message must have communicative power, otherwise it becomes a form of hermetism (Eco, 1990: 27f). Understanding is the beginning of fictions, although their political goal may be the provocation or dissent. Understanding and consensus must be therefore distinguished. Legitimation fictions seek to approach and understand the legal rules and language of legality. Fictions are a feedback of law, a reflection of the living law and all that a political society experiences and accepts as law. Fictions are to translate legality into a condition of everyday life for members of political society.

Common sense cannot be identified with the notion of norms of correct thinking or the metaphysical concept of human nature as the foundation of any legitimate community. Common sense is rather an open framework of conversation proceeding in the pluralistic space of *forum.*[4] This space may not be therefore identified with truth, but rather with tolerance of the otherness of those entering into conversation with us.

There are three structural limits of legitimation fictions: 1) their *topic* is law and justice; 2) their *purpose* is legality; 3) their *communicative* framework is common sense. These limits and the demand of comprehensibility reduce the plurality of the space of legitimation fictions and give it the features of *the contractual model.* In order to support legal legitimacy from the outside, a legitimation fiction must win against the other fictions and its meaning is always the subject of many negotiations.

From the perspective of legality, the space of legitimation fictions represents *a continuum* in which the question of legitimacy constantly repeats itself together with attempts to answer it. Due to its limits, this continuum can never be entirely chaotic, and it is typical of the process of 'wild' semiosis which does not have a systemic character (Eco, 1999: 250, 256). Understanding the meaning of a particular legitimation fiction for a system of legality is a result of a never-ending process of negotiations and 'double communication' between different legitimation fictions and between a fiction and the system of law.

The contractual model embraces individual actions and decision-making practices which one assumes that others have comprehended even if they do not agree with them (Davidson, 1994: 14-6). The social contract therefore cannot survive as the grand project of modern politics and legitimation fiction of the system of law. Nevertheless, the contractual model manifests certain structural features which still make it an attractive model for contemporary political communities, their system of political domination and legal legitimacy. Conversation as a process setting up the internal limits of the legitimation space is hardly conceivable without the contractual model.

The whole analysis of relations between legality, legitimacy and legitimations may therefore be concluded by saying that the legitimacy of law and political domination must be the subject of permanent negotiation

[4]Common sense is politically ambivalent and its meaning may be both critical and conservative. From the position of common sense, it is possible to criticise the technologies of political power, economic exploitation and the expansion of instrumental reason and capital into the public sphere. At the same time, it is also possible to refer to common sense as a traditional and persisting structure of society, which resists the consequences of modernisation (for historical philosophical and humanist context of this rich concept see, for instance, Gadamer, 1975: 19-29).

with its limits being permanently redefined. This legitimation process, moreover, is an unconditional obligation of people living in the contemporary liberal democracies.

Bibliography

Ackerman, B. (1992), *The Future of Liberal Revolution*, Yale University Press, New Haven.

Alexy, R. (1989), *A Theory of Legal Argumentation,* Clarendon Press, Oxford.

Amselek, P. and MacCormick, N. (eds), (1991), *Controversies about Law's Ontology,* Edinburgh University Press, Edinburgh.

Arato, A. (1993), 'Dilemmas Arising From the Power to Create Constitutions in Eastern Europe', 14 *Cardozo Law Review*, n. 3-4, pp. 673ff.

Arendt, H. (1956), *The Origins of Totalitarianism*, Harcourt, Brace, Jovanovich Books, New York.

Arendt, H. (1958), *The Human Condition*, The University of Chicago Press, Chicago.

Arendt, H. (1990), *On Revolution,* Penguin Books, London.

Bankowicz, M. (1991), 'Czechoslovakia - from Masaryk to Havel', in S. Berglund and J.A. Dellebrandt (eds), *The New Democracies in Eastern Europe*, Edward Elgar Publishers, Aldershot.

Barthes, R. (1993), *Mythologies,* Vintage, London.

Bataille, G. (1967), *Le Part Maudite*, Editions de Minuit, Paris.

Bauman, Z. (1993), *Postmodern Ethics*, Blackwell, Oxford.

Bauman, Z. (1995), *Life in Fragments: essays in postmodern morality,* Blackwell, Oxford.

Bauman, Z. (1998), *Globalization: the human consequences*, Polity Press, Cambridge.

Beatty, D. M. (ed.), (1994), *Human Rights and Judicial Review: A Comparative Perspective*, Kluwer, Hague.

Beck, U. (1992), *Risk Society: towards a new modernity*, Sage, London.

Bělohradský, V. (1988), *Krize eschatologie neosobnosti. [The Crisis of Impersonality]*, Rozmluvy, London.

Bennington, G. (1991), *Introducing Lyotard*, Routledge, London.

Bentham, J. (1983), *Constitutional Code*, vol.1 (edited by F. Rosen and J.H. Burns), Clarendon Press, Oxford.

Berger, P. and Luckmann, T. (1967), *The Social Construction of Reality: a treatise in the sociology of knowledge*, Penguin, Harmondsworth.

Berglund, S. and Dellebrandt, J.A. (eds), (1991), *The New Democracies in Eastern Europe*, Edward Elgar Publishers, Aldershot.

Berlin, I. (1969), *Four Essays on Liberty*, Oxford University Press, Oxford.

Boyne, R (1990), *Foucault and Derrida. The Other Side of Reason*, Unwin Hyman, London.

Brink, A. (1983), *Mapmakers: Writing in a State of Siege*, Faber and Faber, London.

Brzezinski, M.F. (1993), 'Constitutionalism Within Limits', 2 *East European Constitutional Review*, pp. 42-4.

Brzezinski, M.F. and Garlicki, L. (1995), 'Judicial Review in Post-Communist Poland: The Emergence of a Rechtsstaat?', 31 *Stanford Journal of International Law*, pp. 13-59.

Bútora, M. (ed), (1997), *Slovensko 1997*, IVO, Bratislava.

Calvino, I. (1996), *Memos for the Next Millenium,* Vintage, London.

Campbell, T.D. (1996), *The Legal Theory of Ethical Positivism,* Dartmouth Publishers, Aldershot.

Camus, A. (1971), *The Rebel,* Penguin, Harmondsworth.

Carbonnier, J. (1988), *Flexible droit. Pour une sociologie du droit sans rigueur*, L.G.D.J., Paris.

Casper, G. (1991), 'European Convergence', 58 *The University of Chicago Law Review*, pp. 441ff.

Castoriadis, C. (1997), *The Imaginary Institution of Society*, Polity Press, Cambridge.

Certeau, M. (1988), *The Practice of Everyday Life*, University of California Press, Berkeley.

Cohen, J. (1999), 'Reflections on Habermas on Democracy', 12 *Ratio Juris*, pp. 385-416.

Connolly, W. (1984), *Legitimacy and the Modern State*, Blackwell Publishers, Oxford.

Cornell, D. et al. (eds), (1992), *Deconstruction and the Possibility of Justice*, Routledge, London.

Cornell, D. (1992), 'The Relevance of Time to the Relationship Between the Philosophy of the Limit and Systems Theory', 13 *Cardozo Law Review,* n. 5, pp. 1579-603.

Cotterrell, R. (1983), 'Legality and Political Legitimacy in the Sociology of Max Weber', in D. Sugarman (ed.), *Legality, Ideology and the State*, The Academic Press, London.

Cotterrell, R. (1989), *The Politics of Jurisprudence: A Critical Introduction to Legal Philosophy*, Butterworths, London.

Cotterrell, R. (1995), *Law's Community*, Clarendon Press, Oxford.

Cotterrell, R. (1996), 'The Rule of Law in Transition: Revisiting Franz Neumann's Sociology of Legality', 5 *Social and Legal Studies*, pp. 451-70.

Cotterrell, R. (1998), 'Why Must Legal Ideas Be Interpreted Sociologically?', 25 *Journal of Law and Society*, pp. 171-92.

Dahl, R.A. (1971), *Polyarchy*, Yale University Press, New Haven.

Dahrendorf, R. (1990), *Reflections on the Revolution in Europe,* Chatto & Windus, London.

Davidson, D. (1994), 'The Social Aspect of Language', in B. McGuinness, and G. Oliveri (eds), *The Philosophy of Michael Dummett*, Kluwer Academic Publishers, Dordrecht.

Day, B. (1999), *Sametoví filosofové (The Velvet Philosophers)*, Doplněk, Brno.

Deflem, M. (ed), (1996), *Habermas, Modernity and Law*, Sage Publ., London.

Derrida, J. (1976), *Of Grammatology*, The Johns Hopkins University Press, Baltimore.

Derrida, J. (1978), 'Violence and Metaphysics: An Essay on the Thought of Emmanuel Levinas', in J. Derrida, *Writing and Difference*, Routledge and Kegan Publishers, London.

Derrida, J. (1986), 'Declarations of Independence', 15 *New Political Science*, pp. 7-15.

Derrida, J. (1992a), 'Before the Law', in J. Derrida, *Acts of Literature*, ed. D. Attridge, Routledge, New York.

Derrida, J. (1992b), 'Force of Law: The 'Mystical Foundation of Authority'', in D. Cornell et al. (eds), *Deconstruction and the Possibility of Justice*, Routledge, London.

Derrida, J. (1992c), 'Mochlos: or, The Conflict of the Faculties', in R. Ran (ed), *Logomachism*, University of Nebraska Press, Lincoln, Nebraska.

Derrida, J. (1995), *The Gift of Death*, The University of Chicago Press, Chicago.

Derrida, J. (1996), *Archive Fever. A Freudian Impression*, The University of Chicago Press, Chicago.

Deutscher, I. (1949), *Stalin: A Political Biography*, Penguin Books, Harmondsworth.

Dews, P. (1995), *The Limits of Disenchantment*, Verso, London.

Douzinas, C. and Warrington, R. with McVeigh, S. (1991), *Postmodern Jurisprudence*, Routledge, London.

Douzinas, C. and Warrington, R. (1994), *Justice Miscarried: Ethics and Aesthetics in law*, Harvester Wheatsheaf, London.

Douzinas, C., Goodrich, P. Hachamovitch, Y. (1994), *Politics, postmodernity and critical legal studies: The legality of the contingent*, Routledge, London.

Duguit, L. (1970), *Law in the Modern State*, Howard Fertig Publishers, New York.

Durkheim, É. (1964), *The Division of Labour in Society*, Free Press, New York.

Dworkin, R. (1995), *A Matter of Principle*, Oxford University Press, Oxford.

Dworkin, R. (1986), *Law's Empire*, Fontana Press, London.

Dyzenhaus, D. (1991), *Hard Cases in Wicked Legal Systems*, Clarendon Press, Oxford.

Dyzenhaus, D. (1994), 'The Legitimacy of Law: A Response to Critics', 7 *Ratio Juris*, pp. 80-94.

Dyzenhaus, D. (1997), *Legality and Legitimacy: Carl Schmitt, Hans Kelsen and Hermann Heller in Weimar*, Clarendon Press, Oxford.

Dyzenhaus, D. (1998), *Judging the Judges, Judging Ourselves*, Hart Publishers, Oxford.

Eco, U. (1988), *Opera Aperta*, Tascabili Bompiani, Milano.

Eco, U. (1990), *The Limits of Interpretation*, Indiana University Press, Indianapolis.

Eco, U. (1999), *Kant and the Platypus*, Secker and Warburg, London.

Ehrlich, E. (1975), *Fundamental Principles of the Sociology of Law*, Arno Press, New York.

Eliade, M. (1965), *The Myth of the Eternal Return or, Cosmos and History*, Princeton University Press, Princeton.

Elster, J. (1991), 'Constitutionalism in Eastern Europe: An Introduction', 58 *The University of Chicago Law Review*, pp. 447-82.

Elster, J. (1995), *The Round Table Talks in Eastern Europe*, The University of Chicago Press, Chicago.

Feher, F. (1993), 'Voice and Text in Constitutionalism', 14 *Cardozo Law Review*, n. 3-4, s.705-9.

Ferguson, A. (1996), *An Essay on the History of Civil Society*, Cambridge University Press, New York.

Fish, S. (1989), *Doing What Comes Naturally: Change, Rhetoric and the Practice of Theory in Literary Studies,* Duke University Press, Durham.

Fish, S. (1994), *There's No Such Thing as Free Speech ... and It's a Good Thing Too*, Oxford University Press, Oxford.

Fitzpatrick, P. (1991), 'The Abstracts and Brief Chronicles of the Time: Supplementing Jurisprudence', in P. Fitzpatrick (ed.), *Dangerous Supplements: Resistance and Renewal in Jurisprudence*, Pluto Press, London, pp. 1-33.

Fitzpatrick, P. (1992), *The Mythology of Modern Law*, Routledge, London.

Foerster von, H. (1960), 'On Self-Organizing Systems and their Environments', in M.C. Yovits and S. Cameron (eds), *Self-Organizing Systems*, Pergamon, Oxford.

Foucault, M. (1990a), *The History of Sexuality I: the will to knowledge*, Penguin, London.

Foucault, M. (1990b), 'On Power', in M. Foucault, *Politics, Philosophy, Culture: Interviews and other writings 1977-1984*, Routledge, London.

Fukuyama, F. (1992), *The End of History and the Last Man*, Hamish Hamilton, London.

Furet, F. (1981), *Interpreting the French Revolution*, Cambridge University Press, Cambridge.

Gadamer, H.G. (1975), *Truth and Method*, Sheed & Ward, London.

Garros, V., Korenevskaya, N. and Lahusen, T. (eds) (1997), *Intimacy and Terror (Soviet Diaries of the 1930s)*, The New Press, New York.

Garton Ash, T. (1990), *We The People*, Granta Books, London.

Gellner, E. (1974), *Legitimation of Belief*, Cambridge University Press, London.

Gellner, E. (1995), *Condition of Liberty*, Penguin, London.

Gerth, H. and Mills, Ch.W. (eds), (1958), *From Max Weber: Essays in Sociology,* Oxford University Press, New York.

Giddens, A. (1990), *The Consequences of Modernity*, Polity Press, Cambridge.

Goodrich, P. (1990), *Languages of law: from logics of memory to nomadic masks*, Weidenfeld Publishers, London.

Goodrich, P. (1995), *Oedipus Lex: Psychoanalysis, History, Law*, University of California Press, Berkeley.

Goodrich, P. (1996), *Law in the Courts of Love*, Routledge, London.

Grimm, D. (1994), 'Human Rights and Judicial Review in Germany', in D. Beatty (ed.), *Human Rights and Judicial Review: A Comparative Perspective*, Kluwer, Hague.

Habermas, J. (1968), *Knowledge and Human Interests*, Beacon Press, Boston, Massachusetts.

Habermas, J. (1976), *Legitimation Crisis*, Heinemann Educational, London.
Habermas, J. (1984), *Vorstudien und Erganzungen zur Theorie des kommunikativen Handelns*, Suhrkamp Vlg., Frankfurt.
Habermas, J. (1987a), *The Philosophical Discourse of Modernity: twelve lectures*, Polity Press, Cambridge.
Habermas, J. (1987b), *The Theory of Communicative Action, Volume Two: Lifeworld and System: A Critique of Functionalist Reason*, Beacon Press, Boston, Massechusetts.
Habermas, J. (1989), 'Towards a Communication-Concept of Rational Collective Will-Formation. A Thought-Experiment', 2 *Ratio Juris,* pp. 144-54.
Habermas, J. (1990), *Die nachholende Revolution*, Suhrkamp Vlg., Frankfurt.
Habermas, J. (1992), *Faktizitat und Geltung*, Suhrkamp Vlg., Frankfurt.
Habermas. J. (1996a), 'Coping With Contingencies - The Return of Historicism', in J. Niznik and J.T. Sanders (eds), *Debating the State of Philosophy: Habermas, Rorty and Kolakowski,* Praeger Publishers, Westport, Connecticut.
Habermas, J. (1996b), 'Paradigms of Law', 17 *Cardozo Law Review*, n. 4-5, pp. 771-84.
Habermas, J. (1997), *Between Facts and Norms*, Polity Press, Cambridge.
Habermas, J. (1999), 'Introduction [to the seminar 'A Discursive Foundation for Law and Legal Practice']', 12 *Ratio Juris*, pp. 329-35.
Hart, H.L.A. (1994), *The Concept of Law. [Revised edition]*, Clarendon Press, Oxford.
Hart, H.L.A. (1983), *Essays in Jurisprudence and Philosophy*, Clarendon Press, Oxford.
Hašek, J. (1974), *The Good Soldier Švejk: and his fortunes in the world war*, Penguin, Harmondsworth.
Hausmaniger, H. (1995), 'Towards a 'New' Russian Constitutional Court', 28 *Cornell International Law Journal*, vol. 2.
Havel, V. (1985), 'The Power of the Powerless', in J. Keane (ed), *The Power of the Powerless: Citizens against the state in central-eastern Europe*, Hutchinson Press, London.
Havel, V. (1989) 'Příběh a totalita' [Narrative and Totality], in V. Havel, *Do různých stran*, Lidové noviny, Praha.
Havel, V. (1991), *Hry [Plays],* Lidové noviny, Praha.
Heller, A. (1987), *Beyond Justice*, Blackwell, Oxford.
Heller, A. a Feher, F. (1989), *The Postmodern Political Condition*, Polity

Press, Cambridge.

Hobbes, T. (1952), *Leviathan*, Encyclopaedia Britannica, Chicago.

Hofmann, H. (1986), *Recht-Politik-Verfassung: Studien zur Geschichte der politischen Philosophie,* Metzner Vlg., Frankfurt.

Holländer, P. (2000), *Nástin filosofie práva: úvahy strukturální [An Ouline of Philosophy of Law: structural notions],* Všehrd, Praha.

Holt, R. (1997), *Wittgenstein, Politics and Human Rights*, Routledge, London.

Honneth, A. (1993), *The Critique of Power: Reflective Stages in a Critical Social Theory*, The MIT Press, Cambridge, Massachusetts.

Honneth, A. (1994), 'Pathologien des Sozialen. Tradition und Aktualitat der Sozialphilosophie', in A. Honneth (ed), *Pathologien des Sozialen. Die Aufgabe der Sozialphilosophie,* Fischer Vlg., Frankfurt.

Hunt, A. and Wickham, G. (1994), *Foucault and Law: Towards a Sociology of Law as Governance*, Pluto Press, London.

Jaspers, K. (1987), *Die Schuldfrage; zur politischen Haftung Deutschlands*, Piper Vlg., Muenchen.

Kant, I. (1970), 'Perpetual Peace: A philosophical Sketch', in I. Kant, *Political Writings,* edited by H. Reiss, Cambridge University Press, Cambridge.

Keane, J. (1985), *The Power of the Powerless: Citizens against the state in central-eastern Europe,* Hutchinson Press, London.

Kelsen, H. (1922), *Der soziologische und der juristische Staatsbegriff*, J.C.B. Mohr, Tübingen.

Kelsen, H. (1945), *General Theory of Law and State*, Russell and Russell Publishers, New York.

Kelsen, H. (1965), 'Professor Stone and the Pure Theory of Law', 17 *Stanford Law Review*, pp. 1128-57.

Kelsen, H. (1971), *What is Justice?: Justice, law and politics in the mirror of science*, University of California Press, Berkeley.

Kelsen, H. (1980), 'Die Funktion der Verfassung', in I. Stewart, 'The Basic Norm as Fiction', *Juridical Review*, pp. 199-224.

Knapp, V. (1959), *Předmět a systém československého socialistického práva občanského [The Outline and System of the Czechoslovak Socialist Civil Law],* NČSAV, Prague.

Kronman, A.T. (1983), *Max Weber,* E. Arnold Publishers, London.

Kuhn, T.S. (1970), *The Structure of Scientific Revolutions*, The University of Chicago Press, Chicago.

Kundera, M. (1984), *The Unbearable Lightness of Being*, Faber and Faber,

London.
Kundera, M. (1990), *The Book of Laughter and Forgetting*, Faber and Faber, London.
Kundera, M. (1991), *The Joke*, Faber and Faber, London.
Kusín, V. (1978), *From Dubček to Charter 77*, Q Press, Edinburgh.
Ladeur, K.H. (1986), ''Prozedurale Rationalitat' - Steigerung der Legitimationsfahigkeit oder der Leistungsfahigkeit des Rechtssystems?', 7 *Zeitschrift fur Rechtssoziologie*.
Lempert, R. (1988), 'The Autonomy of Law: Two Visions Compared', in G. Teubner (ed.), *Autopoietic Law: A New Approach to Law and Society*, de Gruyter, Berlin, pp. 152-90.
Lenin, V.I. (1934), 'The Proletariat Revolution and the Renegade Kautsky', in V.I. Lenin, *Selected Works VII*, New York.
Lenoble, J. (1996), 'Law and Undecidability: A New Vision of the Proceduralization of Law', 17 *Cardozo Law Review*, n. 4-5, pp. 935-1004.
Lévinas, E. (1993), 'The Rights of Man and the Rights of the Other', in E. Lévinas, *Outside the Subject*, The Athlone Press, London.
Lévi-Strauss, C. (1985), *Tristes Tropiques – A Peregrine Book*, Penguin, London.
Lévi-Strauss, C. (1992), *The Way of the Masks*, The University of Washington Press, Seattle.
Lévy-Bruhl, H. (1955), *Aspects sociologiques du droit*, Marcel Riviere et Cie, Paris.
Lewis, P.G. (1994), *Central Europe since* 1945, Longman, London.
Lipset, S.M. (1981), *Political Man: The Social Bases of Politics*, Johns Hopkins University Press, Baltimore.
Luhmann, N. (1969), *Legitimiation durch Verfahren*, W-deutscher Vlg., Neuwied.
Luhmann, N. (1975), *Macht,* F. Enke Vlg., Stuttgart.
Luhmann, N. (1981), *Ausdifferenzierung des Rechts*, Suhrkamp Vlg., Frankfurt.
Luhmann, N. (1982), *The Differentiation of Society*, Columbia University Press, New York.
Luhmann, N. (1985), *A Sociological Theory of Law*, Routledge, London.
Luhmann, N. (1986), *Love as Passion: The Codification of Intimacy*, Harvard University Press, Cambridge, Massachusetts.
Luhmann, N. (1988), 'The Unity of the Legal System', in G. Teubner (ed.), *Autopoietic Law: A New Approach to Law and Society,* de Gruyter, Berlin, pp. 12-35.

Luhmann, N. (1990), *Essays on Self-Reference*, Columbia University Press, New York.

Luhmann, N. (1992), 'Operational Closure and Structural Coupling: The Differentiation of the Legal System', 13 *Cardozo Law Review*, n. 5, pp. 1419-41.

Luhmann, N. (1995a), *Das Recht der Gesellschaft*, Suhrkamp Vlg., Frankfurt.

Luhmann, N. (1995b), *Social Systems*, Stanford University Press, Stanford.

Luhmann, N. (1996), '*Quod omnes tangit:* remarks on Jurgen Habermas's Legal Theory', 17 *Cardozo Law Review*, n. 4-5, pp. 883-900.

Luhmann, N. (1998), *Die Gesellschaft der Gesellschaft 1.,2.*, Suhrkamp Vlg., Frankfurt.

Lyotard, J-F. (1984), *The Postmodern Condition: a report on knowledge*, Manchester University Press, Manchester.

Lyotard, J-F. (1985), *Just Gaming*, Manchester University Press, Manchester.

Lyotard, J-F. (1988a) *The Differend: phrases in dispute*, The University of Minnesota Press, Minneapolis.

Lyotard, J-F. (1988b), *Peregrinations: Law, Form, Event*, Columbia University Press, New York.

Lyotard, J-F. (1990), *Heidegger and 'the Jews'*, Minnesota University Press, Minneapolis.

Lyotard, J-F. (1993), *Political Writings*, UCL Press, London.

MacCormick, N. (1978), *Legal Reasoning and Legal Theory*, Clarendon Press, Oxford.

MacCormick, N. (1982), *Legal Right and Social Democracy. Essays in Legal and Political Philosophy*, Clarendon Press, Oxford.

MacCormick, N. (1989), 'The Ethics of Legalism', 2 *Ratio Juris*, pp. 184-93.

Marčenko, A. (1989), *To Live Like Everyone*, I.B. Tauris & Co., London.

Marmor, A. (1992), *Intepretation and Legal Theory,* Clarendon Press, Oxford.

Marx, K. (1976), *Capital: a contribution to the critique of classical political economy*, Penguin Publishers, Harmondsworth.

Máša, A. (1996), *Podivní ptáci (Strange Birds),* ND tisk, Prague.

Mayer, J.P. (1956), *Max Weber and German Politics*, New York.

McCarthy, T. (1996), 'Legitimacy and Diversity: Dialectical Reflections on Analytical Distinctions', 17 *Cardozo Law Review*, n. 4-5, pp. 1083-1124.

Milovanovic, D. (1992), *Postmodern Law and Disorder: Psychoanalytic*

Semiotics, Chaos and Juridic Exegeses, Deborah Charles Publications, Merseyside.

Minkkinen, P. (1999), *Thinking Without Desire*, The Hart Publishing, Oxford.

Morgan, D. and Lee, R.G. (1997), 'In the Name of the Father? *Ex parte Blood:* Dealing with Novelty and Anomaly', 60 *Modern Law Review*, pp. 840-56.

Murphy, W.T. (1997), *The Oldest Social Science?* Clarendon Press, Oxford.

Musil, R. (1990), *Precision and Soul,* Chicago University Press, Chicago.

Musil, R. (1997), *The Man Without Qualities*, Macmillan, London.

Nehamas, A. (1998), *Virtues of Authenticity (Essays on Plato and Socrates)*, Princeton University Press, Princeton.

Nelken, D. (1998), 'Blinding Insights? The Limits of a Reflexive Sociology of Law', 25 *Journal of Law and Society*, pp. 407-26.

Neumann, F. (1964), *The Democratic and the Authoritarian State*, The Free Press, New York.

Neumann, F. (1986), *The Rule of Law*, Berg Publishers, Leamington Spa.

Niznik, J. and Sanders, J.T. (eds), (1996), *Debating the State of Philosophy: Habermas, Rorty and Kolakowski,* Praeger Publishers, Westport, Connecticut.

Norris, Ch. (1983), *The Deconstructive Turn*, Methuen, London.

Orwell, G. (1990), *Nineteen Eighty-Four*, Penguin, London.

Osiatynski, W. (1992), 'Agent Walesa?' *East European Constitutional Review*, pp. 28-30.

Oxley, A., Pravda, A. and Ritchie, A. (1973), *Czechoslovakia – The Party and the people*, Penguin, Harmondsworth.

Parsons, T. (1949), *The Structure of Social Action*, Free Press, New York.

Patočka, J. (1981), 'What Charter 77 Is and What It Is Not', in H. Skilling, *Charter 77 and Human Rights in Czechoslovakia,* Allen and Unwinn, London.

Patočka, J. (1996), *Heretical Essays in the Philosophy of History*, Open Court, Chicago.

Patterson, D. (1996), *Law and Truth*, Oxford University Press, Oxford.

Pelikán, J. (1971), *The Czechoslovak Political Trials, 1950-54*, Stanford University Press, Stanford, California.

Pelikán, J. (1976), *Socialist Opposition in Eastern Europe*, Allision & Beesly, London.

Perelman, Ch. (1963), *The Idea of Justice and the Problem of Argument*,

Routledge and Kegan Publishers, London.

Plamenatz, J. (1968), *Consent, Freedom and Political Obligation*, Oxford University Press, Oxford.

Podgorecki, A. (1996), 'Totalitarian Law: Basic Concepts and Issues', in A. Podgorecki and V. Olgiatti (eds), *Totalitarian and Post-Totalitarian Law*, Dartmouth, Aldershot.

Pogany, I. (ed), (1995), *Human Rights in Eastern Europe*, E.Elgar Publishers, Aldershot.

Posner, R. (1990), *The Problems of Jurisprudence*, Harvard University Press, Cambridge, Massachusetts.

Postema, G.J. (1986), *Bentham and the Common Law Tradition*, Clarendon Press, Oxford.

Preuss, U. (1964), *Legitimitat und Pluralismus: Beitrage zum Verfassungsrecht der Bundesrepublik Deutschlands*, Suhrkamp Vlg., Frankfurt.

Preuss, U. (1993), 'Constitutional Powermaking for the New Polity: Some Deliberations on the Relations Between Constituent Power and the Constitution', 14 *Cardozo Law Review*, n. 3-4, pp.639-660.

Prins, G. (ed.), (1990), *Spring in Winter: The 1989 revolutions*, The Manchester University Press, Manchester.

Přibáň, J. (1995), 'The Constitutional Court of the Czech Republic and the Problem of the Sovereignty of the Law', in I. Pogany (ed), *Human Rights in Eastern Europe*, E.Elgar Publishers, Aldershot, pp. 135-48.

Přibáň, J. (1997), *Suverenita, právo a legitimita [Sovereignty, Law and Legitimacy]*, Karolinum, Prague.

Přibáň, J. and Young, J. (eds), (1999), *The Rule of Law in Central Europe*, Ashgate Publishers, Aldershot.

Putnam, H. (1981), *Reason, Truth and History*, Cambridge University Press, New York.

Putnam, H. (1990), *Realism With a Human Face*, Harvard University Press, Cambridge, Massachusetts.

Radbruch, G. (1950a), *The Legal Philosophies of Las, Radbruch and Dabin* (translated by K. Wilk), Harvard University Press, Cambridge, Massachusetts.

Radbruch, G. (1950b), *Rechtsphilosophie*, 4. Auflage, K.F. Koehler, Stuttgart.

Radbruch, G. (1950c), *Legal Philosophy*, Harvard University Press, Cambridge, Massachusetts.

Radbruch, G. (1959), *Vorschule der Rechtsphilosophie*, 2. Auflage.,

Vandenhoeck and and Ruprecht, Gottingen.

Radbruch, G. (1999), *Rechtsphilosophie,* Hrsg. R. Dreier, S.L. Paulson, Heidelberg.

Rasmussen, D.M. (1996), 'How is valid law possible? A review of Between Facts and Norms by Jürgen Habermas' in M. Deflem (ed.), *Habermas, Modernity and Law*, Sage, London.

Rawls, J. (1972), *A Theory of Justice*, Clarendon Press, Oxford.

Rawls, J. (1987), 'The Idea of Overlapping Consensus', 7 *Oxford Journal of Legal Studies*, pp. 1-25.

Rawls, J. (1993), *Political Liberalism*, Columbia University Press, New York.

Rawls, J. (1999), *The Law of Peoples with 'The Idea of Public Reason Revisited',* Harvard University Press, Cambridge, Mass.

Raz, J. (1970), *The Concept of a Legal System,* Clarendon Press, Oxford.

Raz, J. (1979), *The Authority of Law. Essays on Law and Morality* Clarendon Press, Oxford.

Raz, J. (1984), 'Hart on Moral Rights and Legal Duties', 4 *Oxford Journal of Legal Studies*, pp. 123-31.

Raz, J. (1994), *Ethics in the Public Domain: essays in the morality of law and politics,* Clarendon Press, Oxford.

Reading, B. (1991), *Introducing Lyotard*, Routledge, London.

Rehbinder, M. (1977), *Rechtssoziologie* , de Gruyter Vlg., Berlin.

Reinach, A. (1953), *Zur Phänomenologie des Rechts. Die apriorischen Grundlagen des bürgerlichen Rechts,* Kösel, Munchen.

Rheinstein, M. (ed,), (1954), *Max Weber on Law in Economy and Society*, Harvard University Press, Cambridge, Massachusetts.

Rorty, R. (1980), *Philosophy and the Mirror of Nature*, Blackwell, Oxford.

Rorty, R. (1982), *Consequences of Pragmatism,* The University of Minnesota Press, Minneapolis.

Rorty, R. (1989), *Contingency, irony, and solidarity,* Cambridge University Press, Cambridge, Massachusetts.

Rorty, R. (1991a), *Objectivity, relativism, and truth. Philosophical Papers volume 1*, Cambridge University Press, Cambridge, Massachusetts.

Rorty, R. (1991b), *Essays on Heidegger and Others. Philosophical Papers vol. 2.*, Cambridge University Press, Cambridge, Massachusetts.

Rorty, R. (1998), *Truth and Progress. Philosophical Papers volume 3*, Cambridge University Press, Cambridge.

Rosen, F. (1983), *Jeremy Bentham and Representative Democracy: A Study of the Constitutional Code*, Clarendon Press, Oxford.

Rosenfeld, M. (1998), *Just Interpretations: Law between Ethics and Politics*, University of California Press, Berkeley.

Rousseau, J. J. (1959), *Les Réveries du Promeneur Solitaire* in *Oeuvre Complétes, vol.1*, Gallimard, Paris.

Sajo, A. (1999), 'Socialist Welfare Schemes and Constitutional Adjudication in Hungary', in J. Přibáň and J. Young (eds), *The Rule of Law in Central Europe,* Ashgate, Aldershot.

Santoni, R. E. (1995), *Bad Faith, Good Faith and Authenticity in Sartre's Early Philosophy*, Temple University Press.

Sarat, A. and Kearnes T. R. (eds), (1991), *The Fate of Law*, The University of Michigan Press, Ann Arbor.

Sartori, G. (1987), *The Theory of Democracy Revisited,* Chatham House Publishers, New Jersey.

Schmitt, C. (1963), *Begriff des Politischen,* Duncker und Humblot, Berlin.

Schmitt, C. (1980), *Legalität und Legitimität,*, Duncker und Humblot, Berlin.

Schmitt, C. (1985a), *The Crisis of Parliamentary Democracy*, The MIT Press, Cambridge, Mass.

Schmitt, C. (1985b) *Political Theology: Four Chapters on the Concept of Sovereignty*, The MIT Press, Cambridge, Massachusetts.

Schutz, A. (1994), 'Desiring Society: Autopoiesis beyond the Paradigm of Mastership', 5 *Law and Critique,* pp. 149-64.

Shils, E. (1975), *Center and Periphery: Essays in Macrosociology*, The University of Chicago Press, Chicago.

Shiner, R.A. (1994), 'The Morality of Legal Positivism', 7 *Ratio Juris*, pp. 41-3.

Shklar, J. N. (1964), *Legalism,* The Harvard University Press, Cambridge, Massachusetts.

Sieyes, E. J. (1963), *What Is the Third Estate?*, Pall Mall Publishers.

Simmel, G. (1964), 'Interaction in the Idea of 'Law'' in G. Simmel, *The Sociology of Georg Simmel*, Free Press, New York.

Simmel, G. (1987), 'Der Konflikt der modernen Kultur', in G. Simmel, *Das individuelle Gesetz: philosophische Exkurse*, Suhrkamp, Frankfurt.

Skilling, H.G. (1966), *The Governments of the Communist East Europe,* Crowell Comp., New York.

Skilling, H. G. (1981), *Charter 77 and Human Rights in Czechoslovakia,* Allen and Unwin, London.

Spencer, G. H. (1969), *Principles of Sociology,* Macmillan Press, London.

Stammler, R. (1925), *The Theory of Justice,* The Macmillan Press, New York.

Stewart, I. (1980), 'The Basic Norm as Fiction', *Juridical Review*, pp. 199-224.
Stokes, G. (1993), *Walls Came Tumbling Down,* Oxford University Press, Oxford.
Sugarman, D. (ed.), (1983), *Legality, Ideology and the State,* The Academic Press, London.
Sumner, C. (1983), 'Law, Legitimation ant the Advanced Capitalist State: The Jurisprudence and Social Theory of Jürgen Habermas', in D. Sugarman (ed.), *Legality, Ideology and the State,* The Academic Press, London.
Šimečka, M. (1990), *Obnovení pořádku [Order Restored]*, Atlantis, Brno.
Tamanaha, B. (1997), *Realistic Socio-Legal Theory,* Clarendon Press, Oxford.
Taylor, C. (1991), *The Ethics of Authenticity,* Harvard University Press, Cambridge Massachusetts.
Teubner, G. (ed.) (1987), *Juridification of Social Spheres: A Comparative Analysis in the Areas of Labor, Corporate, Antitrust and Social Welfare Law*, de Gruyter, Berlin.
Teubner, G. (ed.) (1988), *Autopoietic Law: a new approach to law and society,* de Gruyter, Berlin.
Teubner, G. (1992), 'The Two Faces of Janus: Rethinking Legal Pluralism', 13 *Cardozo Law Review*, n. 5, pp. 1443-62.
Teubner, G. (1993), *Law as an Autopoietic System*, Blackwell, Oxford.
Teubner, G. (1996), '*De Collisione Discursuum:* Communicative Rationalities in Law, Morality, and Politics', 17 *Cardozo Law Review*, n. 4-5, pp. 901-18.
Ulč, O. (1972), *The Judge in a Communist State: A View From Within,* Ohio University Press, Ohio.
Unger, R. M. (1976), *Law in Modern Society,* Free Press, New York.
Unger, R. M. (1996), *What Should Legal Analysis Become?* Verso, London.
Urban, J. (1990), 'Czechoslovakia:the power and politics of humiliation', in G. Prins. (ed.), *Spring in Winter: The 1989 revolutions*, The Manchester University Press, Manchester.
Vaihinger, H. (1924), *The Philosophy of 'As if',* Routledge and Kegan, London.
Van de Kerchove, M. and Ost, F. (1994), *Legal System Between Order and Disorder*, Oxford University Press, Oxford.
Vattimo, G. (1988), *The End of Modernity*, Polity Press, Cambridge.

Von Mohl, R (1844), *Die Polizei-Wissenschaft nach den Grundsatzen des Rechtsstaates*, Laupp Vlg., Tübingen.

Vyshinsky, A.T. (1949), *Voprosy teorii gosudarstva i prava*, Academic Press, Moscow.

Ward, I. (1992), *Law, Philosophy and National Socialism,* P. Lang Verlag, Bern.

Weber, M. (1978), *Economy and Society: an outline of interpretive sociology*, The University of California Press, Berkeley.

Weinberger, O. (1996), 'Basic Puzzles of Discourse Philosophy', 9 *Ratio Juris*, pp. 172-81.

Welsch, W. (1996), *Vernunft*, Suhrkamp Vlg., Frankfurt.

Willke, H. (1991), 'The Autopoietic Theory of Law: Autonomy of Law and Contextual Transfer', in P. Amselek and N. MacCormick (eds), *Controversies about Law's Ontology*, Edinburgh University Press, Edinburgh.

Wittgenstein, L. (1980), *Philosophical Investigations*, Blackwell, Oxford.

Yovits, M.C. and Cameron, S. (eds), (1960), *Self-Organizing Systems*, Pergamon, Oxford.

Žižek, S. (1991), *For They Know Not What They Do*, Verso, London.

Žižek, S. (1995), 'Ideology between Fiction and Fantasy', 16 *Cardozo Law Review*, n. 3-4, pp. 1511ff.

Index

For Product Safety Concerns and Information please contact our EU representative GPSR@taylorandfrancis.com Taylor & Francis Verlag GmbH, Kaufingerstraße 24, 80331 München, Germany

Batch number: 10725941

Printed by Printforce, the Netherlands